OPTIONS TO CHANGE YOUR FUTURE!

An Educational Program for the Currently or Recently Incarcerated

By Wendy Kirkland

WENDY KIRKLAND

Copyright © 2024 by Universal Financial Independence, Inc.

All right reserved under International and Pan-American Copyright Conventions. By payment of the required fees, you have been granted the nonexclusive, nontransferable right to access and read the text of this e-book on screen or in a publisher-produced printed form. No part of this text may be reproduced, transmitted, downloaded, decompiled, reverse-engineered, or stored in or introduced to any information storage and retrieval system, in any form or by any means, whether electronic or mechanical, now known or hereafter invented, without the express permission of Universal Financial Independence or the authors.

Dedication

To my nephew Courtney - May this book guide you to a new path and an amazing future!

TABLE OF CONTENTS

Author's Preface
Shape Your Truth
Believing IS Seeing
Is Fear Holding You Back?
The Law of Attraction
Positive Expectation Brings Connection
Welcome. Let's Get Started
Understanding Wall Street from the Inside Out
Concrete Example of How a Put Works
Bullish or Bearish
Quick Analysis: Calls and Puts
Trade with the Trend
Story Illustration of How an Option Works
Option Premium
Making Sense of Strike Prices
More on Option Premiums
Volatility: The Movement of Price
How Do I Know Which Option to Buy?
Limiting Risk
One More Way to Limit Risk
Trade with Confidence
Navigating Change Your Future
Scanning the Horizon
Chart Reading Can Be an Art
Candles Tell Their Own Story
Support and Resistance
Fibonacci Patterns in Everything
Pivot Points
Average Directional Index (ADX)
Chart Set-up
CYF- Pattern for Puts
Entry Signal and Hold Confirmations
Exit Indications
Recap of Entry and Exit Alerts and Confirmations of a CYF+
Recap of Entry and Exit Alerts and Confirmations of a CYF-
Option Chain
Change Your Future Day-Trading Option Guidelines

Day-Trading Requirement Recap
Overnight Strategy
   <u>Cash versus Margin Account</u>
Fine Tuning Purchase Prices: Placing Trade Orders
   Market Orders
   Limit Orders
Following Through and Trading the Strategy

AUTHOR'S PREFACE

Hi there.

Let me explain how this book came about. I have been writing to a family member who has been incarcerated for a few years. He still has a few more years before there's a chance for probation or eventually release. In addition to the letters that I write to him, I have shared a spiritual book I wrote that explains who he really is, who we all are. He appreciated and continues to absorb these truths and has shared with me what prison is like from the inside looking out and its limitations. Some prisoners get their GED or take college classes, learn skills, and participate in work programs offered through the prison system, but he shared 75% of released prisoners struggle finding a job, slip back into old habits, and end up being reincarnated.

He also shared that he realized for his life to get better, he had to get better. Bemoaning his past wouldn't get him to a brighter future while he was still incarcerated or when he was released. Complaining about his current stressful circumstances wouldn't help either. Neither would hoping his luck would change or wishing on a star.

When it comes to you, who you are and your future, only you can make critical decisions. Because, in the end, you must live with the results that your decisions create.

With this awareness, we realized I could teach him and others while they were incarnated or once they were released about trading stock options, which are traded over the internet, so they could trade once they were home.

An interesting aspect of the stock market is that it doesn't matter how old you are as long as you are over 21. The stock market doesn't care where you live. You can trade from anywhere as long as you have a computer and internet connection. Your physical condition isn't important. Your work history and job experience doesn't matter. College or level of education isn't an issue as long as you know how to trade stock options, and that is what I am going to teach you. And, let me stress that it doesn't matter if you have a past that includes incarceration.

Before I get started, let me share who I am. I'm an everyday person without a college degree, but I have been trading stock options and teaching people to trade for 15 years.

In 2004, Hurricane Frances came through our area of Western North Carolina. It flooded the entrance to Biltmore Estate and all of Biltmore Village, including Legacies, a gift shop my husband Jack and I had owned for 22 years. Five feet of water and mud filled the building, destroying merchandise, art, and equipment.

We didn't have flood insurance. It doesn't flood in the mountains! Yet, I can assure you it does. The area filled up like a bowl.

Two weeks later, it happened again when Hurricane Ivan came through. We'd no more than start to clean and dry out when the building was filled with water and mud a second time.

We were devastated. Our entire financial world was tied up in the shop. It was the source of day-to-day living and our retirement. We were a few months from being homeless with no source of income and being in our mid-fifties, we certainly were not at a prime age for finding new employment.

A friend invited me to lunch for my birthday to cheer me up. While we ate, she told me she had taken a series of classes to learn option trading. The closest I'd ever come to thinking about the stock market were the *Wall Street Journals* that were stacked on two dining room chairs as booster seats for my youngest siblings when we were growing up.

Inspired by this discussion and potential, I took the money Jack and I had set aside for the electric bill - the electricity was turned off anyway - and enrolled in the option trading classes.

Option trading was a good fit for me. Those few classes certainly didn't give me instant success, but I won some, lost some, and won a little more - enough to help pay our bills at the time, plus the cleaning and repair expenses at the shop.

During this transition, I realized I was not only overcoming money-issues and struggling to learn something new, but I also had much deeper belief issues that needed to be worked on... Such as:

- I am too old to learn something new like option trading.
- I am an artist, not a techie or numbers person.
- I'm afraid to put so much time and energy into something that might not work. Lord, I'm already dead tired.
- What about failure? What would my husband Jack and the kids think if I lost the little money I had earned?

My course of study took many paths, but eventually I whittled away at the trading jargon and discovered what was necessary for trading success, and I learned the ABCs of "being enough" and 100% responsible for my life and my own thought-created world.

Sometime later, the friend I mentioned earlier came to me for advice, and I realized she needed help in two areas. For one, she needed additional support in learning to trade to supplement or replace her income like I had. But she also needed help with her attitude toward money and her future. I feel this is also an important aspect for people who are or have been incarcerated.

I could easily have shared one of the books I had purchased after the flood to help her financially, but equally important was her need to shift her attitude toward wealth and life expectations. This same issue is behind 75% of released prisoners being reincarcerated.

Money problems and often eventual reincarceration are primarily "mindset" problems.

Let's start right here and go to the "very" beginning. You were born, which is a miracle within itself. There is a special reason for that, and it is important. You are unique; you are one-of-a-kind. You are important, even if you are not currently aware of being that unique asset.

Adjust your definition of failure. The first step in redefining yourself is to forgive yourself for past mistakes. Truly forgive yourself! Failure doesn't have to be a negative. It means it wasn't right at that moment or in that exact way. If it is still important, try again with what you have learned or change how you do it. Or, perhaps, you did it and it truly wasn't right for you. Congrats for trying with the realization that you learned something, now move on.

So, you are where and who you uniquely are right now. How and why did this happen? What is the reason?

Self-awareness is the point at which you become conscious of being stuck, and you realize what you have done, what you are doing or not doing. You observe yourself, notice your reactions, actions, and choices as if you are watching a stage play about your own life. Awareness is the first step toward change because you can't make a change unless you are aware that a change needs to be made in the first place.

Look back, forgive yourself, truly, forgive yourself! Make amends if you can and then move on. New chapter!

Once you are aware that you want a change, you can then begin to understand why you did or do what you do. It then becomes difficult not to bring about change (of some kind) because you are no longer asleep to the truth that has guided your behavior and choices. You also begin to realize you are not only the instigator behind the "causes" of your behavior, but you are also the creator of all changes that you now want to take place.

There is a freedom that comes with awareness. Rather than thinking you are stuck in a maze or repetitive cycle where there is no escape, you begin to realize you truly are the play-writer and main actor, and you have the lead role in creating your life—not as a reactor, but as an actor. Whether you realize it or not, your reactions and choices are always yours to make. Understanding this is an enormous growth point for many. When you choose to be aware, your past and what is currently present in your life no longer must dictate your future. You are then free to move beyond your self-imposed limits and are allowed to make new choices; it's up to you to take different actions and further expand your understanding. Once you begin the awareness process, your path can't help but bring you forward, paving the way for new experiences that open the door to personal growth and understanding.

Awareness allows you to *consciously* evolve.

Are you ready? Let's do this! Let's plunge in and expand your understanding of your awareness, including spiritual awareness.

Likely you have a preconceived idea of who or what God is based on what you have been told since you were a child. Then, through this lens, your understanding builds through what you experience, read, digest, and absorb, and it solidifies as your own truth.

Your thoughts are very specific and will create that exact thing as back-up confirmation or verification. Therefore, if you look for God outside of yourself, you won't find it. Your mind and thoughts create what you think and feel God is or should be, but this is a limited, changing concept that you have manufactured.

You are also often swayed by other peoples' beliefs. At least for the moment, you believe you grasp who or what God is; it seems real, until it doesn't. You absorb a fraction of what you think is the truth, and you stop searching since it seems out of the realm of real understanding or proof and needs to be accepted on faith. The truth is you can't find something where it isn't.

Eventually, you likely give up and feel even more confused and perhaps empty because you conclude that knowing God is abstract, beyond proof or certainty.

It is difficult to decide where to start in this personal, yet universal discovery. Do I start with the answer as to who or what God is and how we both fit in, or do I start with the steps to the discovery? Perhaps, the best place to start is at a beginning, like the first words in the Bible, but written as clearly and directly as I can manage.

The first words in the Bible are: *In the beginning God created the heaven and the earth. And the earth was without form, and void; and darkness was upon the face of the deep.*

God creates through thought. There is nothing else, but God. As stated above, in the beginning, God's mind was all that existed. Our physical world didn't exist. It hadn't yet been thought of. The power of God's mind was all that existed and, when there was a thought, that thought was created instantly, and yet the development of that thought creation may have taken what you know as years, centuries, decades, or eons and longer. Instantly is subjective. Its creation happens as soon as it is thought, but formation, evolution, or development takes as long as it takes.

Perhaps, before there were any physical creations, abstracts were thought of, yet these basic concepts could have taken millions or billions of years. Here is a long list of abstract concepts to consider: center and beyond center, right and left, top and bottom or above and below, layers, dimensions, first and next, same, in front of and behind, time, now or then, finite and infinite, in and out, clockwise and counterclockwise, together or apart, bright or dark, heavy or light, long or short, wide or narrow, straight or twisted, stretched or slack, symmetrical or asymmetrical, forward or backward, high, medium or low, vertical, horizontal or circular, leading or behind. I could go on and on. These ideas were only concepts until thoughts of physical creations appeared.

The vastness is mind blowing.

It took 13.8 billion years for this moment that is in front of you as your ready to come into existence for you to experience it. Amazing.

To illustrate, let's jump forward from before creation to September 3, 2003. On that day, the Hubble telescope was in space, and it came to a spot where it became stationary. It focused a telescopic camera on an area that was about a tenth of the size of our full moon. If you take our thumb and index finger and put them together so they create a circle and hold it up to the sky, that is about the area of the sky that it focused on. It stayed in place without moving for a little over four months, keeping the camera fixed on the same spot. When it first zeroed in on the spot, the area looked black and empty.

At the end of the photographic period, it produced a camera image that looked like a clear night sky that was full of stars—like looking up at our Milky Way. Each of the glowing dots in the photo is an entire galaxy. Each galaxy contains up to one trillion stars. Each star may have a system of planets. One photo the size of a circle created by your thumb and index finger contains or reveals more than 10,000 galaxies. Imagine what is beyond the stars you see and the rest of the sky surrounding our planet and beyond.

The photo captured galaxies 13 billion light years away, which is the most distant area of space our current technology allows us to photograph. Given the leaps in technology we've seen in our lifetime, what might we see when we leap forward again? One galaxy in the photo contained eight times as many stars as our Milky Way. It is so large it technically shouldn't exist according to current theories in physics.

Whew!

As mentioned, at some point, God thought of physical creations like all those galaxies, and they were projected from thought into existence. God creates through *every* thought. The heavens, cosmos, galaxies, universe, planets, and earth were and are created, developed, and evolved through thought.

God is all there is, and its essence is a part of everything. It creates from Itself because It is "all there is." A thought from God about the universe, planets, and the earth evolving becomes oceans and eventually dry land, plants and trees, variations happening through weather. Life essence expanding starts in the oceans, and ultimately, it crawls out onto the land to become animals in various forms. Because God is all there is, it is then within all of creation. There isn't yet a definitive answer as to how long this process has taken. All said and done, you are a divine creation, an aspect of God. You are divine.

So, you were this miracle who came to be where and who you uniquely are right now. Where do you want to go and what do you want to create for yourself next?

Since this book ultimately will be about option trading on the stock market, let's discuss money and what it has to do with God. (Meaning with you because you are an aspect of God.)

Life has programmed most of us to consider both wealth and poverty in negative terms. Consider the terms "filthy rich" and "dirt poor". Most people, if asked, would agree that money changes people or possibly that rich people are evil or self-serving. Why would money change a person's character? Or push them to make bad choices? Or hurt other people? Why would anyone want money if that were the case? Our beliefs shape the way we live our lives.

You must change your negative beliefs to bring real change into your life.

The first thing you need to do when you enter prison or as soon as you become aware that changes need to be made is to forgive yourself for whatever circumstances brought you to prison. It is important to do a lot of self-evaluation. How or why did you get to this point, why did you do whatever brought you here, and what wrong choices did you make? Prison gives you a lot of time to consider the past and reevaluate yourself, but you must want to do it.

My goal is to not only teach you to trade options, so you can earn a living when you are released, but to also help you change the way you think and build new expectations for yourself based on who you truly are. I have written a book called *Knowing Is Seeing!* that clearly reveals this information, so I am struggling with how to share the details of "who you truly are" without rewriting the whole book. I hope to help you discover who you are and that you have all that is needed to make lasting, life-evolving transformations that will totally change your future, including learning to trade options.

I don't want to go down a negative path, but you need to know and recognize your triggers and when they come up, be able to deal with them whether it is going outside to the yard if that is a choice, read a book, exercise, or work out, or talk to someone. It is wise to surround yourself with positive people. Becoming aware of who you truly are and who they truly are is beyond important. That said, sometimes, you will need to feed your spirit. That little voice inside of you will ask, "What's up with this? Why is this happening?"

You'll need to discover, believe, and support the spiritual part of who you are, and I am going to cover this in bits and pieces throughout the book, so that the growing awareness helps to support and develop your recognition of who you are and your positive option trading strength. Learn how to be positive, expect amazing results no matter what your circumstances are as you begin to trade. It could be that right now you are in a box, and that is okay. Think outside the walls. Be positive. See yourself at your favorite place, visiting family, at the beach walking in the sand, sitting on a ridge looking out over a valley, driving through the country, imagine yourself successfully trading options and living a good life. Know that you are consciously, intentionally, bringing about positive changes that will brighten your future.

Remember the friend I mentioned? She learned to trade options while she looked for and found a new employment position in her field. She decided to trade options part-time and then do what she loved and felt destined to do. But, more than that, she now focuses on what she wants to do with money… what it will bring … and how it makes her feel. She does not focus on money itself and never on the lack of it. And she no longer harbors negative beliefs like everyone in her family is destined to be poor and live an unsatisfying life.

We all are what we believe and know ourselves to be. You are now taking steps on the path toward creating an amazing life.

SHAPE YOUR TRUTH

First, you form your beliefs, and then your beliefs form you and the world you live in.

You might be eager to jump into the *Change Your Future* strategy, but take a moment to reflect on this. We are all our own self-fulfilling prophecies. We live the lives that we believe we are capable of living. But what if we let ourselves imagine a life of freedom, abundance, and prosperity? Can we truly make it happen? The answer to this is YES!

Look at the life you have created. Likely, it is exactly as you expected. You are a creator. It is time to become aware of your creative abilities and strength. Consciously choose what you want in life. Let me share how this is possible.

Throughout this book, I am going to insert "Joy reminders". When things get hard, it is easy to lose focus or postpone your goals and dreams. Finding your joy keeps you on track.

Learning to trade options is the easy part.

My dad used to always tell us that "Believing is Seeing" unlike the more commonly shared, "Seeing is Believing." If you believe something is possible, it is! If you believe you can do it, YOU CAN!

BELIEVING IS SEEING

Before we launch into the trading strategy, I want to explore the concept of beliefs more deeply, zeroing in on how to use their influence to make your ability to create or manifest your will more effective.

Since our beliefs - whether acceptance- or fear-based - are often felt most profoundly in personal experience, I'd like to focus our discussion on that area. After helping an untold number of people develop and attract conscious, healthy relationships with abundance, positive expectations, and joy, I have developed an unshakeable confidence in the power of positive expectation to create your personal reality.

There is one principle that stands out from all the others from my work within the trading community and traders' feelings about money and abundance. *The barrier to a lasting, positive relationship with money or any other form of abundance is a part of ourselves that we are unable or unwilling to accept.* An aspect of ourselves that we have never accepted and embraced keeps us from forming and keeping genuine abundance in all its forms - financial, positive emotions, love, joy, confidence, awe, acceptance, appreciation, time, gratitude, kindness, and security in all its aspects.

Since this book will focus on option trading and the money it can earn, I am going to zero in on financial abundance, but, if there are other areas in your life that need to be refurbished, change the word, and apply these "rethinking" techniques to that part of yourself.

Here is why that is so important. If you do not love or accept some aspect of yourself, you will always be looking for someone else to take care of it for you. This never works out. People who do not accept some aspect of themselves seem to attract similar situations or people who are more than willing to support and confirm the validity of that belief. A broken person is always looking for just the right person or situation to fix their circumstances when the real solution can only be found inside of themselves. Without discovering the solution within yourself, the same stuff keeps happening, over and over, and over again.

If you love and accept yourself unconditionally for everything you are and everything you are not, you will attract similar circumstances and people who also love and accept themselves.

Only a moment of loving and accepting yourself unconditionally will do the job of manifesting or creating your desired expectation.

IS FEAR HOLDING YOU BACK?

Earlier I listed some of the programming we have all heard about. Have you ever said or thought one of these while you were in prison or out?

- I am a failure.
- Nothing I ever do turns out right.
- The first of the month is a dread because the rent or mortgage is due.
- If something bad is going to happen, it happens to me. I'm a magnet.
- I'll put off maintenance on the car until I can afford it.
- I always feel guilty when I make money. I don't deserve it.
- I'll never be at peace when it comes to the subject of money.
- My family said being rich was evil.
- Prison is exactly where I belong.
- I can't afford this.
- I always avoid paying bills until the last minute.
- I am just like my father or mother, always broke and one step behind.
- Geez, I live in a poor man's world.
- My neighborhood sucks and I fit right in.
- No matter how hard I work, it is never enough.

Most of us spend our lives running from certain parts of ourselves, never realizing that they are fixable. When we finally zero-in on them, we discover the root is fear. It is usually a particular fear, and there are only a few fears that come into play when we are considering financial abundance.

One fear is rooted in the expectation of betrayal because there is never enough. You can probably see why this fear could destroy money relationships. It certainly did in my early trading years before I became aware that fear was driving my money troubles.

Both Jack and I worked long hours running the gift shop, but there was never quite enough to pay all our obligations. We juggled bills, paying one and holding another a little longer. We never took a vacation. When you're afraid of being broke or "know" there will never be enough, you'll either keep money distant so it won't hurt so bad if you don't have it, or you'll cling to money, so it won't disappear without dragging you with it, kicking and screaming.

Another big fear is the dread of being consumed, wounded, or changed by money. When you are in the grip of this fear, you're worried that your uniqueness and freedom will be lost if you surrender to full appreciation and acceptance of financial wealth. So, you stay at arm's length, just as a person who is afraid of drowning might never stick a toe in a lake or sit on the edge of a swimming pool.

The thing to know about fear is that it is not real. It is a feeling that you create within yourself. It is nothing more than the pulsating queasy sensation in the pit of your stomach. You can control it. You can experiment to prove the truth of this. Think of something unpleasant, something you really dread. Hold on to it for just a second. Feel the emotion that you created.

Now realize, you just made yourself feel that way. It is not real, and you can just as easily and quickly make it disappear by realizing it does not have substance. It never did.

I like a quote I once read from Dr. Fritz Perls that says, "Fear is nothing more than excitement without the breath." Breathe. Breathe into fear and watch what happens. Like a caterpillar whose body no longer serves him, it twitches and emerges from its cocoon complete and new. The butterfly flutters out of hiding and flies away. When you realize the truth of fear, know it is not real, and embrace it directly, you can truly feel the fear disappear.

In the place where fear used to be, you now feel a big open space into which a wonderful new relationship can enter. That's what happened for me, and that's what I've seen happen to a lot of people when they gather the courage to accept themselves, including their fears. Then they can change their expectations for themselves.

THE LAW OF ATTRACTION

Let me share a personal example with you. I struggled with self-esteem for the first 40 years of my life. I was the oldest of seven kids by parents who struggled with divorce, remarriage, and more kids, and, no matter how I helped them, it was never enough or done right. I found an escape by getting married at eighteen and having my first child at nineteen. We worked hard but never managed to get ahead. I had two more children, went through bankruptcy, and numerous residential moves. My effort to escape had in fact recreated the life I thought I was trying to escape from.

I would silently judge others and compare my insides to their outsides, which always resulted in a tidal wave of negative self-talk.

However, I finally found a way to make fruitless striving and dissatisfaction disappear *through loving myself instead of hating myself for not being enough.*

When I finally gave myself that split second of unconditional love, I felt free for the first time in my life. How liberating it was to love myself for something that had moments before been unlovable!

In that moment, I also realized that I tended to push away love and acceptance because deep down inside I didn't think I deserved it, and, to console myself, I pushed myself harder and harder, trying new things, and then tore myself down for my efforts not being enough.

What I discovered in that moment of acceptance of myself was that life was too beautiful to be upset all the time - constantly comparing, competing, thinking this is right and that is wrong. Life was too unpredictable to disrespect others and myself with faulty judgements and erroneous interpretations.

Life was to be enjoyed, not to be suffered through. I had a craving to feel present, to enjoy my family, and appreciate my place within it.

I made a new commitment to love and accept myself every time I felt those negative feelings. I also realized that gratitude opens us up for receiving. Every time I felt "poor me", I consciously became thankful for what I had in my life. I discovered that, if I appreciate and know that what I desire will enhance my life even more, bringing more joy for which I will be forever grateful, then life keeps evolving, getting better and better.

Now I focus on what I want to do with money, what it will bring, and how it will make me feel. I don't focus on money itself and never on the lack of it. Focusing on money itself is restrictive and limiting. To get or obtain what I desire might come from another source. I might not need to spend a penny. My desire might be gifted to me or traded, or I might find it or inherit it. Take money out of the equation. Focus on the joy of abundance without focusing on the source. I am in the heart of that feeling right now as I write this book, my nephew Courtney, and others who are reading. My joy comes from sharing who you truly are and explaining and teaching option trading.

The trick is to ask not from a place of lack and shortcoming, but rather focus on what you want to do with what you desire, how it will make you feel, and the gratitude you will have when it arrives.

It takes conscious effort and persistence to stop thoughts of lack in their tracks and immediately replace them with positive thoughts grounded in gratitude.

Instead of thinking, "I'm not deserving." "I am a criminal." "I spend money faster than I make it. I'm just no good at it. Never have been. All I need is an extra thousand bucks." Replace it with, "I am flooded with abundance. I am learning to manage my money responsibly, always paying my bills thankfully and on time. I am grateful for what I have." "I am an awesome individual." "I am unique and special."

We have all heard of the law of attraction – Like attracts like. Positive belief in your own abundance in all its forms will draw the resources you require toward you like a magnet.

Think of money as a form of energy. This is a give-and-take universe. It is two-sided. You must give to receive. You don't always have to give money, obviously. Instead, you can give energy, effort, wisdom, skills, talents, help, an empathetic ear, kindness, understanding, knowledge, support, and sharing your joy.

The ideal situation is to do what you love. If you are not quite there yet then change your attitude about where you are or the job you don't like. Be grateful for what you are learning and the opportunities it does offer to grow, share, and expand. Be happy with what you have rather than dissatisfied with what you don't have.

Be glad you are contributing within your prison community and working toward helping your family.

Personally, I quit pushing away love and acceptance. I allowed others to help me. I openly shared my feelings. I quit pretending I was independent and that I knew it all. As if by magic, a world of love, confidence, and abundance in all its forms opened before me. Soon I was surrounded by love and financial freedom, completely encircled by it. It had been there all the time, waiting for me to change my mind and let it in. I realized who I truly was and started routinely reminding myself. I am an aspect of God.

POSITIVE EXPECTATION BRINGS CONNECTION

As I loved myself, I suddenly found myself making another shift of consciousness. Up until that moment, I'd always felt slightly disconnected from other people and the world around me, but I hadn't been aware of feeling that way. I was disconnected and didn't know it - I thought that was just the way everybody felt. Disconnection was the way life was.

Here Jack and I owned and operated a gift store. We were there seven days a week and had little or no time for friends. That said, hundreds of people visited the shop each week, but everyone was a tourist or a stranger, and, though we talked about gifts and art, there was an arm's distance between us. Suddenly, through my change in how I thought about things, a shift occurred deep within me, and I felt connected to other people and to the world around me. A wall disappeared... one I hadn't even known I was behind. We are all part of the same whole, an aspect of God.

Part of this shift came about because of the flood that swamped our store twice. I felt like I was drowning, but at the same time, it was as if the water broke through barriers and washed away debris that was holding me back. I discovered option trading, stretched myself and formed a trading community. Like attracted like. And now you are knowingly a part of that community.

It was a physical shift I could feel. I can compare the feeling of disconnection to having a tiny rock in my shoe. I'd walked so long with the irritation of the rock in my shoe that I'd lost consciousness of that fact that I was uncomfortable and irritated. Suddenly the rock was removed and, for the first time in my memory, I took a step without the soreness. Now the shoe feels comfortable, and my steps are joyful.

That's what loving and accepting ourselves, feeling gratitude, and positive expectation can do. It frees us to walk through the world feeling at one with ourselves and other people. It's a new way to be, a way of being that brings abundance in all its forms and makes every step of the journey richer and more joyful.

You have the ability within you. Create the life you truly want.

WELCOME. LET'S GET STARTED

Welcome to *Change Your Future*. We're going to have a lot of fun together!

My strategy can be used on any timeframe chart. It will be up to you to decide how much time you want to put into option trading. Some people enjoy the pace of day-trading, while others prefer watching a trade unfold in their spare time in the evenings or weekends for weeks or months at a time. Also, I am going to discuss this information as if you have been released from prison and are sitting in front of a computer studying the charts and patterns.

To understanding the complete cycle of this strategy, we are going to zero in on and discuss trading on very short-term charts so you can experience the entire set-up - the cycle from entry to exit within a few hours ...or sometimes even overnight. To make sure that you see how this works for any schedule, you should also practice the same process in other timeframes...15 minute and less for day-trades...30-minute, 60-minute, and daily for swing trades...day, week, and month for longer term. The principles and patterns remain the same. The difference is the length of time it takes to flow through the pattern stages. Each candle on the chart represents how much time that candle incorporates of the equity's move. Three-minute candles are what it did in 3-minutes and the next candle is the next 3-minutes. A 10-minute candles shows 10-minute moves, a daily candle shows daily-moves, etc.

Life throws us curves periodically. Where once actively trading throughout the day might seem perfect, there are times when it doesn't work perfectly - during the summer months when the kids are home, while you travel, or when you tackle another project. Flexibility is important. The same patterns and concepts you learn on a 10-minute chart work on a 30-minute, 60-minute and daily chart. Once you master the principles, you master your own fate through the time you devote to trading!

Through this book, I'm going to remind you to stay positive and truly remember who you are. You are awesome. I will move those section headings off to the left. The centered headings will relate to trading.

UNDERSTANDING WALL STREET FROM THE INSIDE OUT

This book, *Change Your Future*, has been in the works since 2023. My introduction to options trading, *Exploring Your Options,* was published in 2019. The books are designed to work together. *Exploring Your Options* covers the basics of option trading and the importance of chart reading, as well as how to open a brokerage account and how to read an option chain. That basic information will only be briefly repeated here. *Change Your Future* is a strategy book. It will cover specific indicators to place on your charts and how to read and use the information they provide.

The stock market routinely changes. Yes, the market rises for a while and then drops, losing value, but overall, that doesn't change what I do, which is to help people to trade what the market hands out each day. When you are trading options, the market can be traded when it goes up or down. When the market or an equity goes up in price, you select "Call" options, and, when the market or an equity goes down in price, you select "Put" options.

So, what exactly is our strategy based on? Let's call it the "CYF pattern," which is a rare combination of events or circumstances, creating an unusually bad or powerful result, but, in our reference, it is set of opposing conditions from which you can benefit in a powerful way.

Change Your Future is a general, but apropos title, relevant on several levels. What are your "options.?" During February of 2020, the market reached all-time highs and was primed for a pullback. Pullbacks give the market time to release steam, flatten, and then slowly recover, which is a normal and natural event. Now, in mid-2023, the market has risen with small swings up and down along the way but is zeroing in on the all-time highs of 2020.

Routinely, the market swings from being overbought to being oversold and back to overbought again. The image below is a three-and-a-half-year view of the Dow Stock Exchange. Even without knowing how to read a stock chart, you will be able to easily see how routinely the Dow swings from being overbought (the upper shaded peaks) and oversold (the lower shaded peaks).

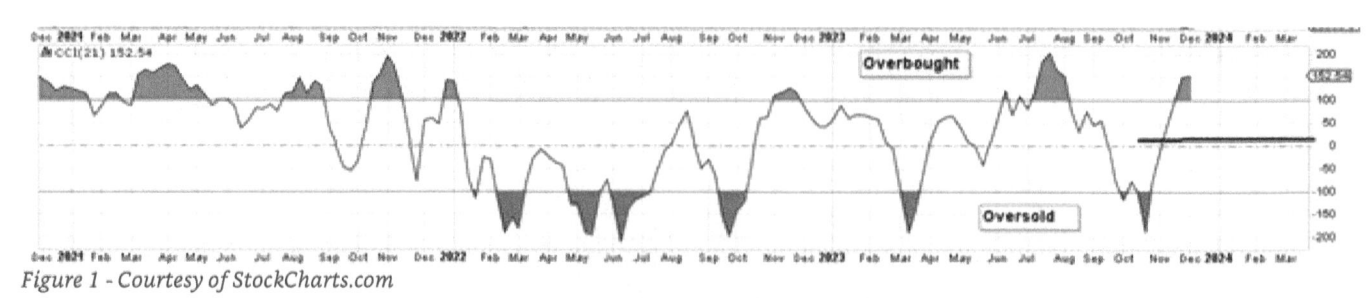

Figure 1 - Courtesy of StockCharts.com

Global and domestic political events, including the COVID-19 pandemic, set up the perfect atmosphere for an unprecedented market correction, as well as turning the personal lives of most of the world's population 180 degrees. Few people imagined in mid-February 2020 how life would change by the end of March 2020.

On the chart above, the shaded lower peaks during that Covid period were the lowest, and they were the widest and lasted for the longest period without change. During 2022 and 2023, there were numerous drops that I call fins, like a dolphin fin. There were drops that rose for a while and then dropped again, back, and forth into 2023,

For option traders, the market's pullback/correction set ups are unusual and periodic, yet they create remarkable trading prospects. Daily, there were regular 3-10% drops in price, recoveries, and then price drops again, back, and forth. These waves up and down presented unprecedented trade opportunities.

Yes, there are aspects of trading that are often just glanced at during these turbulent times, that need to be considered, like implied volatility that can elevate premiums and skew spreads between Bid and Ask premiums. We will explore these concepts in detail.

Yet, despite these challenging times, knowledgeable traders who considered these elements in their trade decisions were able to ride the waves in market pricing brought on by the volatility.

When you own stock outright and it goes up in price, you earn a profit. When stock drops in price, you take a loss. In *Change Your Future*, you can profit when stock prices go up or down. Call options are purchased when you expect prices to go up for whatever reason. Put options give you the opportunity to earn a profit when an equity's value drops.

CONCRETE EXAMPLE OF HOW A PUT WORKS

Because a Put is unique in the option trading world, most people struggle to understand how it is possible to make money when the market goes down. Let me give you an example outside of the option world of how they work.

In simplest terms, imagine that someone promises to buy from you an item at a fixed price. Let's say they promise to pay you $100 for a life raft whenever you want to sell it within the next 90 days. It doesn't matter what the life raft looks like or its condition, the buyer promises to pay you $100 any time during that 90-day period. For this promise of purchase, you pay him $5.

Now it is possible that the life raft's value could increase during that 90-day period. Perhaps, life raft use has grown in popularity during a stormy season, and it is now worth $120 because life rafts are scarce now.

Hopefully, you would have considered this storm season before entering the trade agreement, but, if things happened as a surprise, you would walk away from the trade and would be out the $5 you paid him for his promise to purchase the raft. It wouldn't make sense for you to buy a life raft for $120 only to turn around and sell it for $100.

Imagine, on the other hand, the life raft you planned to purchase then resell has taken a beating through roughhouse play in the community swimming pool. It is cracked and discolored when you are ready to make your purchase. The value of the life raft is now $60. Despite its low value, the buyer must pay you the agreed-upon price because of your agreement. You purchase the life raft for $60 and sell it to the buyer for $100.

You made $35 profit. ($100 less $60 to make the purchase = $40 less $5 for the contract = $35 profit or 700% over your original $5 investment)

Having two types of options to purchase - both Call and Put - you can earn a profit no matter what the market dishes out. It doesn't matter if the price goes up or down, yet the key is for you to understand how to determine the direction before deciding which way to trade.

Not only that, but option premiums are also a small percentage of the actual cost of the stock. You benefit from the price movement of 100 shares of stock since each option contract covers 100 shares of a stock (or other type of equity), and, to benefit from the price movement of these 100 shares, you pay a premium that is equivalent to a small percentage of the equity's price. The price of an equity might be $50 or $5,000 to own the 100-shares of stock and yet, the option's premium is $.95 a share or $95 for one option contract to benefit from its price moves on those 100-shares over the next 3-weeks. Therefore, it is important to learn to read charts to be able to make an informed decision as to the direction of the equity's price's move.

Again, you determine direction of the equity's probable price move (based on learning to read its price chart and patterns) because the person or market-maker who is in the trade with you is expecting the opposite trading conditions to happen, or at least expecting you to mishandle the trade, so that, in the end, he will win and profit. It is the reason that he entered the trade.

Market-makers figure that most traders don't have a clue and trade based on wishful thinking.

However, if you can read the conditions correctly, you can find the correct direction. So, let's put you on the winning side of *Change Your Future*.

BULLISH OR BEARISH

If General Mills or some other major industry comes to your town and brings new jobs and adds money to the economy, then, chances are, the other businesses in your area will experience an increase in business as well. If your town loses a major employer, the other local businesses may report a decrease in business because less money is circulating. In the same way, economic trends and current events like the COVID-19 pandemic or a conflict between countries influence Wall Street, and stocks have a "herd effect".

This is easy to understand when you realize major banks, financial institutions, and market-makers team up when a positive or negative news event takes place, and together they begin to sell or buy shares from retail customers (like you and me). You can think of it like a wholesaler like a grocery store and its retail customers.

From here on, I will refer to these "wholesalers" - the groups of banks, financial institutions, and professional buyer/sellers - as "market-makers". They are "making a market" (a two-sided trade) with you and me and other individual traders.

When economic trends are on the rise and equities are increasing in value because investors are confident in the economic future of the market, then we are said to be in a "bull market", or traders are said to be "bullish". On the other hand, in times of great economic uncertainty or during a dramatic event, the market becomes "jittery," and then stocks may decline in value. Analysts would then say we are in a "bear market", or traders are "bearish".

As mentioned earlier, there are two perspectives to trading. The easiest way to understand this is to think of a store owner. He is a seller of merchandise. His perspective of the sale transaction is the opposite of yours, the buyer. He has purchased and is holding inventory that he hopes to sell to prospective customers at a price that is higher than what he paid for those products that line the shelves.

In much the same way, it is easy to see that the wholesaler/market-maker's point of view is the exact opposite of the trader. When the trader is jittery and sells his shares, the market-makers are happily buying them up at ever-decreasing prices. Or in a bull market, the market-makers are gladly selling to excited traders at ever-increasing prices.

Stocks rise and fall daily, and you don't assign the terms "bull" or "bear" based on one day or a week's performance. The terms are relative as well. The market can be "bearish" for a period when other economic forecasts seem uncertain. On the other hand, the market can turn "bullish" when certain indicators point to economic expansion. (These indicators and trends are a study in themselves, but for now, the general definitions will do).

A great many other terms are part of the language of the broad and specialized world of option trading and investing, but for now, these basic definitions are enough material to begin understanding where option trading fits into the big picture.

Joy Reminder:

As we explore the trading world and how it fits into your personal situation, marvel at each new moment with a sense of awe. Begin to discover new opportunities for excitement and joy. Strive to feel happier and more carefree, even when you must focus on life's serious issues.

By embracing gratitude and joy and choosing to see your world with new eyes, you can turn even the smallest moment into something valuable.

CONSCIOUSLY MAKE A CHANGE

Before you are released from prison, making a change doesn't really have anything to do with getting your GED or learning a skill like upholstery and running a machine to create a license plate or even learning to trade options. Real change has to do with discovering your own humanity and being aware that your true self is an aspect of God. If you haven't done that, it won't matter what you have studied and learned, it won't do you any good or change your future. Because if you haven't touched on your own humanity, your Godliness, being an important part of it all, then you are apt to slip right back into the crime that sent you to jail in the first place.

If, on the other hand, you rediscover your own humanity and that you are an aspect of God at your core, your mind, your psychology starts to change because you are now a human being who is connected to every other human being. You are part of the same whole. This truth doesn't just include people in your community, but also people in other countries who are going through their own hardships, as well. You open your heart and mind to accept and start caring for other people. That is true rehabilitation.

People who manage to stay out of prison once they are released are those who have re-discovered humanity and know that everyone is spiritually connected. These people take care of their kids; they are well-respected; they are not living a criminal life; they are happy and filled with self-respect.

All this said, once you are released, it is important not to carry a grudge. I am not sure exactly how this book will be received or will play out, but my hope is that once it is published, perhaps, the prison system will be open to classes where a teacher or trading coach might be able to hold sessions and openly look at charts on a computer screen and answer questions. I hope this information, this option trading knowledge will bring about a change, and a reduction in returning prisoners. I totally get that you can get a released inmate a job, an apartment, a car, but unless he is ready to make a change and stay out of prison, then it is likely all for nothing.

I feel there is a short four-to-six-month period after an inmate is released when they are full of enthusiasm, but not long after, they start getting beat down by the world and their former acquaintances who are still involved in criminal-whatever. They get sucked back in.

In today's world, if you go to a job interview and say you have a criminal record, you likely won't be hired. If you don't tell them and they find out, they will let you go. In a sense, you must fight to stay out of prison by making the right choices and putting in the work. The way I see it, there are two positive choices for you to stay out of prison and to earn a living. 1) You can create your own business. It is very unlikely that anyone will ask or think you have a record if you're operating your own business. It doesn't matter what type of business (some require a license): plumbing, electric, insulation, landscaping, lawn mowing, etc. 2) You can learn to trade stock options.

Once you are released, it isn't about playing catch-up by trying to experience all you missed. The day you get out is about the moment, now, right this minute and tomorrow. How do you make tomorrow better for yourself?

QUICK ANALYSIS: CALLS AND PUTS

You will recall that options are vehicles that you buy and sell to take part in the exchange of equities, just like the life raft trade we discussed. An option is defined as "the right, but not the obligation, to buy or sell an equity at a certain price before a certain expiration date".

There are choices in many different arenas where option trading is carried out, including exchange-traded funds (ETFs), stocks, indexes, future contracts, commodities, securities, and so forth.

However, you don't need to concern yourself with all the possible areas in which you can trade options. I'll keep the discussion to three areas - stocks, ETFs, and indexes. In general, I refer to them as equities.

We briefly discussed the two types of options earlier. Simply stated, there are only two types of options - Call Options and Put Options, or more commonly referred to as a Call and a Put.

Call Options are "contracts that give the owner the right, but not the obligation, to buy a specified number of shares of an equity at a specified price, called the strike price, on or before a specified date, called the expiration date". Call options are purchased when the price of the underlying stock is expected to go up.

Put Options are "contracts that give the owner the right, but not the obligation, to sell a specified number of shares of an equity at a specified price, the strike price, on or before a specified date, the expiration date". Put options are purchased when the price of the underlying stock is expected to go down.

During recent periods when businesses were closing their physical offices or reducing size, and citizens and workers are encouraged to work from home. Online meetings conducted through Zoom (ZM) or Cisco Webex (CSCO) soared. Zoom's stock went up to $580 and today as I type it is $67. While Zoom (ZM) was zooming back in 2020, Darden (DRI) owned by General Mills (GM), who operates Olive Garden and Red Lobster and other chain restaurants, had DRI stock drop from $125 per share to $35 and now back to $155. In any set of circumstances, there are always winners and losers, but in *Change Your Future*, using both Call and Put options, they all have the potential to be winners.

It is hard to know during unknown world events how the world and life will settle out, but as mentioned earlier, for option traders, little has changed. We can work from our computers at home, study, and learn option trading if this is a new concept or jump into the waters of amazing opportunities presented during any unsettled, stormy period and any sunny period that follows.

TRADE WITH THE TREND

The "bulls" and "bears" concept become relevant here. In a bull market, when the overall market is going up, successful option traders buy and sell their Call Options. They recognize the beginning of the upswing when market-makers are cranking up the excitement level. It is counterproductive to go against the flow of the market. You want to get in near the beginning of the move, or after a pause or pullback, and not wait until every other trader who is interested has entered, and the move will soon be over.

Likewise, in a bear market, when the overall market is trending to lower stock prices, then successful option traders consider purchasing and selling their Put Options at the beginning and end of the move. I'll limit our discussion for now to Call Options and, other than general information, I will save an in-depth look at Put Options for a later section.

Remember: You are buying and selling *options* to buy and sell stock, but you do not have to exercise that option. In other words, you will not own shares of the stocks on which you purchase options unless that is what you choose to do. Most option traders buy and sell their option contracts without the intention of ever owning the stock itself. It is the option itself that has the most value, highest percentage gain, and a smaller investment. I'll explain this leverage more fully over the next few pages, but for the moment, think of it as if you are renting a business or company for a specific period, and you benefit if it increases in price during the time, you rent it.

STORY ILLUSTRATION OF HOW AN OPTION WORKS

Imagine you have a friend who wants to sell his vintage sailboat. You are familiar with the model of boat, and you feel it would be a good investment, but you don't have the $20,000 to purchase the boat as an investment now, so you offer another proposal.

"If you'll give me a piece of paper saying I can purchase your boat for $20,000 any time over the next six months," you say to your friend, "I will pay you a $1,000 fee now." Your friend accepts your proposal because it is not important that he sells today. In essence, you have bought an option – the option to purchase the actual boat later.

Three months later, you go to a boat show and meet someone, who is anxious to find and buy the same vintage sailboat that your friend wants to sell. He is willing to pay $25,000. You hold up your paper—the option—and wave it in front of interested buyer, saying, "I have access to the perfect boat and will accept your offer of $25,000."

You go back to your friend, and the trade is made. Here's what happened:

- Your friend receives the $20,000 he wanted for his boat, in addition to the $1,000 you paid for the option to purchase his sailboat. He is happy.

- The new buyer purchases the vintage sailboat for $25,000. He is happy.

- And you make $4,000 for the sale of the boat at the higher price ($5,000 profit on the price difference less the $1,000 cost of the option contract), a 400% increase on this initial investment. You are happy.

This story, just like the life raft example earlier, illustrates in a simple way the crux of the world of trading options. In the story, you see the boat, the owner, and the buyer. They are all tangible to you. In the world of Wall Street, it is all like invisible pieces of paper, so to speak, especially when the transactions take place online. However, the principle is the same. You control enough of a desirable stock to make a great deal of money with essentially only a down payment.

Most of us cannot go out and simply plunk down $20,000 to invest in an underlying instrument like a vintage sailboat or a block of stocks. But you can benefit from the leverage of controlling the "underlying" with a fraction of the cost by using options. The leverage of options allows you to profit by an exaggerated amount, in the same way a pulley leverages weight so you can lift more than physically possible.

Options give you profit leverage that builds wealth.

Joy Reminder:

The beauty of learning, experiencing, and developing is that we sometimes discover we have made mistakes. There are times we wish we could just let someone else decide for us what is real and true, yet this is clearly not a practical option. However, we benefit from this evaluation as we hone the ability to make up our own minds about what is real, taking everything that comes our way as truth with a grain of salt.

I am not suggesting that we ignore information from outside sources. On the contrary, we need to trust in our inner ability to weigh what we see or hear to decide whether we agree with it. Input provides us with the opportunity of deep regard. As we provide ourselves with time to reflect, taking our own experiences into consideration, we find that making up our minds and weighing pros and cons is a meaningful process through which we grow into more grateful, connected, and joy-filled human beings.

HEART-CENTERED THINKING

As mentioned earlier, you are a creator. According to Dr. Joe Dispenza, who trained in fields of neuroscience, "Every thought you think produces corresponding chemistry within your body equal to that specific thought, which in turn creates an emotion. Therefore, you only relate to the thoughts equal to your emotions." It is known when we, you, and I, are heart-centered and feel our wholeness, (let's connect this to you) -- your connectedness, your oneness, God-connectedness, you are less separate from your goals, dreams and desires.

According to Dr. Dispenza, when you feel gratitude, mental freedom, connectedness, love, appreciation, and kindness, all those emotions open the door to your mind so that you can program your body with the thoughts of your new future, what you are creating. The next moments agree. If you live in the feeling of fear or lack, but try to think you are abundant, you can't produce a measurable result because change can only happen when thoughts are aligned with the emotions that are playing out in your body. You can think positively all you want, but, if you don't truly accept and believe it, you will be unable to draw those created results ultimately to you.

You can repeat the affirmations, I am abundant, I am fearless, and I am always successful to yourself, but if what you are internalizing is the opposite, your goal will never make it past your brain to your heart, which means, as a human creator, you are not creating those results. You are sending mixed messages.

It is only when you change your energy to the positive that you can create more consistent results. Spending time putting your energy toward your future good outcomes trains your mind and body to produce that result. That's because, according to Dr. Dispenza, your body believes that the emotion you are feeling is coming from an experience in your current environment. It is a situation of practice makes perfect. When you invest time in this creative space, your body responds as if it's in the future experience and begins to create or draw in the desired results.

Take time to focus on activating positive emotions rather than waiting for something to happen to stir up the emotions. By taking control, you then become who you are supposed to be, your divine self. When you are living through the heart, you are creating the positive energy to produce and sustain these feelings, and draw in positivity, including the trade results you are seeking. You will act toward your own good.

Again, if you feel or know things never work out for you, then that will be the result. You are the creator. Realize who you are and change your expectations!

OPTION PREMIUM

The option's premium is the amount you pay to control the underlying equity. This option premium increases in a magnified way when compared with the underlying equity's price.

As the equity's price goes up, your Call option increases in value or for a Put as the equity decreases in value, and then you sell your option to someone else well before the expiration date. In that way, you trade the option, but never actually buy or sell the underlying stock. If your requests are in line with Bid/Ask prices, it is all handled behind the scenes by your broker, dealing with market-makers and you reap the results.

Try to remember these two crucial points:

1. As an option trader, you make money by purchasing the "right" to buy or sell a "thing," and that right in itself has value and gives you, the trader, leveraging power.

2. You never need to worry about finding an interested buyer; through the option contract itself, the sale is guaranteed the moment that you decide to sell, providing you have purchased an option with a level of open interest. (This will be explained and covered in greater detail.) You just don't want to be the only one in the trade.

Most of us are accustomed to thinking of the stock market as an exchange, where you buy and own actual shares of stock, and then decide to sell for various reasons. Therefore, it sometimes requires a new mindset to fully appreciate the value of an "option."

The deal you managed on the sailboat—your $4,000 profit in three months—probably sounds pretty good. Let's see what it would look like with a stock option.

If you buy an option on a stock, you can think of the option as a down payment on that stock. Imagine purchasing an option on 100 shares of Boeing (BA) stock to control the financial power of those 100 shares.

To make this even more clear, let's compare a stock purchase to an option purchase:

- If Boeing's stock price is $225 per share, 100 shares of stock would cost $22,500. If next month the stock price goes up $2, and you sell the stock, you have a profit of $200 on your 100 shares. Your profit is .88%, less than 1%.

- But, if you buy a Call Option on those same 100 shares of BA stock, you will pay approximately $5.10 per share. (This is a good estimate, but the actual option prices vary greatly). This $510 investment controls all 100 shares of BA stock.

- If Boeing's stock price goes up $2, your option may go up half that amount or more. Let's use 50% or $1. (This, too, varies according to the underlying option).

- This $1 increase or $100 profit is 19.6% of the initial price you paid for the option, $510. Using the leverage of options, you've made 19.6% profit on the same underlying equity that only realized a .88% profit when the actual stock was sold.

100 shares @ $225 = $22,500

$2 increase x 100 shares = $200

New Value = $22,700

Gain .88%

Or

1 Option contract on 100 shares @ $5.10 per share = $510

$1 increase in option price x 100 shares = $100

New Value = $610

Gain 19.6%

It is evident that options provide traders with two benefits:

1. You can begin trading with a small amount of money.
2. You can turn a high percentage of profit.

There is increased leverage. As you begin to practice trading, your confidence increases, and you can earn even greater profits. With my strategy, a $200 profit can become $400, $400 can become $800, and before long, a trading account will increase, showing exponential or "compounded" profit.

MAKING SENSE OF STRIKE PRICES

Leverage is an exciting concept. An important element is the price you pay for an option contract. As you will see in the chart below, options come with lots of options. (LOL)

Let's first expand on your understanding of an option chain and the pricing of an option contract.

Once you've decided to purchase a Call Option, you have the choice to buy your option "In-the-money," "At-the-money," or "Out-of-the-money". (You have these same choices on Put Options).

"In-the-money", like it sounds, is the amount by which the price of the underlying equity exceeds the strike price.

If Alibaba (BABA) stock price were to be $94.39, and you decide on a Strike Price of $90, with an August expiration date of the year 2023. The option contract would read BABA Aug 2023 90 Call.

This August option is $4.39 in-the-money, which is the difference between the actual stock price and the strike price ($94.39 minus 90.00). The 90 is the strike price of $90 and the expiration date is the third Friday in August 2023. Again, the expiration is always the third Friday of the expiration month for "monthly" expirations. There are also weekly and daily expirations on some equities.

"At-the-money" is when the price of the underlying equity matches the strike price, or nearly so.

If BABA's actual stock price is $94.39, and you buy a Strike Price of $95, the option contract would also read BABA August 2023 95 Call.

However, this August 2023 option is at-the-money since the strike price nearly matches the stock price. (It is $0.61 out-of-the money, but it's said to be at-the-money since it nearly matches).

"Out-of-the-money" is the amount by which the price of the underlying equity is below the strike price.

If BABA's stock price were to be $86.50 instead of $94.39, and you bought a Strike Price of $90, the option contract would still read BABA Aug 2023 90 Call.

However, this option is $3.50 out-of-the-money since the stock price is below the strike price.

This terminology may seem to indicate that the strike price moves. This is not the case. You may think the strike price has moved from out-of-the-money to in-the-money, but it is the equity's price that has moved. The strike price remains constant, consistent with the price of the option purchased.

The BABA August 2023 90 or 95 Call remains a $90 or $95 Call Option no matter if BABA's stock price moves above or below $90 or $95 (depending on which you selected.) The premium or cost to buy the BABA August 2023 Call options will change as the price of the stock changes.

All options available to purchase, whether they are in-, at-, or out-of-the-money, are listed on an option chain. An example of a chain appears below.

Please don't worry about over-analyzing it. I just want you to begin to grasp the terminology and to recognize the appearance of these tables and charts. I will cover the specifics of this table as we go along.

The option chain below shows an Ask premium of $5.40 for BABA's 90 strike that expires Sept. 8, 2023. This is likely to be the price you would pay if you were to open a trade on the 90- strike. Had you opened the trade several days or weeks ago, $5.20 is the current Bid premium and the amount you would likely receive if you were to close the trade.

Note on the chart below that the Call premiums and information are on left side of the column of strike prices and the Put premiums are on the right side of the strike column.

The current date isn't shown on this image, but the option chain information that is being looked at is September 8th, and is a weekly option expiration, expiring the week before the monthly expiration of the 15th, the expiration we have been discussing.

The option chains on your broker's site will list "all" the expirations available. The further out the expiration is, the more expensive it will be. Time has value. Think of this as the expiration date on a carton of milk. If the milk expires in 2 weeks, it has less time value, and its price will be on sale when compared to ultra-filtered milk with an expiration date of 8 weeks out in time.

Symbol	Name							Implied Vol	Historical Vol	Price	Change
BABA	ALIBABA GROUP HOLDING LIMITIED							0.354	0.488	95.01	2.11

September 8, 2023 - Calls | September 8, 2023 - Puts

Symbol	Bid	Ask	Price	TPrice	Volume	OI NS	Strike	Symbol	Bid	Ask	Price	TPrice	Volume	OI NS
BABA	11.95	12.25	12.20	12.16	1	25 W	83.00	BABA	0.02	0.03	0.03	0.03	32	808 W
BABA	11.00	11.25	10.11	11.18	0	38 W	84.00	BABA	0.03	0.04	0.04	0.05	5	1033 W
BABA	10.00	10.20	10.24	10.21	25	172 W	85.00	BABA	0.03	0.04	0.04	0.08	230	613 W
BABA	9.10	9.25	9.22	9.26	1	12 W	86.00	BABA	0.04	0.05	0.05	0.13	59	288 W
BABA	8.05	8.30	8.25	8.33	108	339 W	87.00	BABA	0.06	0.07	0.07	0.19	212	353 W
BABA	7.15	7.30	7.17	7.43	45	154 W	88.00	BABA	0.09	0.10	0.09	0.29	806	1077 W
BABA	6.20	6.35	6.37	6.56	107	653 W	89.00	BABA	0.13	0.14	0.13	0.42	482	523 W
BABA	5.20	5.40	5.30	5.73	568	1265 W	90.00	BABA	0.21	0.22	0.21	0.59	1591	1713 W
BABA	4.40	4.55	4.35	4.95	81	356 W	91.00	BABA	0.32	0.35	0.33	0.81	551	1003 W
BABA	3.55	3.70	3.68	4.23	417	1639 W	92.00	BABA	0.50	0.53	0.51	1.09	2323	760 W
BABA	2.85	2.98	2.95	3.57	1048	1760 W	93.00	BABA	0.78	0.80	0.78	1.42	2853	1019 W
BABA	2.25	2.30	2.35	2.97	1357	1478 W	94.00	BABA	1.15	1.19	1.16	1.83	1582	352 W
BABA	1.75	1.80	1.78	2.44	4467	5131 W	95.00	BABA	1.63	1.68	1.64	2.29	2976	290 W
BABA	1.34	1.38	1.34	1.98	8180	2082 W	96.00	BABA	2.22	2.26	2.25	2.83	1246	64 W
BABA	1.02	1.05	1.04	1.58	6880	1667 W	97.00	BABA	2.89	2.94	2.85	3.43	188	171 W
BABA	0.78	0.81	0.81	1.24	5030	930 W	98.00	BABA	3.60	3.75	3.62	4.09	118	110 W
BABA	0.60	0.62	0.60	0.96	2938	1524 W	99.00	BABA	4.40	4.55	4.52	4.81	18	121 W
BABA	0.45	0.47	0.47	0.74	21268	11883 W	100.00	BABA	5.25	5.45	5.27	5.58	29	129 W

Figure 2 - Courtesy of optionistics.com

Take a deep breath. This and the information that follows may seem like a lot to take in all at once, and it may even seem like a foreign language. In a sense it is, but in a short time, you will be able to evaluate the information given in all these charts, tables, and graphs as quickly and easily as scanning a recipe. Remember, I'll always provide examples to illustrate, so read through the definitions, and don't be concerned if you don't yet grasp the full meaning.

MORE ON OPTION PREMIUMS

An option's complete price, its premium, is comprised of two things – intrinsic value and time value. It is also shadowed by another aspect - volatility.

Intrinsic value is the in-the-money value (Price of Equity less Strike Price). An out-of-the-money option's intrinsic value is zero. Look at the chart above, the strike prices in the darker area, those above 95 on the upper/eft - Call side are in-the-money and on the Puts side, lower left are also in-the-money. The strikes in the lighter colored areas are out-of-the-money.

The time value of an option's price decreases as time passes. Out-of-the-money options are comprised entirely of time value, while a deeply in-the-money option is comprised almost entirely of intrinsic value. Another name for time value is extrinsic value.

To clarify this, let's think of the gallon of milk we mentioned earlier.

The milk itself has intrinsic value, and the longer the time left before it reaches its sell date, the more time value it has. The combination of these two factors makes up an option's full value (intrinsic and extrinsic value), just like they make up the reasoning behind the milk's price. As the milk closes in on its sell-by date, its time value decreases. At expiration, it has zero time-value and maintains only the intrinsic value of the milk itself.

So why consider paying for extra time? Sometimes time is needed for a trade to play out. Let's say two extra months. What is the probability of a price change in the underlying equity? Is it more likely that the equity's price will move $2 in one month or in two months?

Since option premium change is largely driven by the change in the underlying equity's price, having more time for the change to happen will be to your advantage, and you would expect to pay a higher premium for the benefit of added time. In a sense, it is buying extra security, giving more time (if needed) for your stock options to reach your goal. If they should get there sooner, you can sell them earlier than you may have expected.

Now, I will remind you that we are discussing trading concepts in a general way. I want to give you a solid base to stand on before we dig into the details of this *Change Your Future* (CYF) trading strategy.

In this general understanding of option values and expirations, we have been talking about weeks or months out in time. However, as we begin to discuss the CYF trade strategy, we are going to be working in short timeframes for you to see the pattern's beginning and end. To do so, you will be considering out-of-the-money options and shorter expiration dates.

We will cover the specifics of the strategy once you have a good footing on solid ground.

VOLATILITY: THE MOVEMENT OF PRICE

The "shadowing effect" mentioned above is the historical and implied volatility of an equity. Volatility in the stock market refers to movement or swings in price on either side of the average price. Volatility is often given as a statistical measure, a numerical amount.

Historical volatility refers to the actual price movement of an equity over specific periods of time in the past. Implied volatility is an estimate of future price movement, which is considered in the volatility component of option premium pricing.

This math is not something that you need to figure out. It is incorporated within option chain pricing, but a general understanding is advantageous. For example, if an equity moves $1.30 in one day, it is more volatile than a stock that typically moves $1.30 in a week.

Equity price movement benefits from this higher volatility, so you must pay a higher premium for the associated option. This is why an option contract on one $80 stock might cost $3, while an option contract on another $80 stock might cost $5 to purchase. The price is higher because the probability of a premium increase within the lifespan of the option for the faster-moving underlying equity is higher. Your chance of making more money faster grows with higher volatility.

The optimum time to purchase an option contract occurs while a stock is in a time of calm (low volatility) when the option premium is lower than it might be at other times, and then sell when it has increased in value and moves into a period of higher volatility where premiums increase rapidly and sell before they start to decline.

Okay, let's move on to some additional discussion of the stock market.

HOW DO I KNOW WHICH OPTION TO BUY?

This is one of the first questions new option traders ask. Everyone wants to know how to decide what stock options to buy. The obvious answer is to only purchase options that are expected to achieve a substantial return on your investment. And how do you know that?

Once you understand the principles of option trading, then it is time to learn how to carefully consider the underlying equity upon which the option is based. I will get to that a little later, I promise. I will provide a complete discussion about a method to select great underlying equities and discuss other selection strategies. Clearly, that is at the heart of this discussion.

LIMITING RISK

Let's discuss the issue of risk and limiting risk because it's closely connected to making good choices in selecting ripe, sound equities as underlying assets for your option positions.

One basic way to reduce risk is by purchasing options on only the very best underlying equities - what I call high Average True Range (ATR) equities. ATR is how much an equity moves each day on average. I look for equities that move consistently 2% or higher. This consistency is a key to limiting risk.

Average True Range (ATR) is an indicator that can be placed on a chart. The indicator will point to a value of the average move of the equity. Based on the chart below, CVS Health Corp.'s (CVS) ATR is 1.45. Two percent (2% or .02) of CVS's stock price is 1.31. An average move of 1.45 per day is well above 2%, so it would be a good day-trading candidate.

Notice the image below is a daily time frame chart because we want to know its average move per day.

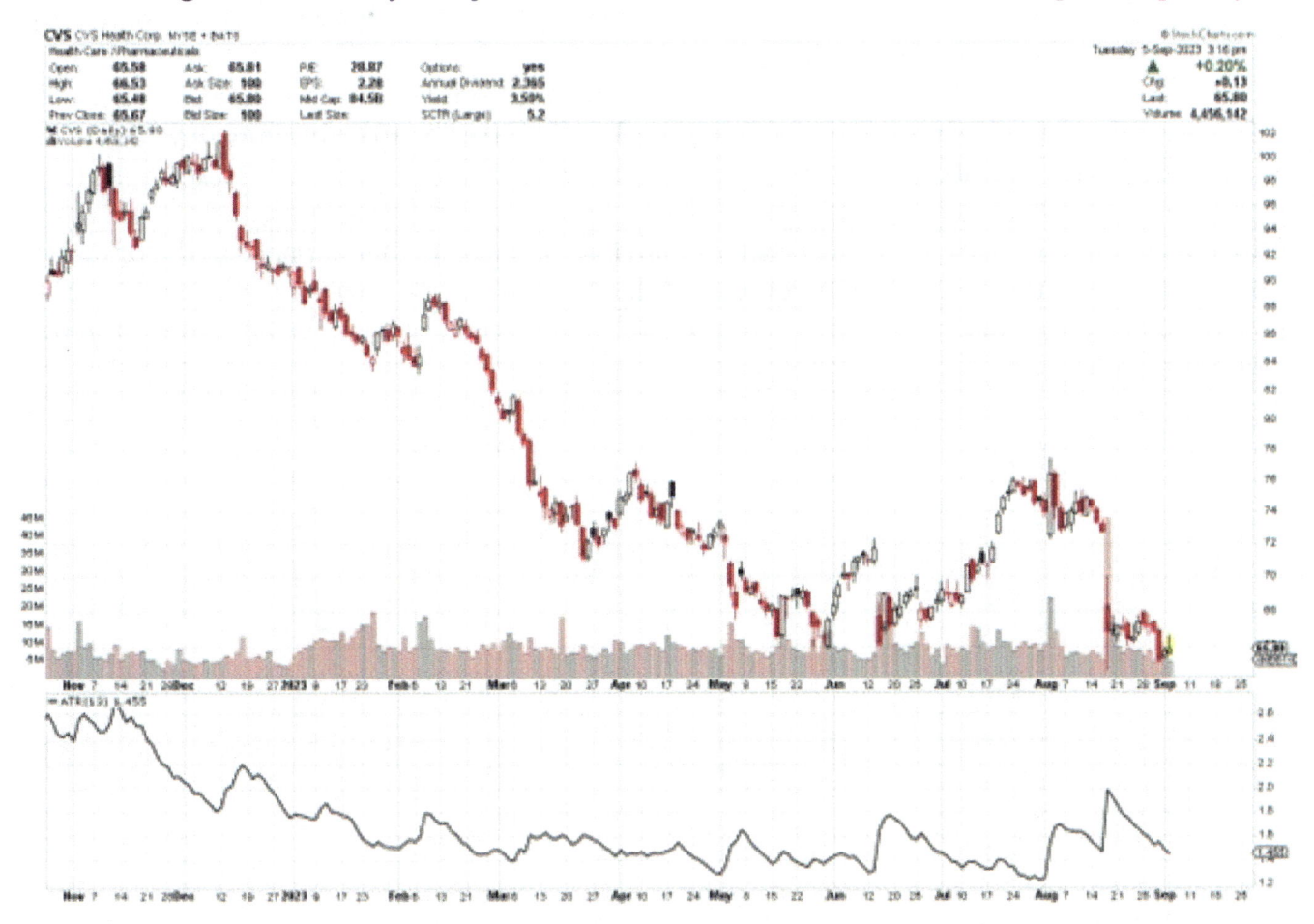

Figure 3 - Courtesy of StockCharts.com

You can manually perform this calculation on equities that are of interest to you, or you can collect the symbols from one of my routinely updated public charts that are kept on Stockcharts.com at this link. https://stockcharts.com/public/1366433

This list is a collection of 30-minute charts, but you can make a list of the symbols that have been verified as 2%+ movers that offer options, and then create your own candidate list. The hard work has been done for you.

Okay, besides candidate selection, what potential risks must you consider?

Overall, options are less risky than stocks because the amount that can be lost is limited, and you know the total amount you can lose the moment you choose to purchase an option. Let me say that again, you can never lose more than your initial investment, and you decide what that will be.

The leverage of options is an all-important characteristic. Those who buy options limit their risk but have potentially unlimited reward.

Let's say you decide to buy an option from the option chain below for Coca Cola (KO).

For this example, you'll purchase a Call option. This is an August option on Coca Cola's stock, when the stock price is $59.31, and a strike you select the $60 strike, which is $0.69 out-of-the-money.

This option will cost us $0.30 (Ask Price) per share. Since options are in lots of 100 shares, the total will be $30 per contract. They are moderately priced. Let's make it worthwhile and buy 10 contracts or 1,000 shares for a total of $300.

With options trading, this is the most that you can lose no matter what happens to the underlying stock ($300). Coca Cola's stock can become worthless, and what you have risked is $300 to control $59,310.00 of Coca Cola's stock for a given period. In this case, September 22, 2023, or about 3 weeks from now.

CHANGE YOUR FUTURE

Symbol	Name						Implied Vol		Historical Vol		Price		Change
KO	COCA-COLA CO						0.117		0.146		59.31		-0.52

September 22, 2023 - Calls							September 22, 2023 - Puts						
Symbol	Bid	Ask	Price	TPrice	Volume	OI NS	Strike Symbol	Bid	Ask	Price	TPrice	Volume	OI NS
No data							51.00 KO	0.00	0.95	0.75	0.75	0	5 W
No data							52.00 KO	0.00	0.03	0.04	0.01	0	94 W
No data							53.00 KO	0.02	0.03	0.02	0.00	0	132 W
No data							54.00 KO	0.03	0.04	0.03	0.00	2	262 W
KO	4.25	4.45	4.77	5.19	1	7 W	55.00 KO	0.05	0.06	0.03	0.00	0	41 W
KO	3.35	3.50	3.45	4.21	10	101 W	56.00 KO	0.08	0.10	0.09	0.01	11	47 W
KO	2.35	2.48	3.34	3.26	0	51 W	57.00 KO	0.15	0.17	0.16	0.04	18	183 W
KO	1.48	1.57	1.45	2.36	12	5 W	58.00 KO	0.32	0.34	0.32	0.13	48	599 W
KO	0.68	0.80	0.75	1.57	70	61 W	59.00 KO	0.64	0.69	0.65	0.33	94	300 W
KO	0.25	0.30	0.28	0.94	195	101 W	60.00 KO	1.23	1.29	1.24	0.68	27	386 W
KO	0.06	0.10	0.10	0.50	474	597 W	61.00 KO	2.00	2.27	2.12	1.22	40	70 W
KO	0.03	0.05	0.05	0.23	443	1683 W	62.00 KO	2.98	3.15	3.13	1.94	1	46 W
KO	0.02	0.03	0.03	0.09	5	672 W	63.00 KO	3.95	4.20	2.41	2.78	0	9 W
KO	0.00	0.03	0.02	0.03	9	168 W	64.00 No data						
KO	0.00	0.03	0.02	0.01	0	125 W	65.00 KO	5.95	6.20	6.14	4.67	2	0 W
KO	0.00	0.03	0.01	0.00	0	3 W	66.00 No data						
KO	0.00	0.75	0.03	0.00	0	1 W	67.00 No data						
KO	0.00	0.75	0.18	0.00	0	1 W	68.00 No data						

Figure 4 - Courtesy of optionistics.com

As a stock increases or decreases in price, it seldom does so in one fell swoop. It ticks up and down in penny/nickel/dime increments. At any point, if you decide that the market hasn't cooperated with your option choice, you can sell, cutting your loss short.

In such a case, as in our example, the stock price of Coca Cola's stock might rise, say, $2.10 to $61.41, but, for the sake of our example, let's say it had dropped $2.10. In turn, your option has become less valuable. Maybe its value now has dropped from $0.30 to $0.21 for each of the 100 units of stock in each of your option contracts, or $21 for each of your 10 contracts (1,000 shares) or $210 in value.

43

You have the choice of selling and taking a loss of $90 or holding on to the option. You bought a longer expiration and have several weeks before expiration. If your chart reading tells you this is a reaction to the news, and just a bit of profit taking by the big players, the stock is apt to continue its trend up. Or you may decide it is time to cut your losses.

Just so you see how the Bid and Ask premiums work, let's go back and say price did go up to $61.41 (a 20%+ move up in price happens; that is a nice move likely over a week+) and your premium rose by 50% (we will talk more about premiums and Delta after a bit.) So, your premium rose $1.05 (half of the $2.10 move in price) ($0.30 paid premium plus $1.05 = $1.35) or $135 for each contract, and you bought 10 contracts or a total of $1,350. You paid $300 for the 10 contracts and made $1,050 profit above that price.

Part of the *Change Your Future'* success strategy involves maximizing profit and minimizing loss. You'll learn when to sell and walk away and when to hold because you have time, and this is what your technical analysis tells you. Finally, you'll learn when to take profits off the table.

ONE MORE WAY TO LIMIT RISK

If you're worried that you will miss a pullback or the market dropping (or rising in the case of a Put) and leave yourself no time to get out of a position, there is a protective device in place for that—a safety net. This device allows you to set "stops" on your options, which will close the position if it drops below the point set. We will go over this in more detail later.

The only exception to this working effectively is when the equity drops beyond that point the moment the market opens. Then, it is as if the price jumps over the stop before it can be triggered. Like a child's game of hopscotch, the price can leap over the stop as it gaps down or up.

TRADE WITH CONFIDENCE

Learning how to trade options in a systematic way leads to confident investing, and confidence is a key to wealth building. I see people of all ages, educational backgrounds, and locales taking part in options and changing their viewpoint on trading. I also see these people come to realize and appreciate that they are part of an elite group involved in taking controlled risks.

These same people have stepped up to take charge of their financial futures. I'm sure you would agree that deadliest-catch fishermen or race-car drivers have risky occupations. But imagine a crew of these fishermen or drivers getting together. Do you think they gulp down coffee and agonize about the risks they're taking? Not likely. These risks are no longer foremost in their minds. They have learned through techniques and skill how to minimize those risks. These workers are much more likely to discuss a new tool that helps them perform even better, and they're likely to hang out with those who are successful.

By the time you finish this book and perhaps, decide to step on your trading path, you will see the opportunities and advantages of seeking out other option traders, either through chatrooms, (I'll post a link later to a service) or through face-to-face trading groups in your community.

Like the fishermen and race-car drivers, you'll share the tools and techniques you've found to become a successful option trader who is building their wealth.

Joy Reminder:

Put aside a little time for being positive and happy today. By doing so, you might be able to ease the sense of obligation, negativity, and pressure you feel. You might think of ways to bring a little lightness into your normal routine, like taking short breaks throughout the day to read something humorous, chat with a buddy, take a shower, or head outside to enjoy the sunshine. By periodically shifting your perspective to positivity or focusing on more pleasurable activities, you will be able to joyfully concentrate on your tasks and complete them with ease.

Check out a one-word attitude change. Negative to positive: You are not lonely; you are enjoying private time.

THE POWER OF CONNECTION

With that connection we discussed between what you believe in your heart and what you know in your mind, you are capable of more than you know. Knowing everything is always for your benefit, even if it doesn't feel like it now, is a major step along the personal fulfilment path. Remember the story I mentioned at the start of this book about the flood that wiped out the family business and, yet, that storm and flood turned out to be the most amazing gift that has kept on giving and has brought me to you right now, where I am sharing that same gift of option trading.

Contrary to popular thinking, being worthy isn't something you earn, it is something you recognize within yourself. And once you do, you won't be able to think, speak, or behave in any other way than if what you most wanted was meant to be. You were born worthy and have just forgotten.

Reaffirming to yourself about who you are and what you want from life will recondition your mind, rewire your brain, and give you the ability to create things for your own good from your belief.

This allows you to alter the way you act with others, and to know and expect to be successful in option trading. Dr, Dispenza recommends that you "replace stressful situations with positive experiences that will give you energy, fill your spirit, and leave you with a sense of wholeness, connection, and unity. Your brain may think, but when you operate from the heart, it knows!"

NAVIGATING CHANGE YOUR FUTURE

For many people, chart reading—the nitty-gritty of learning to trade and interpreting the price movement of a business, a company—is also a stage that may cause fear to rise to the surface, at least to some degree. Specifically, I've noticed that too many people become fearful about "messing up". They usually feel this way because all the pieces of this riddle aren't in place yet.

Even so, most people can be very hard on themselves. They've become programmed to expect a great deal from themselves, even instant understanding, and immediate perfection. These high expectations can lead to fear of making a mistake.

Please understand that if you're afraid to make a mistake, you're destined to interfere with the process that will ultimately make you a successful trader. Blame it on conditioning or the pressure so many people feel to "do it all." It seems this is a tough lesson for many would-be traders. Yet, far from being the end of the world, mistakes are your ticket to new understanding.

Don't fear mistakes. Use them as feedback. So many innovators credit mistakes as contributing to their most worthwhile successes. Earlier I shared how my erroneous thinking had locked me into a life of believing I wasn't enough. Sometimes mistakes can be life changing in other positive ways, such as the day I accidentally reversed my chart indicators and, on that day, discovered the CYF (Change Your Future) pattern you will be learning in the next section or two.

Mistakes can lead to greatness, but only if we stop judging them as negative. By the end of these next sections, you will be able to read and interpret stock charts. You'll be able to practice trading without losing a dime. Some of your choices will be winners and some losers, but each choice will be a teacher, putting you on the path to leveraging your wealth to a higher level.

The chart images posted within the book cover various time periods over the past. They were selected to best illustrate a chart concept or pattern, not to show the most current price information.

The Change Your Future patterns, which I have also called P3 patterns in other materials, were discovered over a period of years. Specific details and their meaning were revealed in layers over time. Through viewing tens of thousands of charts, I developed this strategy based on the equity's price life cycle.

It was recently brought to my attention that the CYF patterns are truly unique in the world of trading. Sure, there are strategies that use a variety of indicators and oscillators that show what a stock's price has done recently. A few predict that there may ultimately be a swing in the opposite direction, but there are none that can be used on EVERY equity and on EVERY time frame chart without exception to show what stage it is experiencing within a price's life cycle, a key component to my strategy.

Just like humans, one person may experience a slightly longer toddler or adolescent stage or pass away prematurely, but overall, we all go through very similar and predicable life stages. The life stages of a stock with slight variations can be identified ahead of time, well before they happen. CYF patterns are exceptional and truly unique.

By the time you move through this information, you will realize you are being given an incredible, very flexible gift. It will never break or wear out. You will be able to use it forever and apply it to any time frame chart, not just a ten-minute chart used in our Change Your Future short-term strategy.

SCANNING THE HORIZON

If you have considered my criteria of using Average True Range (ATR) to identify good trade candidates or visited the link I shared, then you should have a good list of potential stocks. Now you'll run them through technical screens to locate specific patterns.

These technical indicators show where the stock is in its market life cycle, and they explain what the chart is telling you about the equity's price.

Once I've explained the individual indicators, we will put it all together, step by step. Try not to feel overwhelmed. I will explain and layer the information so that it will gradually begin to fall into place for you. Here are some facts to remember:

- As well as giving a picture of individual equities, stock charts contain an abundance of information about what is happening in the overall market.

- Charts can be set up for different time periods: daily, weekly, monthly, yearly and even shorter periods of time, including hourly, thirty-minute, ten-minute, and minute-by-minute.
- Each chart creates a picture of the equity's position within the market, in its sector ranking, and where it stands in its own life cycle. Various indicators help tell the stock's story. We are going to cover the details in stages a little at a time.

Information that can be gleaned from the chart below includes the following and will all be explained as you proceed:

- Daily highs and lows
- Open and close prices
- Volume
- 6 months trading average
- Buying pressure and selling pressure
- Patterns created by candlesticks
- Areas of support and resistance

Figure 5 - Courtesy of StockCharts.com

Let's do a quick review of the details. If you want even more details, they are covered in depth in *Exploring Your Options* available on Amazon. As you read across the top of the chart, it tells you to which stock, ETF, or Index this chart refers. Below the name tells you its sector and industry. In this case, we are looking at Deere & Co. (DE) in the Industrial sector and Commercial Vehicles industry. Many of us think of this company as John Deere.

Following the data from left to right, you see the upper area also shows the date, the open, high, low, closing price for the previous day, last price, volume, and the change in dollars and percent of stock's total price.

Beneath this bar to the left tells you that this is a daily chart, and it repeats the last price and the volume.

You may recall that time runs horizontally from left to right at the bottom of the chart, with the left being the furthest in the past, right being the most recent. The last candle would be what happened in the most recent session for this period.

DE's chart indicates that you are looking at a Daily chart, covering the company's price history over a ten-month period. The price scale is displayed on the right side of the chart.

Across the bottom of the main chart, the bars show volume, usually two bars of different colors, red and gray. Red signifies the times when greater selling took place, while the gray bar shows a buying period, meaning more stock was bought than sold. Notice that the volume's color and size correspond to the color of the candlesticks running through the middle of the chart that depicts price.

You will note that a large volume bar doesn't necessarily create a large price candle. If you look back and study Deere's chart above for March through May, you have a couple super large selling (red) volume bars. In May, there are large red selling volume bars that tie into the downward price movement and eventually, the rise started in June and continued into July. I am sure you get the gist. The volume is the strength of the daily move.

CHART READING CAN BE AN ART

I am going to touch on chart reading. This is one area that all traders are continually refining. Not only do charts vary in their time frames, but they can also be set up in a variety of ways, depending on your trade strategy.

Let's touch on the basics using a chart for the technology company, Nvidia (NVDA). (See below.)

I am not going to repeat all the chart details unless I feel it needs to be emphasized.

The price scale is displayed on the right side of the chart. As you move your eye from left to right studying the candlesticks, you are moving from the oldest to the most recent price information.

Again, across the bottom of the chart, the bars show volume, red and gray. Red signifies the times when greater selling took place, while the gray bar shows a buying period, meaning more stock was bought than sold. Notice that the volume's color and size correspond to the candlesticks running through the middle of the chart that depict price. You will also note that a large volume bar doesn't necessarily create a large price candle.

You will need to understand the candlestick, or candle, which is an important technical symbol on charts in general. They are designed to tell a concise story. You will see candles in red, black, and hollow (white and red).

Candlesticks provide information about the average price of the underlying equity. They reflect the price action over the course of the market session for the period selected (in our case, daily). If it is a daily chart, the candle reflects the movement that day from opening to closing bell. If the chart is a weekly chart, then the candle reflects an accumulation of the week's activity throughout that week.

Figure 6 - Courtesy of StockCharts.com

Thin lines above and below the body of the candle represent the high/low range of the session and are called shadows, or wicks.

How the price movement unfolded for the period, or the relationship between the opening and closing price, is vital information and forms the essence of candlestick symbols. Actual candlesticks are not green and red, but are black and red. Below the current candlesticks on right side, the volume bars on the left, there are several bearish (selling) and on the right, the last two are bullish (buying).

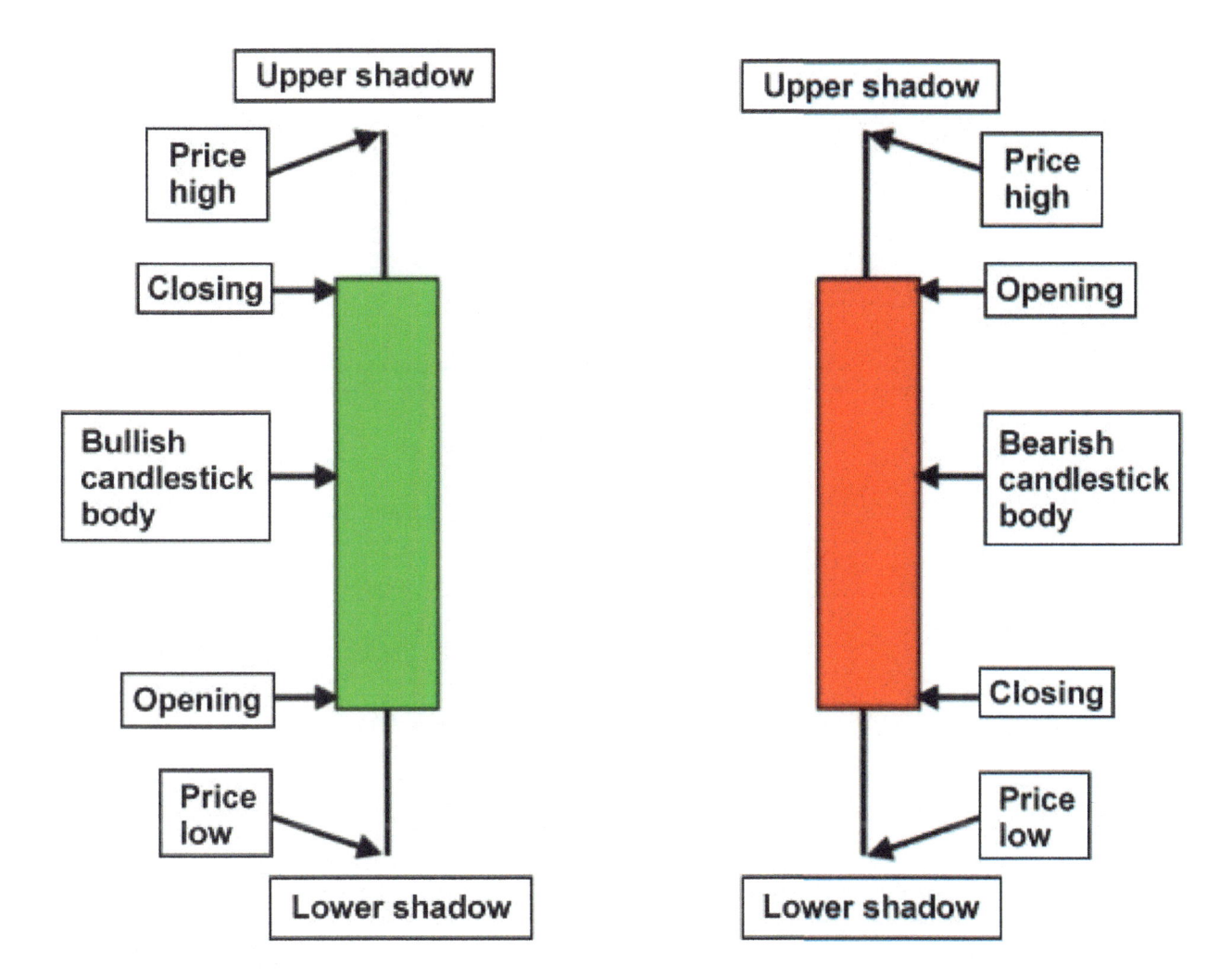

Figure 7 - Courtesy of LiteFinance.org

Notice on the chart above, there are hollow black candles, solid black, hollow red, and solid red. Hollow candlesticks indicate that the *closing price was greater than the open price.* Likely, buying has taken place, driving the price up. Filled candlesticks indicate that the *closing price is less than the opening price.* This probably means that selling has taken place, which drops the price.

If the candlestick is hollow black, this means that the closing price was greater than the previous closing price. Conversely, a red candle indicates that the closing price is less than the previous close.

A longer candle indicates more buying and selling, and short candles reflect little price movement.

Long solid black candles often indicate a bearish period, where the stock opened near its high price and closed near its low. As we discussed earlier, this may be an indication that the stock is moving into oversold territory. A long black candle after a long period of advancement of an equity can suggest that a turning point is on the horizon or mark an area of future resistance.

Long hollow black (white in the middle) candles reflect bullish activity, where the stock opened near its low and closed near its high. This may indicate that the stock is moving into overbought territory. A long white candle after a long period of decline for a stock can indicate that turn may happen in-the-near-future, or it can mark an area of future support.

Shadows, or wicks on candlesticks can also be long or short. The upper shadow marks the high price of the period, and the lower shadow marks the low. If the shadows are long, prices moved in a wide range beyond opening and closing prices. If they are short, prices hover near the opening and closing prices.

CANDLES TELL THEIR OWN STORY

Shadows/wicks are not always of equal size, and this tells a story about trading for that period. Candles measure the market emotion around a stock and the impact of this sentiment on the price movement.

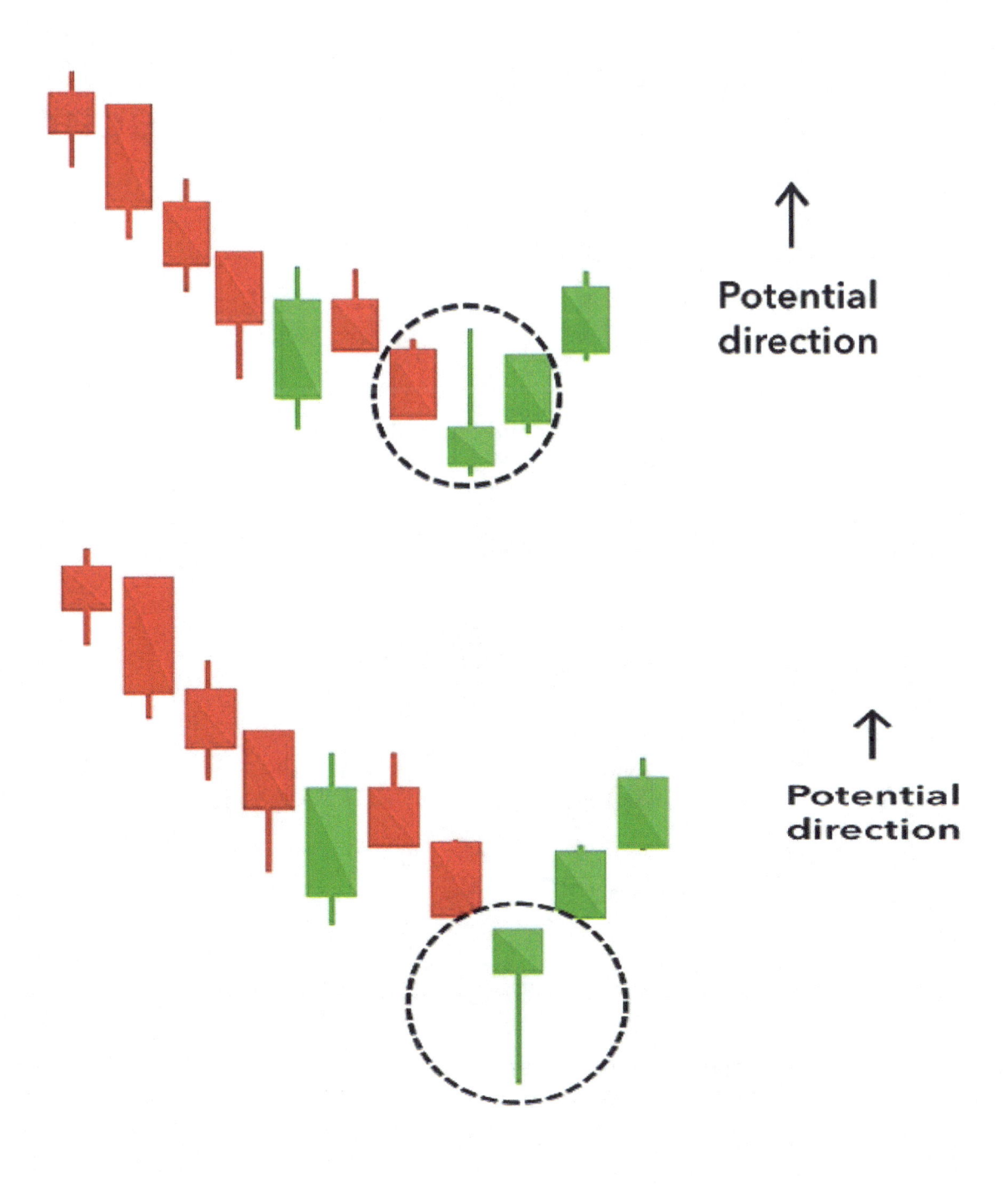

↑ Potential direction

↑ Potential direction

Figure 8 - Courtesy of IG.com

An Inverse Hammer Candle has a long upper shadow, and a short lower shadow reflects a day where buyers pushed prices up; however, the volume of selling drove prices down, closing below the open. A short upper shadow and a long lower shadow reflect a day where active selling drove prices down, but interested buyers purchased enough that the close was above the open. It is called a Hammer.

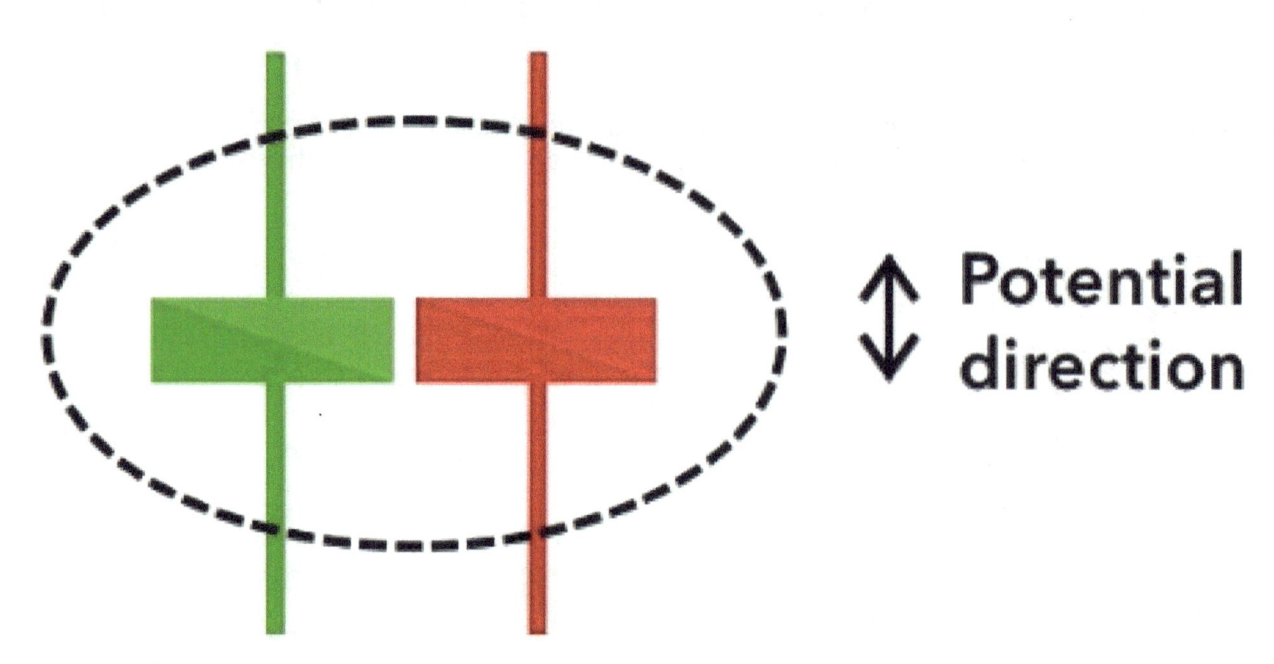

Figure 9- Courtesy of IG.com

Candlesticks with small bodies and long upper and lower shadows are called Spinning Tops. (Can you see how they look like one?) These show significant movement in price in terms of highs and lows, but the range of trading from open to close was tight, marking little actual change. This often represents indecision on the part of buyers and sellers, where neither was able to take control. This could indicate a possible reversal of the trend is coming.

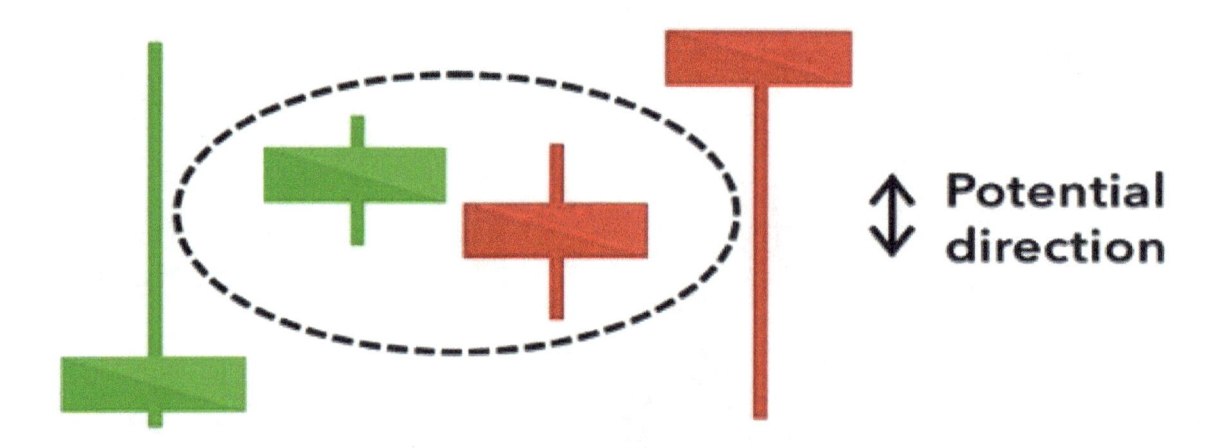

Figure 10- Courtesy of IG.com

Candles with extremely short bodies or even lines are called Doji. They show that the stock opened and closed at nearly the same price. The length of the shadows will indicate the pressure of the buyers and sellers in terms of price movement throughout the day. Shadows can be long, indicating there was a lot of movement, but in the end, price opened and closed nearly even. These really indicate a stalemate.

There are many strategies that compare a Doji candle to preceding candles to determine a trend. For example, after a long black candle, which typically indicates a decline, a Doji would suggest that a change in trend may be on the way. The pressure to sell may be ending, and the bears may be losing control of the decline. Other signals would be needed to confirm the reversal, such as a gap up or a long white candle. The reverse is also an indication of a trend change. A Doji after a long white candle would suggest that buying pressure is ending. A true reversal could be confirmed by a gap down or a long black candle.

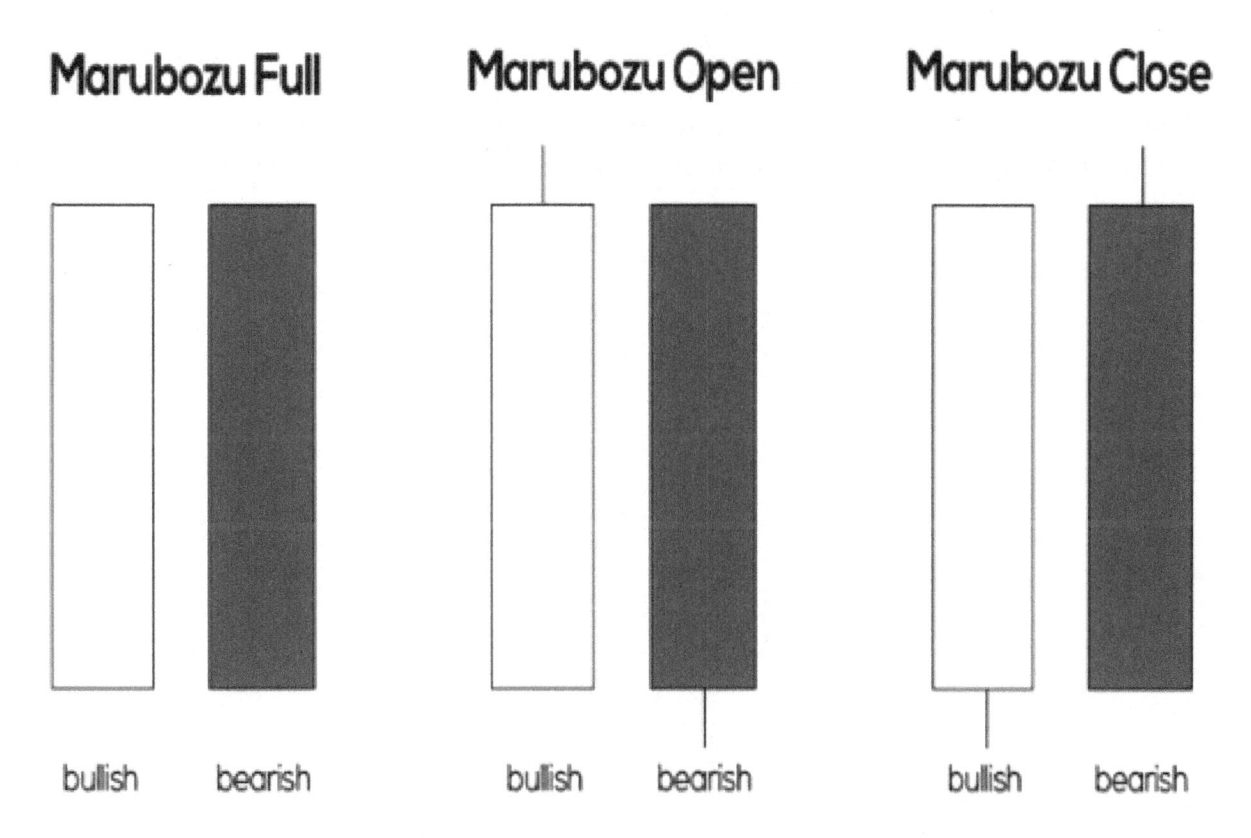

Marubozu Full   Marubozu Open   Marubozu Close

bullish bearish   bullish bearish   bullish bearish

Figure 11- Courtesy of IG.com

It is possible for a candle not to have any shadows or wicks or small ones on open or close. These are referred to as Marubozu candles. The high and the low are shown as the open and the close. A hollow (white) Marubozu indicates that the open was the low for the day, and the high was the close. This would suggest that the buyers (bulls) were in control for most of the day. Conversely, a black Marubozu shows that the open was the high for the day, and the low was at the close. This would suggest that sellers (bears) oversaw the movement of the day.

While candlesticks provide clues about interest and emotion surrounding a particular equity, their information is limited to highs and lows, and open and close. Unless you are using an intraday chart, they do not reflect the actual price movements over the course of the day. Trend directions are more accurately confirmed using trendlines, moving averages, and other forms of technical analysis on longer-term charts that we will touch on below.

It is important to remember that candlesticks provide information about the average price of the underlying equity. They reflect the price action over the course of the market session for the time selected (in the chart above, daily).

Many of the charts in this book will be 10-minute charts where each candle will reflect price movement over a 10-minute period.

The last candlestick (on right) can be a partial period if you are viewing it before the closing bell or the end of the period. These candles are also usually two colors, often red and black, and are either solid or hollow.

Even though much information can be gleaned from candlestick symbols, they don't represent the sequence of events between the open and close, only the ending relationship between the open and close.

The high and low of the period are obvious (top and bottoms of the candlestick including wicks), but the candlesticks cannot tell you which came first. That means that this information doesn't mean as much in your decision to purchase an option as information about where the stock closed at the end of the period.

SUPPORT AND RESISTANCE

As we begin to talk about the lifecycle of an equity, which is essential to the Know Your Future Option strategy, it is important to understand two concepts that every chart can reveal – support and resistance. Successful traders can spot areas of support and resistance as they look at a chart. Two overlays that I add to a chart, which help to identify areas of support and resistance, are EMAs and Pivot Points. We will discuss these in the next sections.

An easy way to think of support and resistance is as floors and ceilings. The floor is called support, and the overhead ceiling is called resistance. Support reflects the supply of this stock, and resistance reflects demand. You can easily think and remember this by thinking about gravity and the support needed to hold things up. Resistance is a barrier that prevents or inhibits something from going higher like a ceiling.

So, these are the two most important principles involved in understanding chart analysis, and subsequently profitable trading:

- Support is a price level to which prices "tend" to descend to but not break through.
- Resistance is a price level to which prices "tend" to ascend to but not pass through.

The key word here is "tend". These imagined lines of floors and ceilings hold through most price movement whether it is daily or intraday charts. It takes something out of the ordinary to happen to break through the support and resistance lines. These could include reporting earnings growth or a large loss in a major contributing company, a major lawsuit against the company, an overall stock market reversal, FDA refused drug approval, sector rotation, or the end of an extended up/down trend.

The shorter the time frame chart, the less effort it takes to break through these support and resistance levels. It makes sense to realize that an earnings report that comes out every quarter would have a major effect on a weekly or daily chart, and yet breaks of support and resistance on an intra-day chart like a 10-minute chart doesn't need a major catalyst like a quarterly earnings report and a Fed meeting for support and resistance to be tested and eventually break into a new trend direction.

Of course, when these major events do happen, the price on a 10-minute chart is apt to have a significant move, so it is wise to be aware of these planned events. A minor test or break of support or resistance on a 10-minute or intraday chart can happen after morning open when the market decides on its morning direction. The daily lunch period can be a time of indecision or the chart leveling out or drifting slowly lower. The afternoon session often resumes the morning's direction up or down and, then late in the trading day, there can be a slight shift as market-makers shake up price, enticing traders to sell and close their trades, either taking profit or closing a losing trade.

Support and resistance lines gain strength as the time frame lengthens. For example, support and resistance lines in a 30-minute chart might hold for a day or two; in a 60-minute chart, they might remain unbreakable for a few days; a daily chart's lines might be steadfast for a week or two. Since we will be focusing on 10-minute charts for our instruction in the Change Your Future strategy, being aware of these support and resistance areas is important because they slow or stop price, but it does so for a shorter period.

You can spot areas of support and resistance without any fancy formulas. They are the tops of peaks, the low point of troughs, and any time there are several candles that consolidate at one price level. These areas can be seen in EMA lines, previous highs and lows, and Pivot Point lines.

By watching for levels of support and resistance, you can find natural trade entry and exit points that go beyond the patterns you are going to focus on in this strategy. They also provide logical exit points. You could consider purchasing an option when a stock starts to come up off the support floor. You then watch closely, being ready to sell as the stock's price comes close to the ceiling resistance before your option's expiration date.

While it's possible that the stock might break through resistance to then go higher, you will stand ready to sell in case the stock doesn't have the thrust-power to do so. In other words, you'll be ready to sell once the stock hits resistance and is likely to descend back toward support.

Support and resistance can also be used for setting price targets that are established at the time that you enter a trade. Right from the get-go, you establish your expectation of where it is going to go to be a profitable trade. You are declaring your intention or expectation for the trade while you are following the indicators in the CYF strategy. Remember, believing is seeing. Price will often hit your expected level.

One of the hardest lessons traders must learn is that it isn't important if you earn every possible cent in a trade. If you earn a profit, it is money you didn't have yesterday and is something to be proud and thankful for. You followed your plan and earned a profit. Congratulate yourself! No regrets allowed. Remember money problems are mindset problems. Change your mind! Be positive and grateful.

EXPONENTIAL MOVING AVERAGES— EMAS

A type of line of support and resistance is shown with moving averages. There are two types of moving averages – simple and exponential. I prefer the Exponential Moving Averages (EMA). These lines can act as ceilings (resistance) and floors (support). Once price gets through a resistance line, that line then can become a future support area. And, when a support line is broken through, it can become a resistance line on the way back up.

When you create a chart, you have the choice of time references to set for the Exponential Moving Average. I most often reference the 8-day, 13-day, 21-day, 55-day, 144-day and 233-day EMAs. For the purposes of this book, I am keeping it simple and only using the 8,13, 21- and 233-EMAs. These are Fibonacci numbers, which I love. I will tell you more about Fibonacci in an upcoming section.

Your chart must be set to a Daily time frame to get Daily EMAs. If you were to have your chart on a 60-minute time frame, your EMAs would represent hours, not days. The 8-EMA on a 60-minute chart would be 8 units of 60 minutes. The 8-EMA on a 10-minute chart would be 80 minutes.

For the Change Your Future short-term day-trading strategy, you will be using super short-term time frames with the intent of being in and out of trades quickly as soon as the price move ends. Therefore, we will start moving in that direction by applying the 8-EMA, 13-EMA, 21-EMA, and 233-EMA to a 10-minute chart. This will also provide you with the opportunity to see the complete cycle of the CYF strategy, which can be used in any time frame.

The 8-EMA on the 10-minute chart will be showing you an average of 80 minutes (an hour and 20-minutes), the 13-minute is showing 130 minutes (2 hours and 10 minutes), 21-EMA is 210 minutes (about 3.5 hours), and 233-EMA 2,333 minutes (just under 39 hours or just over 5 days.)

Price trades above the 233-EMA 70% of the time and below the 233-EMA 30%, so having this EMA on the chart, though price doesn't cross above or below very often, helps to know if the general bias is bullish or bearish.

In the left-hand corner of a chart, the notation will tell you which type of moving averages (MAs) or Exponential Moving Averages (EMAs) are used and the price that moving average reached.

When an equity is trading above any of the moving averages that are incorporated within the chart, watch what happens when the price reaches the support of the EMA. In the same way, if it is trading below, watch what happens when it reaches the resistance of the EMA. Again, I think of these as ceilings and floors. It can be hard to move through a ceiling or break through a floor.

Support as a floor can restrict prices from dropping further. It is not impossible to break through, but it inhibits that movement, and it will often bounce from there. Resistance as a ceiling can restrict prices from going higher. It is not impossible for price to break through, but it also inhibits that continued movement, and it will often pull back from there.

On the chart below, you are zeroing in and getting a close-up view of the price action of the last six days on the right side of Zoom's chart, the end of August 31st through September 8th. September 8th is a Friday. The chart gives the equivalent of a full week.

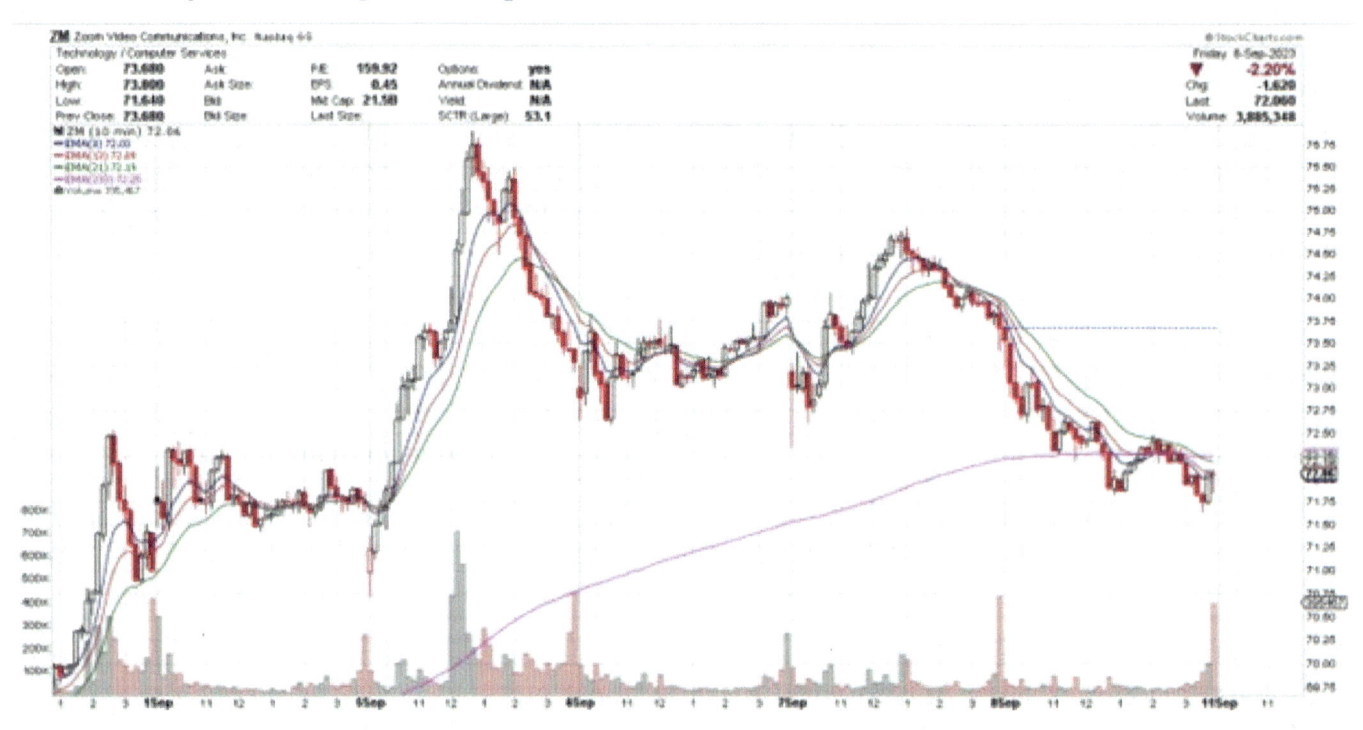

Figure 12- Courtesy of Stockcharts.com

If you set up your charts through Stockcharts.com or some other charting service, the EMA lines will be different colors. Stockcharts' charts are blue, red, and green for the short term EMAs that you will be using, making them easy to follow and identify. The 233 EMA is pink. The EMA lines that have been added to Zoom's candlestick chart above depict the price movement for five days. These lines add additional information for your consideration.

Now each candlestick represents the price movement of a 10-minute period.

Notice the times the candles slipped down to the 21-EMA like on August 31st but the 8 and 13-EMAs dipped down but didn't cross. They moved up from under the 21-EMA on the 6th, down again on the 7th and up on the 8th to touch the 21-EMA but did not cross.

The EMA lines become areas of support and resistance. Ideally, in an uptrend, you want the 8-EMA (blue) to be on top of the 13-EMA and 21-EMA (red). This strong up-trending pattern is shown on the chart from September 5th at 9:30 am (off to the left) until about 12:50 pm on September 5th. Strong downward movement happened when the EMA lines crossed down around 2:00 pm on the 7th and continued down until close on the 8th.

Notice, as the price was rising along the chart, how many times the 8-EMA/13EMA lines and candlesticks dipped down toward the support of the 21-EMA and, like a floor, it got close and then popped up again. Price also broke through. As price was falling, there were numerous areas where the 8-EMA tested resistance (ceiling) from the underside to break through the ceiling and was repelled. The 8-EMA is making a new attempt as I captured this image.

Notice, too, the 233-EMA. There was one cross between 2:00 pm and 2:30 pm on the 8th. While price and the EMAs dropped back below the 233-EMA so the bias or trend is bearish. When the shorter term EMAs crossed below the 233-EMA, the bias or trend was bearish. Above it is bullish.

Eventually, we will dig into price/volume anomalies or disagreement, and it is early to get into that subject, but, for just a second, let me draw your attention back to the first/opening candle on September 1st on the chart above. It is a long solid black candle (long wicks on upside and down and small black body). Solid black and hollow red candles are rare. There are only three solid black candles on this chart, all on the same day and no hollow red ones.

A solid black candle is created when the creation of the candle's body starts at the top, and it closes lower at the bottom of the candle. Most candles start at the bottom of the body of the candle and close higher if they are a bullish black hollow candle. Bearish red candles start at the top and close lower. It makes sense, bullish candles should normally increase in value, and bearish should decrease in value. The anomalies are when a bullish candle remains positive (up) but closes lower than it started. In the same way, a bearish candle remains bearish (down), but it closes higher than it started.

Now look at the volume bar underneath the solid black candle. It is a tall volume bar on the chart; not the tallest, but tall for the size of the candle. Now you would expect that, to create a tall volume bar, the candle would have been a large hollow black candle to reflect the buying taking place. In this case, the candle shows selling and buying took place after the opening. They don't agree or support each other. This suggests that, even though there was a large upward price movement, there was selling taking place to offset the buying on the volume bar.

Price and volume bars should support the information each is sharing. When these anomalies take place, they are warning signals that something is happening under the surface that we aren't seeing and that we should pay special attention. This gives you a glimpse into the market-makers' world.

We will dig into price and volume in another section, but I wanted to share since I spotted this great example on this chart.

Joy Reminder:

It can be beneficial to periodically adopt the mindset of a child and approach life and even its complications with a sense of wonder and awe. By doing so, we can infuse even the simplest moments with joy and gratitude. As adults, we often feel the need to be serious and responsible as we go about our daily routines. While this certainly can be wise, we can also benefit from putting aside our seriousness and adopting a more youthful, open mindset.

As we explore our world and appreciate each new moment with a sense of awe, we begin to discover new opportunities for excitement and joy. We begin to feel happier and more carefree, even when we focus on more serious adult activities. By embracing a light, child-like approach and choosing to see the world with new eyes, you can turn the smallest tasks into

WENDY KIRKLAND

something magical.

YOU DECIDE WHO YOU ARE AND WHAT YOU WANT

Regularly remind yourself that you are an active creator, who continually draws everything into your life, depending on your thoughts, expectations, drive, goals, and emotions. Also, remember that your divine self doesn't know negative words like "can't", "don't", or "hate", all it understands is your focused attention and what you know and believe.

So, imagine what happens when you say or think over and over, I don't want to fail. When I am released, I don't want to be incarcerated again. I don't want to be broke all the time. I don't want to be late. I don't want to screw this up. It is my last or only chance. I don't want to mess this up like I usually do. I hate mean people. I despise disrespect. I hate it when my car doesn't run well. I loathe feeling rushed. I hate it when I can't afford what I want to buy. I hate it when people are mean to me. I hate it when the store doesn't have what I need. I despise it when people disappoint me. I hate negativity. Lord, I'll hate it when I lose a trade.

There is nothing wrong with your mind. Your mind is a tool, and it runs automatically. The problem comes when it continually tells you there is lack in your world – lack of money, lack of friends, lack of success, lack of health, lack of love, lack of support, lack of abilities, or resourcefulness, and lack of resources in general (everything), so there isn't enough to go around.

The mind can be a troublemaker, a trickster. If you believe your mind rather than know you oversee your thoughts, recognizing it as being the creative one, then what it brings up repeatedly, adding strength each time it comes to mind, is exactly what you'll experience. It will reinforce or add solidity to that thought being true. It becomes what you "know". It is a vicious circle because knowing is seeing. Or put another way, if you have a list of things you don't want, you are likely to see many items on that list show up. Your wishes and focused attention are being granted.

Change your mind. Dwell on what you truly want, what you want to experience. Know it will happen in the perfect moment.

FIBONACCI PATTERNS IN EVERYTHING

Before I get too far along into chart reading, our trading patterns, and the rules covering our option trades, I want to step back and discuss how the Fibonacci sequence or Divine Proportion plays into my strategy.

Most traders have at least a basic understanding of a chart to track an equity's price movement. In the various strategies I teach, I use a handful of different chart indicators, but one consistent element is Exponential Moving Averages, which are applied to every chart for every time frame strategy, and I always use Fibonacci numbers. So, let me explain the history behind this choice.

The first record of the Divine Proportion numbers I'm talking about dates to about 200 BC. In the West, they first appeared in 1202, introduced by Leonardo of Pisa, known as Fibonacci. Leonardo puzzled over the reproduction of a pair of rabbits, (which seems to have nothing to do with the stock market), yet it brought about this special number sequence.

Leonardo pondered the end "family" result from this pair of rabbits, and this simple (or not so simple) multiplication introduced a numerical sequence that seems to show up everywhere. I am simplifying here, but as amazing as it may seem, the Universe seems to function by this very sequence of numbers.

These numbers relate to our strands of DNA; they are found in nature in the veins and numbers of leaves on a stem, petals on a flower, tree branches, insects' body joints and legs, human physical anatomy and, in very general terms, in the proportions of the human body.

Broadly speaking, the distance between the forehead, nose and chin, the shoulder, elbow and wrist, or the hip, knee, and ankle all function around Fibonacci numbers.

The number ratios are found in seashells, spirals of galaxies, the harmony of music, the artistic eye, genealogy of a bee, the makeup of chemical elements and the behavior of light and atoms. (This is a quick capsulation. Research for yourself).

Anyway, if in the great scheme of things, the sequence of numbers relates to the movement and formation of all material things, including brain waves, then it stands to reason to me that this equation and sequence of numbers might apply to something as ambiguous as the stock market… and traders' reaction to the market. Why not?

Elliott waves, which is another well-recognized and accepted chart reading principle of counting up and down waves in the market, is based on Fibonacci numbers as well.

So, I ask again, why not? Why can't I settle on a sequence of numbers that ties in with the equation of Divine Proportion?

We see harmony expressed by emotions, feelings, and characteristics present within ourselves. This harmony is viewed within nature as the Divine Proportion. Simply stated, given three parts of an organism or natural occurrence, the ratio of the largest piece to the middle-size piece is the same as the ratio of the middle-size piece to the smaller piece. Simple enough, right? Don't jump ship.

This is going to make sense in a second.

This sequence of numbers is easy enough to figure out. Fibonacci numbers begin with zero (0). Easy math. 0 plus 1 is 1. Now we are going to start adding the number back to itself. 1 plus 1 is 2. 1 plus 2 is 3. 2 plus 3 is 5. 3 plus 5 is 8. 5 plus 8 is 13. 8 plus 13 is 21, and so on, on into infinity. (The ratio between 5 and 3 is the same ratio between 3 and 2… on up the line of numbers. Each set of numbers has the same exact ratio between them and in relationship to their sum, the whole—the Divine Proportion).

0, 1, 2, 3, 5, 8, 13, 21, 34, 55, 89, 144, 233 … on into infinity… and beyond.

Okay, so most traders are familiar with moving averages. Every trading guru or instructor has their favorite combination. I often used 9, 15, 50 and 200 EMAs when I first began studying the market. But for my instructional classes and for our Change Your Future strategy, I use a special set of EMAs (Exponential Moving Averages). I use the Divine Proportion (Fibonacci numbers).

We will cover how to use these EMAs as part of the strategy, but, for now, I want to express my amazement at how often these numbers are not only close to support and resistance levels, but they nail these number points to the penny. It is crazy accurate.

I am beyond the point of trying to justify why these numbered EMAs work so well, I am at the point of acceptance. As you begin to use them, the Divine Proportion lines will leave you astonished as well.

After a great deal of study, I have left off the first five Fibonacci numbers -- 0, 1, 2, 3, and 5. There is so little space between these lines that they are not helpful in trading. So, the numbers we will be using are 8 and 13 and the 233-EMA for the sake of overall trend, keeping it simple on our e10-minute chart. When you place them on a chart, they look like colored ribbons. This sequence gives a short-term, mid-term, and a longer-term view of an equity's price action.

You don't need to remember the numbers now. You will come to know them intimately as we proceed.

So, let's begin our next section by establishing some common ground.

VOLUME

We touched on volume earlier when we discussed the volume bar that didn't correspond with the price candle.

The volume bars that run beneath the candlesticks show the buying and selling volume that took place during the creation of that price candle. Of course, during any given period, there isn't going to be 100% buying or 100% selling. Perhaps, most traders or institutions are buying, but there will always be others who are ready to take their profit and see this as a selling opportunity. Or the reverse, the majority are selling off their shares and taking profit or closing losing trade positions, and still others will see this selling as a buying opportunity to pick up cheap stock.

Here are three things to be learned about volume:

1) Volume is relative. Let's say you went to visit two different auctions. If this had been your first visit to either of the two auctions, it would be hard to gauge whether the activity being observed was average, above average, or below average.

    If you were a regular visitor, you would be able to gauge instantly whether there were more attendees or less than usual. Based on this perception, you could make a judgement on the bidding that would be likely to take place.

    This is part of the reason that volume is such a powerful indicator. You, as a trader, can judge relative sizes and heights rather quickly. It is this relationship of volume and price or effort and result in relative terms that is important.

2) The second point is volume without price is meaningless. Imagine an auction taking place with no bidding. The whole process would be little more than a show-and-tell exhibit.

    Remove the price from a chart and all you have is volume bars. Volume reveals interest without any correlation with price action.

    It is only when you have the chemistry between the two that you have the power of volume and price analysis.

3) The third element you should take away from the auction scenario is that time is a key component.

    What if, in the auction room, instead of the bidding taking place over a few minutes, it lasted for hours? This would tell us that interest in the item was minimal at best. Hardly an enthusiastic bidding war.

    To illustrate this further, let's say the door to the auction house was to open at 9:55am, and the auction was to start promptly at 10:00am. Potential bidders were lined up around the building. We have the same price action when the bidding starts, but the entry door is the volume control. If the door is left open, the price's move will continue steadily with no great rush of enthusiasm.

However, as soon as the door begins to close, pressure increases, and bidders are attempting to come into the room in the same amount of time, but the pressure of urgency has increased.

Now that you have begun to understand the nuances of volume and price and their correlation, it must be stressed that trading is an art, not a science, and, therefore, analysis must consider other influencing circumstances. Technical analysis is also an art, and interpreting it is no different.

It takes time to learn and to analyze quickly.

As you will see in this book and as you continue to study, you will find the analysis process is a subjective one, requiring discretionary decision making.

The starting place to this discretionary decision making is whose perspective are we using when we talk about buying and selling?

Are we gauging from the auctioneers (market-makers) or from the bidding customer's (trader's) perspective? Using this auction analogy, you can ask yourself if the volume/price correlation represents the wholesaler's perspective or is it the retail customer?

As traders or investors, the whole reason for studying the process, including price and volume, is to see what the insiders - wholesalers or market-makers - are doing. We want to understand and view the process through their eyes.

So, it is their perspective we will use and come to understand as we move through the concepts, charts, indicators, and patterns discussed throughout this book.

We want to follow or take advantage of the circumstances being orchestrated by the wholesaler or market-makers. Manipulation has a negative connotation, but it is wise to be aware of, and to see the market-makers actions when they are taking place and to have coordinated moves, taking advantage of their lead.

Before we dig deeper into the market-maker's mindset, let's cover more basic information, like indicators and chart set-up.

PIVOT POINTS

Earlier I mentioned that there are two overlays that reveal areas of support and resistance. In addition to EMAs, I use Pivot Points on every chart. According to StockCharts, Pivot Points are "significant levels that can be used to determine directional movement and potential support/resistance levels. Pivot Points use the prior period's high, low, and close to estimate future support and resistance levels. In this regard, Pivot Points are predictive or leading indicators."

These were originally calculated manually by the market-makers, setting key levels that they would use throughout the day. At the beginning of the trading day, they would look at the previous day's high, low, and close to calculate a Pivot Point for the current trading day. With this Pivot Point as the base, further calculations were used to set Support 1, Support 2, Resistance 1, and Resistance 2. Now these are calculated automatically by most charting services.

On short term charts of 15 minutes and under, the Pivot Points are set using the prior day's high, low, and close. They remain the same all day. For timeframes between 30 and 120 minutes, the Pivots are calculated using the prior week's high, low, and close. They don't change until the end of the week. Daily charts are calculated on the previous month's high, low, and close. They are the same for the entire month. We don't often discuss monthly or yearly charts, but their Pivots would be calculated on the prior year's information.

We are focusing on 10-minute candles on the charts, so they are there for the day and will be adjusted the next day.

The Pivot is the average of the high, low, and close. Two Support levels (S1 and S2) and two Resistance levels (R1 and R2) are derived from the Pivot Point in their own calculations. Moves above each line indicate strength and moves below each line shows weakness.

Looking at the chart below, the lines from top to bottom are labeled Resistance 3 (R3), Resistance 2 (R2), Resistance 1 (R1), Pivot Point (P), Support 1 (S1), Support 2 (S2), and Support 3 (S3). These resistance and support levels are calculated every day by the charting company to reflect areas where prices rose and fell over previous periods that may no longer be seen on the chart. It has a 3rd Pivot Point, because I put an F in the Parameters box which stands for Fibonacci.

Price action in relation to these lines can provide you with information about the price direction of an equity. If price drops to support and holds, a bounce back up is likely. If price hits resistance and goes no further, it is likely to drop further until it can get the strength to push through. As you begin to look at more and more charts, you might be surprised how often prices rise or drop right to these levels.

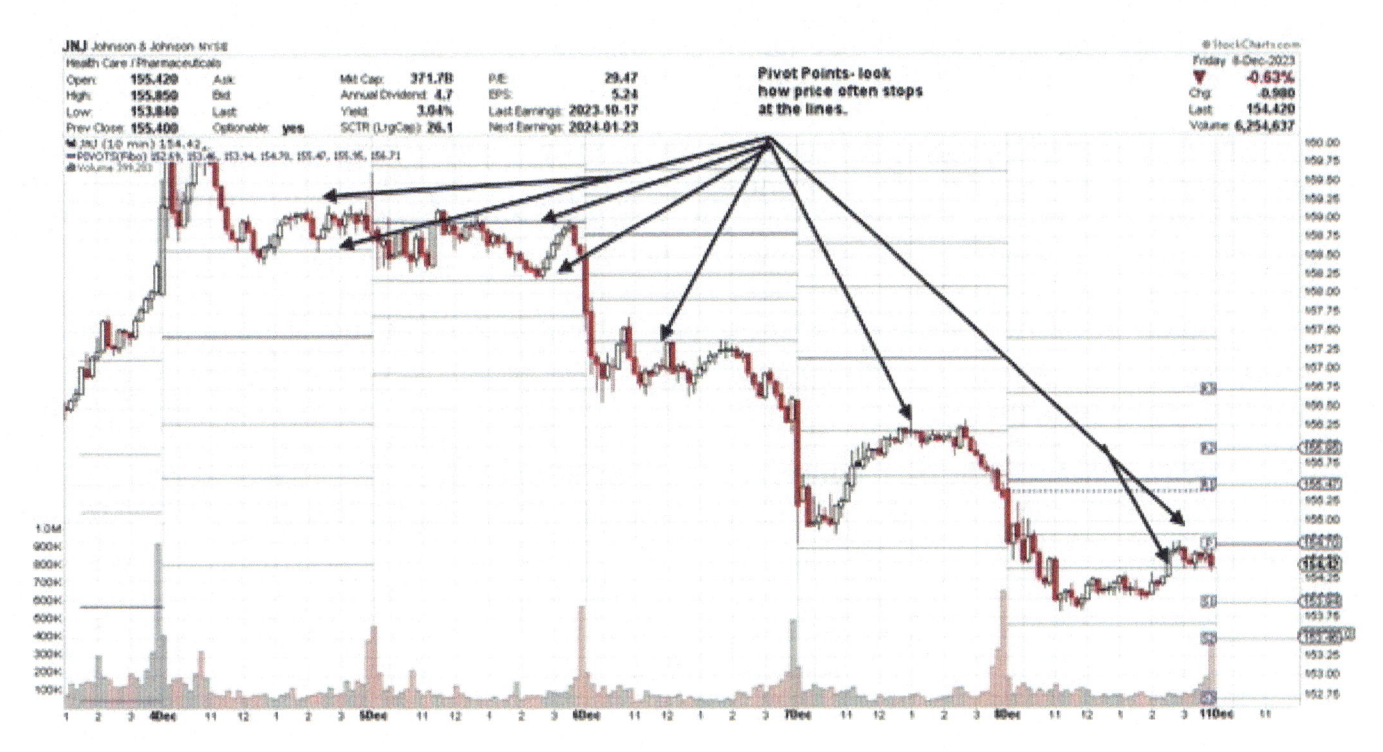

Figure 13- Courtesy of Stockcharts.com

On the chart below are noted major support and resistance lines that are used by price over the course of a day or two and minor support and resistance lines that are used as consolidation areas at support and resistance where the price bounces back and forth over the course of minutes.

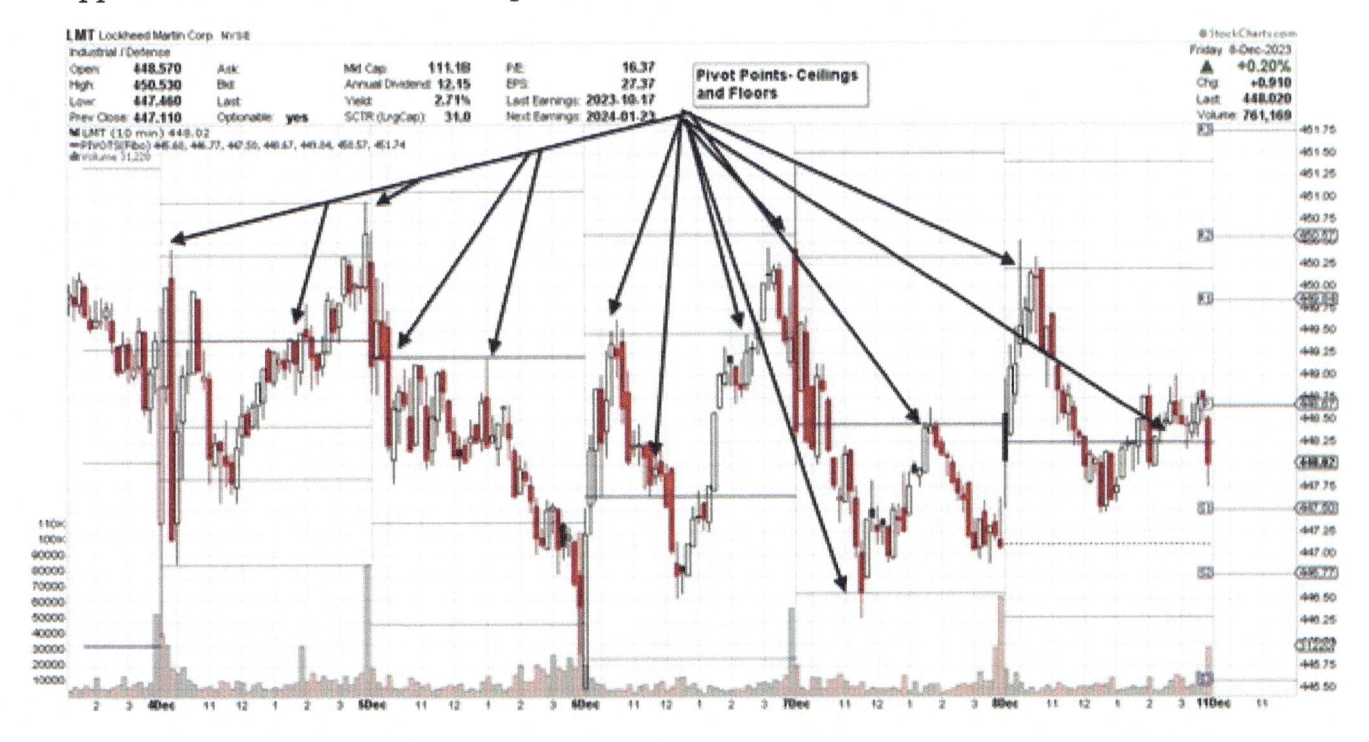

Figure 14- Courtesy of Stockcharts.com

You will note on the chart above for Lockheed Martin (LMT) that the EMAs can act as support or resistance and so can the Pivot Points. Look at the light colored, solid or dotted horizontal lines running in sections across the chart. These areas are not made of concrete, and yet they often slow down prices, causing it to pause long enough to rest, and regain strength and recover. At other times, after testing this area, it will break into a new direction.

Look at December 8th throughout the day, ten candles tried to drop through the pivot point and when traders couldn't be enticed to continue buying beyond this point, market-makers dropped the price, traders panicked, started selling, taking prices lower. Market-makers snapped up the inventory at decreasing prices, taking it down below S1.

The wick on the last candle says there are also some buyers. It could be that these new buyers will

be trapped in a losing trade if price drops when the market reopens on December 11th, even after it started to recover from the drop.

Now that you are aware of the basic concepts of support and resistance as you look at charts in the next segments, pay attention to those areas where you see those areas (Pivot Points and EMAs) on the charts.

AVERAGE DIRECTIONAL INDEX (ADX)

We are going to add some other indicators to our chart. These indicators will help to create very specific patterns. Once the patterns form on a chart, I will go through the details of how to recognize these patterns and how they are read.

The Average Directional Index (ADX) determines the strength of a trend, whether it's trending up or down, or trading sideways. As an oscillator, the ADX fluctuates between 0 and 100, but readings above 60 are relatively rare. Low readings, below 20, indicate a weak trend and high readings, above 40 indicate a strong trend.

Studying the ADX, you'll note that the ADX indicator does not rate the trend as bullish or bearish, but merely assesses the strength of the current trend. In other words, a reading of 40 can indicate a strong downtrend as well as a strong uptrend.

To determine in which direction the trend is flowing or to indicate a change in direction, two other lines are added to the graph. Usually two different colors, green for bullish and red for bearish; they represent respectively a Positive Directional Index (+DI) or Negative Directional Index (-DI).

As these green and red lines cross each other and the ADX trend line, we can determine not only the strength of the trend, but in which direction it will head before it fully takes place.

- When the green +DI crosses upward over the red -DI and/or the black ADX trend strength line, we can expect the trend will be up.

- When the green +DI line crosses downward and the red –DI moves upward and crosses over the black ADX trend strength line, we can expect the trend to fall.

- On occasion, it happens that the DI lines will touch each other prior to crossing, and they will act as resistance and will bounce off each other, resuming the previous trend direction.

- There are other times that the DI lines braid as they swim up and down struggling to be the dominant direction. When this happens, the price most often goes flat and trades in a tight range.

The ADX is special enough that it will be added twice to our chart. The full chart set up will be covered before long.

As these indicators are applied to our charts, their movement, and the information they impart will become crystal clear. Hang in there. These indicators are going to create a picture that you will be able to spot as it is forming.

The default is 14 periods, and I am going to tweak this to 13, which is one of our Fibonacci numbers.

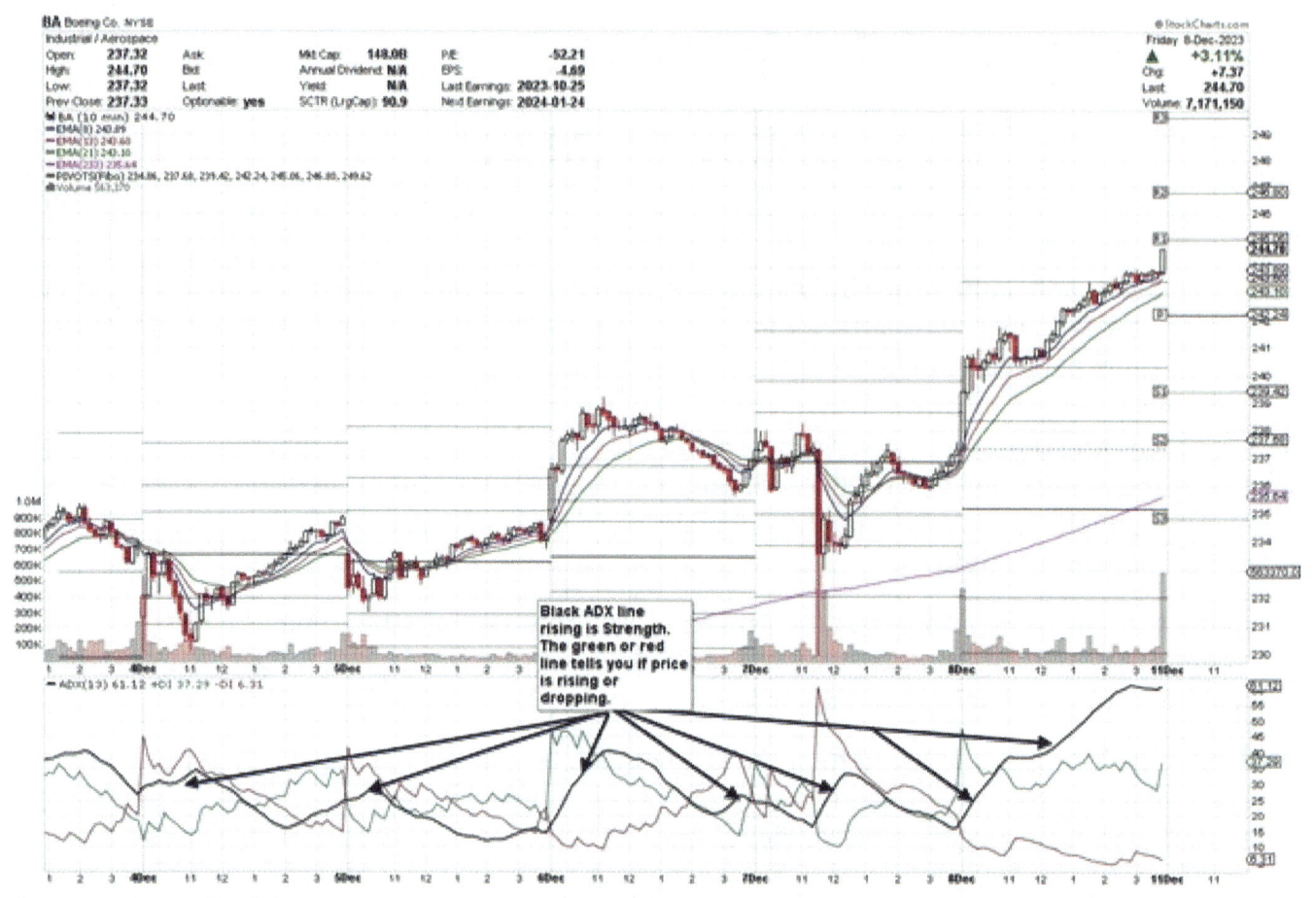

Figure 15- Courtesy of Stockcharts.com

I will post the chart again without the arrows and lines, so you can get a better view of the information and how the different indicators work together. Notice that the DI lines foretell a change in direction before the actual change, but on occasion, they can braid, and the price goes flat because the two directions are battling it out.

Figure 16- Courtesy of Stockcharts.com

Notice the areas where the blue 8-EMA either comes close or touches the red 21-EMA and bounces back or crosses above or below it. An upward cross happened on December 7th at 1:30 pm, pulled back at the Pivot Point. Notice ADX that the +DI touched the -DI near the same time and pulled back until the next morning. The next day, the price broke above the 7th's pivot point and the EMA rose in up trending order. The EMA lines spread out and climbed, putting space between them.

When the ADX is heading up and the +DI is up and in control, price and the EMAs will rise. When the ADX is heading up and the -DI is up and in control, price and the EMAs will drop.

Remember, the ADX line is a strength line. Anytime the ADX line is rising it is showing strength, and momentum is supporting the DI line that is in control or on top. Look at the chart below as an illustration of this.

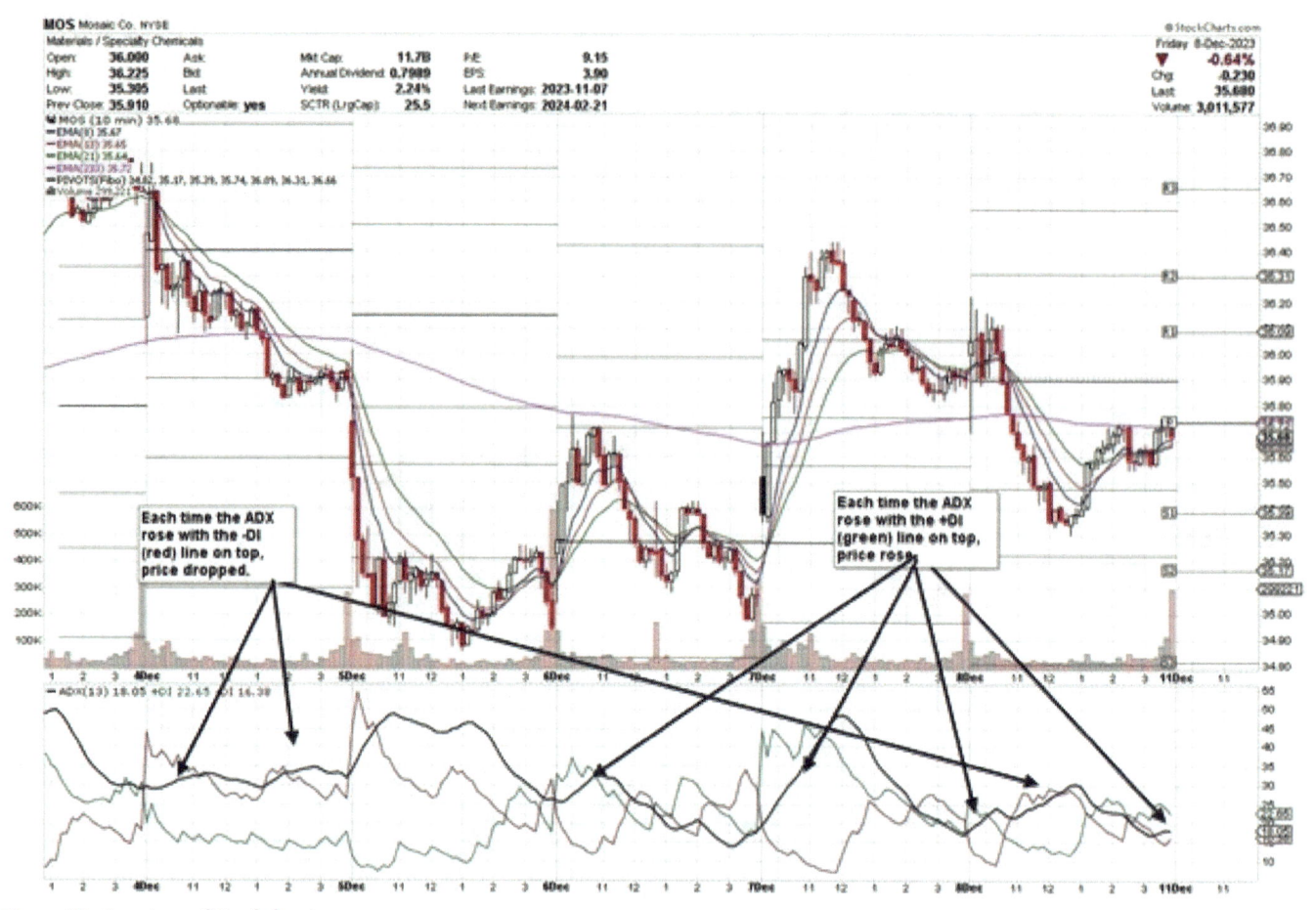

Figure 17- Courtesy of Stockcharts.com

This might seem like a lot of information to absorb. Take it slow. Before you know it, your eyes will be circling around the chart in quick motions, gathering the information that your mind's eye will absorb and analyze instantly. Then, it will slow and zero in on the important portions.

In the same way that your eye and mind work together to look at a Monet painting, your eyes swirl over the details, putting them together to take in the whole picture. It is only when your eyes settle on the small details of a ripple of water that the small dots and minute nuances become evident. This analyzing ability comes rather quickly when you spend just a little time looking at charts. One day they seem to be foreign and confusing to you, and, within a short time, they become old friends that comfortably share their story. Hang in there. It will happen!

Okay, the PPO indicator is next, and then the CCI, and we are done with the elements for the creation of our patterns. From there, we will tie all the pieces together.

PRICE PERCENTAGE OSCILLATOR (PPO)

I present this oscillator as one of the main components of the Change Your Future patterns for our strategy. For traders who are familiar with the MACD and prefer to use that indicator instead of the PPO, they are welcome to do so. I prefer the PPO. The PPO is like the MACD but uses a more complex and a more reliable formula; it's based on the percentage difference between two moving averages over a given period. It uses two lines, one thicker and one thinner, to display its information as well as a series of blocks located beneath the lines called the histogram.

The PPO is an indicator that either confirms or contradicts the signals given by the Exponential Moving Averages that we have inserted into our charts. As a momentum indicator, it's one of the simplest and most reliable indicators available.

The PPO is a lagging indicator, meaning it uses information based on a stock's past performance. This lagging indicator turns into a momentum oscillator and functions by tracking the amount of difference between the short-term moving averages and a longer-term moving average, often the (default) 12-day MA and the 26-day MA. The results form a line that oscillates above and below "zero," without any upper or lower limits.

This equation is represented by a thick line. The other period is included as a reference point, seen as a thinner line. If the PPO is positive and rising, then the gap between the referenced time periods widens.

- When the thicker line moves up, positive (bullish) momentum is building for that underlying stock or index.

- When the thicker line moves downward, then the negative gap widens, so we see negative price (bearish) momentum.

- When the thicker line crosses upward over the thinner line, we see that as a signal to buy. This buy-signal will often confirm other buy signals depicted on the chart.

- But, when the thicker line crosses the thinner line in a downward slope, we see a signal to sell, depending on the option's expiration time frame.

You'll see two graphs within the PPO chart. One is formed by moving averages and the other is a histogram, which notes what has transpired previously on a shorter trigger Exponential Moving Average (EMA).

The histogram is the bar chart along the bottom of the PPO graph. The size of the bars fluctuates above and below the zero line. These bars are another way of expressing the relationship between the PPO equation and an equation using a 9-day (default) exponential moving average.

- If the shorter moving average (the thicker, dark line) is above the longer moving average (the thinner, lighter colored line), the PPO histogram will be above the zero line, or positive.

- If the shorter moving average is below the longer moving average, the PPO histogram will be below the zero line, or negative.

- The PPO histogram compares the PPO number equation with the 9-day EMA. If the value of the PPO is greater than the 9-day EMA, the histogram will be above zero, or positive.

- If the value is less than the 9-day EMA, the histogram will be below zero, or negative.

Again, we are going to tweak the PPO parameters to 8, 13, 9 periods, which partially ties into our Fibonacci numbers. Nine is not a Fibonacci number, but rather than have two 8 periods on the same indicator I upped it to 9.

The histogram of the PPO can give you a heads-up or alert to what may soon take place.

Signals in the histogram to watch for:

1. Positive divergence that precedes a Bullish crossover on the PPO. A positive divergence (ever higher lows) in the histogram indicates that the PPO is strengthening and could be on the verge of a crossover. Divergence means disagreement. Therefore, if the histogram blocks are getting smaller, and the PPO hasn't yet crossed up, the histogram is suggesting that a cross may happen soon.

2. Negative divergence (ever lower highs) that precedes a Bearish crossover. A negative divergence in the histogram indicates that the PPO is weakening in momentum. Divergence means disagreement. Therefore, if the histogram blocks are getting smaller, and the PPO hasn't yet crossed down, the histogram is suggesting that a cross may happen soon.

3. Broadly speaking, a widening gap indicates strengthening momentum, and a shrinking gap indicates weakening momentum. Usually, a change in the histogram precedes any change in the PPO.

4. The main signal generated is a divergence on the histogram followed by a moving average crossover.

5. Keep in mind that a centerline crossover on the histogram represents a moving average crossover for the PPO.

The size of the histogram bars and the shape they create give visual clues, representing the expected movement of the moving averages.

If you are feeling overwhelmed, just let this basic indicator information settle in. We will get into the specifics and how to use the information when we apply the indicators to actual chart set-ups. Once you begin to absorb the basic information, you can come back and reread the specifics. It is all part of the detail-layering process.

The drawbacks or downside to the PPO's histogram is that it is a second derivative, based on the PPO's equation of the price action of the underlying stock or index. The further removed an indicator is from the underlying price action, the greater chance of a false signal.

Because the histogram was designed to anticipate the PPO's signals, the temptation exists to paddle beyond the wave, getting in too soon. But, by acting only on a short-time frame chart signals that agree with the next time frame up, we are assured of trading with the longer trend and not against it.

You will see this in action as we proceed. But please understand, the histogram signals need to be taken as part of a whole evaluation. Don't be tempted to plunge in on just the histogram information.

Again, we are going to tweak the default numbers to 8, 13, 9 for the PPO indicator.

As I mentioned earlier, the histogram blocks within the PPO are a leading aspect of the indicator. Notice on the 14th around 3:00pm the PPO cross suggested the rise was over, along with the dropping CCI and the EMAs and price struggling with the 233 EMA. It is like price rose and hit its head on the 233 EMA line.

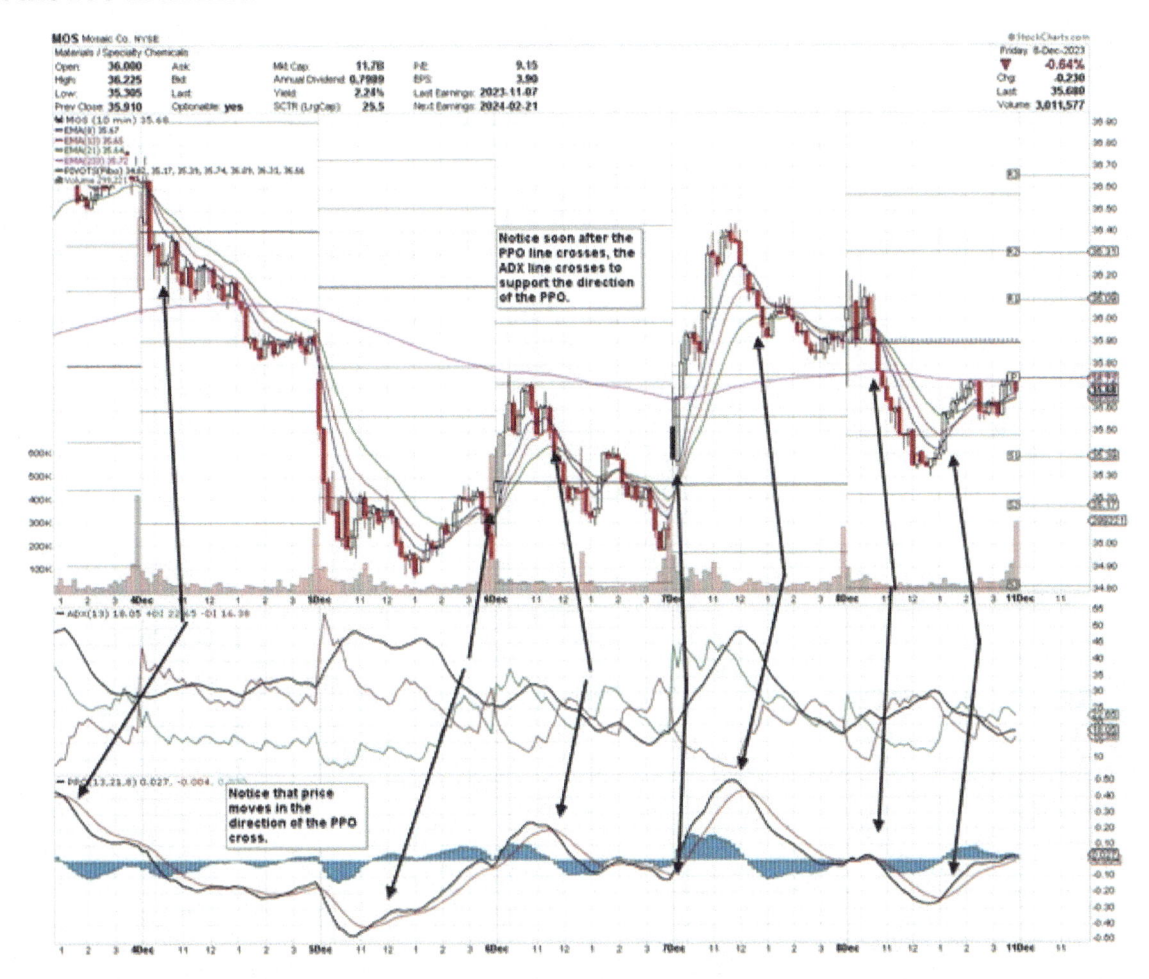

Figure 18 - Courtesy of Stockcharts.com

Study each indicator to see which one gave the first hint that a change was forming. Then which one happened next? Which one followed? How about the PPO and the EMAs? The 8-EMA crossed down and over the 13 and both sat on the 21-EMA, so now they are pushing in up-trending order in one quick burst at 1:00 pm.

Also notice how it is struggling at the 233 EMA (the pink line).

Now that we have the PPO in place, we are going to add another ADX indicator. Yes, we want two of them, one above the PPO and one below. This will be explained further. But for now, just know that the line-up of indicators is an important element to the strategy, allowing us to ride a wave of strength up and down.

Figure 19 - Courtesy of Stockcharts.com

I am not going to explain the use of the second ADX indicator just yet. We will get into that when we start discussing specific patterns and the stages they flow through. Now we are going to add our last indicator to our chart.

COMMODITY CHANNEL INDEX (CCI)

CCI measures the current price level relative to an average price level over a given period. CCI shows as high when prices are far above their average and shows as low when prices are far below their average. In this manner, CCI can be used to identify overbought and oversold levels.

Remember that overbought refers to an equity that has experienced such a high level of demand that the price of the stock has moved beyond the actual value of the stock until the market corrects itself. This means that the price of the stock is likely due for a reversal, or at least a pullback. A stock is considered oversold when the price of the stock has fallen below the actual value of the stock. This can be caused by an overreaction on the part of investors, or more than typical selling, which has brought about a drop in the price where the stock fell too far, too fast and may be due for a reaction rally.

Figure 20 - Courtesy of Stockcharts.com

This indicator can give us a quick picture of the areas you heard described in our discussions about an auction and buying customers when their selling efforts had gone up as far as they were likely to go (overbought by their customers), and it was time for them to start buying back their merchandise. Once they had shelves stocked with merchandise, the CCI indicator would signal a pattern of being oversold by their customers, and it would be time for them to rest and then start selling to their customers again.

CCI creates a chart image that is easy to read. You have the peaks or upper waves, breaking the upper surface above the 100-line. On a chart shown in color, they are green. This is a period when the equity is overbought by traders. From the market-maker's perspective, their shelves are bare or are starting to become bare from selling inventory.

The lower peaks or tidal under currents are created by a drop below the lower level of the -100-line. On a chart shown in color, they are brown. This is a period when the equity is oversold by traders. From a market-maker's perspective, their shelves are full or are starting to fill up as they buy back inventory.

The natural path of equities and the market is to swing from overbought to oversold, going from buying periods to selling periods. You can think of this as a turbulent sea created by the perfect storm where it goes from tornadic waves to a strong undertow current. It is then that you Change Your Future.

You will notice on the chart above that there are periods when the CCI line dropped below the 100-line, but it does not actually drop low enough to cross the -100 line, or it peaks below but just barely and then quickly heads back up again. These periods tie in when the 8-EMA dips down below the 13 and 21-EMA and then quickly puts on the brakes and shifts direction.

Extreme overbought and oversold are usually the significant areas to depict trend direction changes. Less extreme peaks can point to shorter term price swings that still can be used in quick day-trades.

Touches or minor swings above or below the zero line often tie in with 8-EMA touches, when it comes close to the 13 and 21-EMA and can act as a confirmation of that movement.

Joy Reminder:

Trusting that we are capable of finishing what we set out to do can make all the difference in achieving a successful outcome. When we believe in ourselves, EVERYTHING becomes positive. Difficulties become challenges to be overcome, and each step toward keeping a positive attitude, along with positive expectations becomes about enjoying every experience before we arrive at our positive result. Because we ward off doubt and worry, we never let those concerns get in the way of our success. Obligations are easy to manage because we trust we can meet them. By trusting that you can accomplish all your tasks successfully, you can have a productive and stress-free day.

INTENTIONAL CREATION

Decide what you want in life, what you want to happen, and focus "knowing" on it.

Here are some examples now or in the future. When you head outside or to eat, know your activity or destination will be reached safely, on time, and will go well. Know you will get a slot in a limited course or program. When you are released and driving a car, know you will find a front row parking space. If you merge into traffic, know there will be half-block of empty road so you can merge across several rows of traffic safely. Know you'll easily find what you are looking for at the store. Know you'll always have the money to make your desired purchases. Know the time you must have to achieve your desired goal will be just right. Know you will always love the people in your life no matter the choices they make.

Knowing your true beliefs creates everything you want because your knowing is unwavering and, through this knowing, creates.

CHART SET-UP

Okay, now let's look to see how you set up the charts with all the needed indicators and overlays.

The chart below is a screenshot of the lower portion of the chart at Stockcharts.com. Not every charting service will use the same procedures, but this will give you the guidelines needed to set up your charts in the right order and with the needed time periods or parameters.

All the indicators below have had their parameters changed to tie back to Fibonacci numbers.

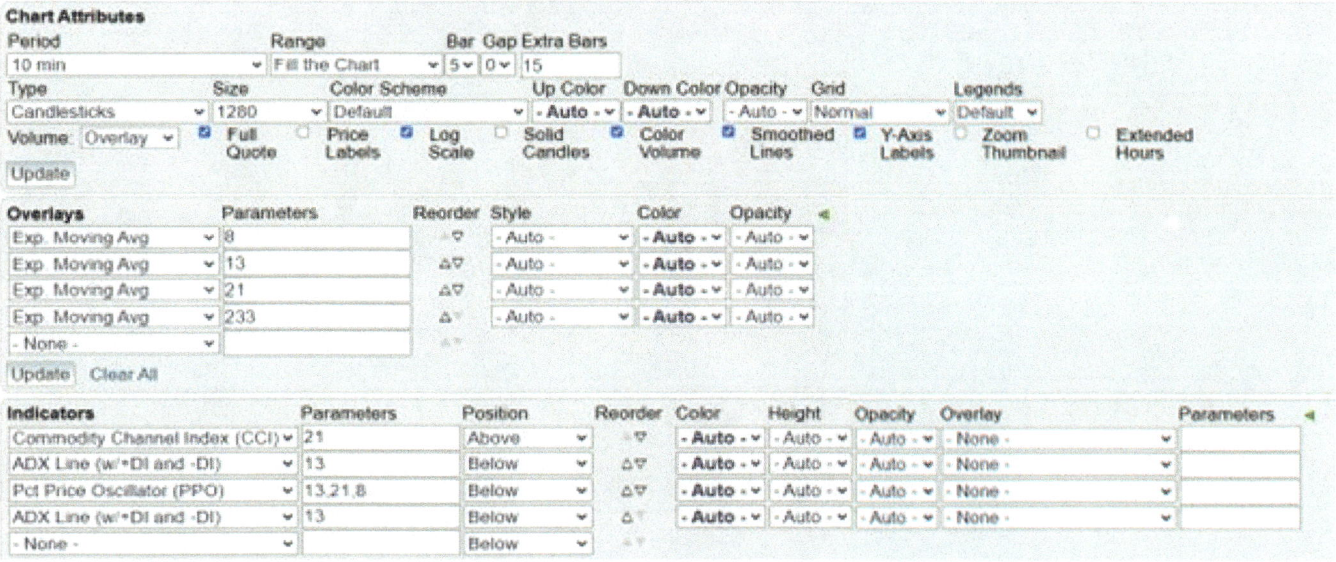

Figure 21 - Courtesy of Stockcharts.com

Starting from the top, you'll see that I added the special EMAs (8, 13, 21, 233 EMAs) and changed each number to be the Fib numbers in order in the Overlay section. Each EMA line will now be a separate color.

Pivot Points is next. Under Parameters, I added an F, which means I want to use Pivot Points based on Fibonacci numbers, which adds a third line of resistance and support.

I have inserted each indicator in the order we discussed them. I placed the ADX indicator in the line-up twice with the PPO in between. Each of the indicators has had their default numbers change to Fib numbers.

The CCI is the last indicator, and its parameter was changed to 21.

For our instruction in the Change Your Future strategy, we will be using a 10-minute setting, where each candlestick represents the price action for 10 minutes. If later you prefer to trade in a different time frame, the set-up is the same.

So, there you have it. This is our chart set-up. Hopefully you can place these chart overlays and indicators on your current chart service or at your broker. If not, then the small monthly fee charged by Stockcharts.com or another service can be deducted as a business expense that will be offset by your gains. I find it well worth the expense. I have nothing to do with Stockcharts.com personally, but I consider it to be one of those "can't do without" tools in my trading arsenal.

SPECIAL CYF+ (PLUS) AND CYF- (MINUS) PATTERNS

Earlier I mentioned the truly unique chart patterns discovered years ago that have slowly revealed aspects of themselves over the course of time. They are the crux of this strategy.

I am going to point out two different patterns that can be visible on any time frame chart, but, as I mentioned, we are going to focus on 10-minute charts. Let's start with the CYF+ pattern that will be used for Call trades. Then, we will discuss the CYF- pattern that will be used to initiate Put trades.

I mentioned earlier that I once messed up my charts by reversing indicators, and it was a fortuitous mistake. At that time, I had the ADX only on the top of the PPO, and I used it only as an indication of strength. One morning, I accidentally deleted my chart set-up and, when I recreated it, I placed the ADX indicator underneath the PPO.

In reviewing my trades that next weekend, I noticed a pattern created by these unrelated indictors that was present every time I located a winning trade when I expected price to go up. Sure enough, it pointed to up-trending moves. Since then, viewing thousands, probably hundreds of thousands of charts, I now recognize the specific stages of this pattern and its counter-pattern that suggests that price is going to drop.

I can look at any chart, regardless of the equity or the time frame and tell you which stage it is in and what is likely to happen next with price movement. And this is what I am going to teach you to do as well.

You have come a long way already. I am proud of you! You've got this.

We have our chart set-up established, so now I want to draw your attention to a pattern that often forms. I will annotate a chart where I circle the pattern - the CYF+ Pattern. This picture on the chart is as close to a guarantee as you can find in the stock market.

It's interesting. The PPO indicator and the ADX indicator have no connection to each other. They are separate indicators, yet when they are set up as you have done with the PPO on top of the ADX, a pattern is formed, and, when this specific picture is created, the stock will ALWAYS go up. Oh, there are times when it takes a few days, and other times when the price pops up like a dolphin, breaking the surface, and then dropping back down for a short period, but in the end, it always comes back up.

I will list a few charts so that you can see the accuracy in what I am showing you. Also, I will point out on a chart or two what happens when this pattern fails after it gets started. When it does fail, the pattern forms again, tightens, and then pops up with even more gusto like a tsunami that has built up steam.

There are times that the lines of the PPO and ADX are drawn together so tightly they almost touch and other times there is a larger bit of space between them. The indicators create their patterns separately, yet together they tell a story about the stock's past and its future. The CYF+ picture is created when a stock has not just dropped, but dropped drastically. The PPO black line reflects this extreme drop, and the ADX black line reflects the strength behind the drop. The pattern combination of these two indicators draws this unique picture that guarantees upward movement.

After we look at this pattern on a few charts, I will show you the second pattern, the CYF-, for Puts. Then, we'll address what you need to look for on the other indicators that will pinpoint exactly when to enter a trade. Also, we'll review an option chain so you can see how to select the option you wish to purchase once you've located a stock that has drawn the picture of an equity that is getting ready to explode.

On the chart below, notice the circle drawn over an area on both the PPO and ADX indicator. Once you study this area, look up on the candlestick portion of the chart and see the uptrend that happens after this picture is formed.

Both the CYF+ and the CYF- pattern go through specific stages. We will cover those stages after you look at a few charts to get the basics.

After this book was fully written, I decide to change the title. You will see KYO+ and KYO- typed on some of the charts below. KYO+ is exactly the same as CYF+ and KYO- is the same as CYF- The important aspect is the + or – symbol. I will type a few reminders of this change before you look at charts.

Here is a chart for Goldman Sachs (GS).

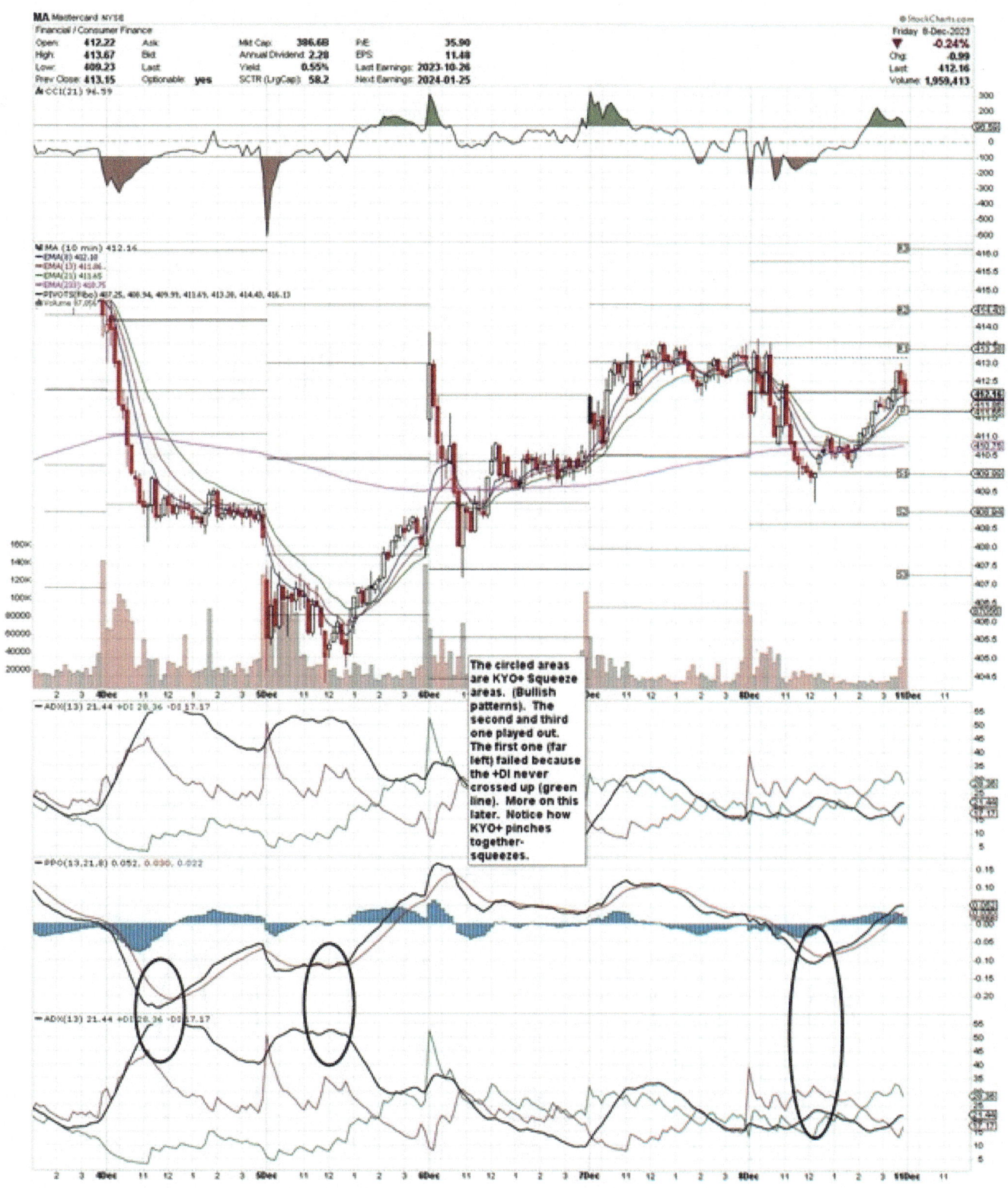

Figure 22 - Courtesy of Stockcharts.com

Here is another image of the same GS chart.

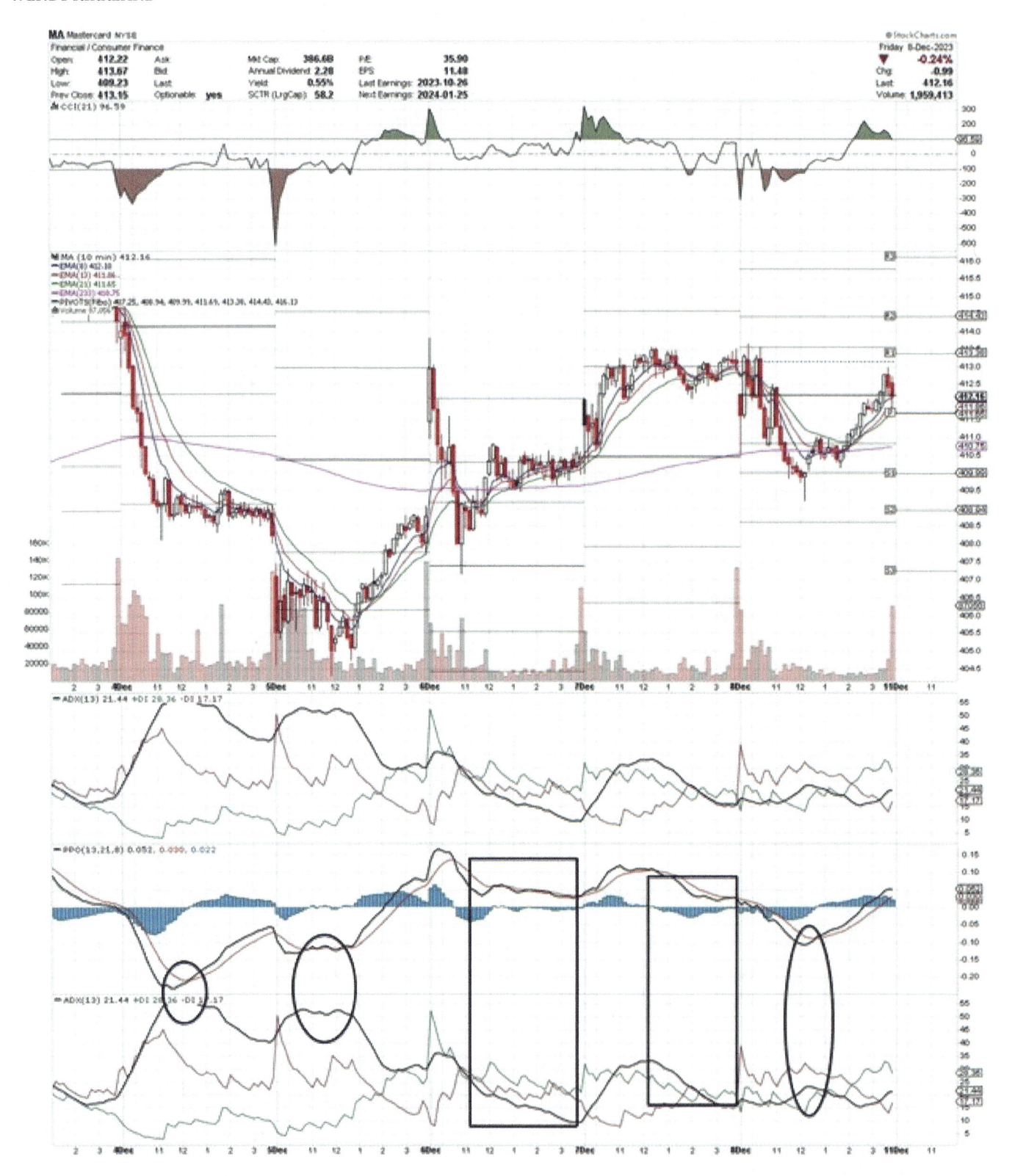

Figure 23 - Courtesy of Stockcharts.com

On this MA chart, I put boxes around two areas that might LOOK like CYF+ patterns at first glance, but they are not. There are certain elements that have to happen for the PPO and ADX lines to create a CYF+ pattern. Namely, there has to be a PPO drop where the ADX line rises supporting the -DI line. Notice in all the marked areas the PPO had crossed down, but only in the three of the circled areas did the ADX line rise while the -DI line was in charge, which created the CYF+ pattern. On the boxed areas, either the -DI was not in charge and was still below the +DI, or the ADX line was heading down (weakening) rather than rising.

On first glance, the peak created by the PPO and the rising peak created by the lower ADX are directly above and below each other. How close is subjective and varies, but they are always "directly" above and below. In the squared areas notice the peaks that should create the CYF+ pattern (lines drawing together) are offset and not directly under each other. I often call the CYF+ pinches or squeezes. The PPO and ADX squeeze together.

On Mastercard (MA) chart below, there are two circled areas marking CYF+ patterns; only those two developed by following through, having a later +DI cross and a rising ADX. The others marked with squares failed, and the PPO crossed down as did the -DI but the ADX never rose to give strength to the pattern and then the CYF- pattern failed when the PPO crossed up again.

This suggests that though the CYF- pattern started formed with the PPO cross down, price wasn't finished rising. The +DI was still officially in charge, or, if the -DI did cross, it still wasn't strong enough to entice the ADX to rise. The -DI cross up and over the +DI is a confirmation that price is ready to move down and hopefully draw the ADX to support the move by rising. If ADX doesn't rise, usually the -DI will weaken, cross back down and the PPO will rise again. It is as if the rise happens in waves, up and down a little, up again, etc.

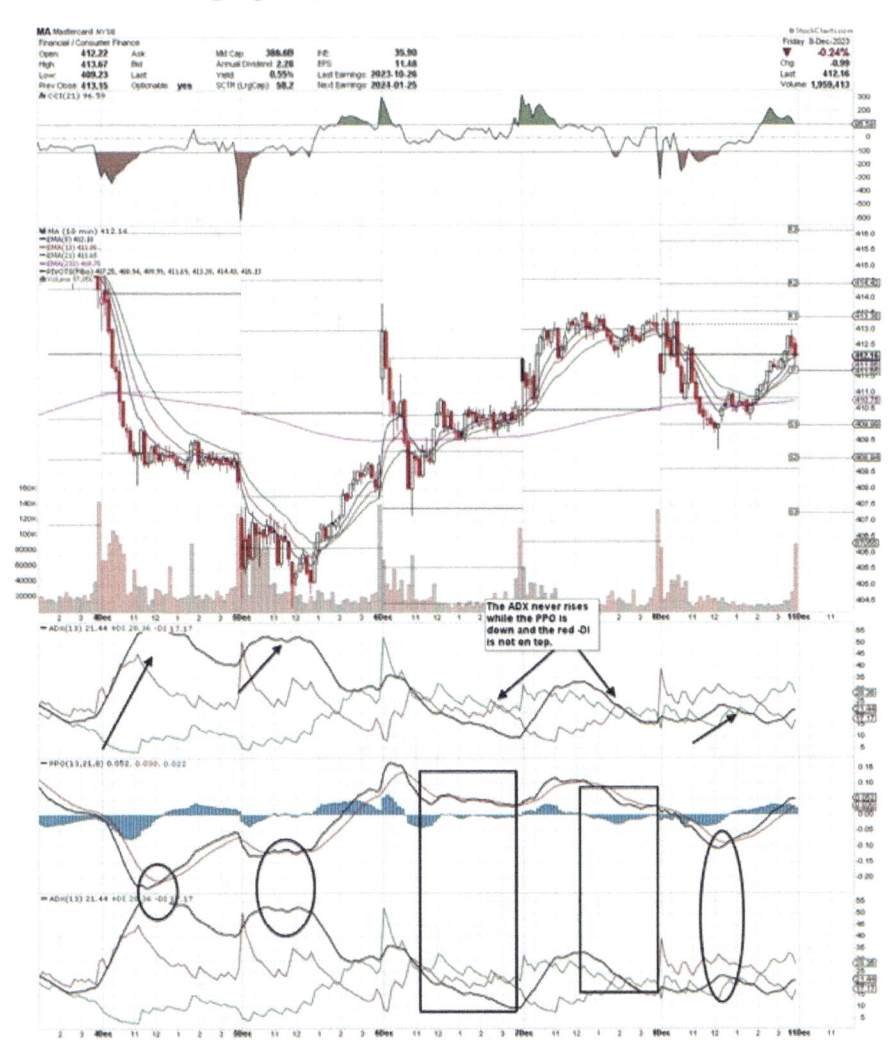

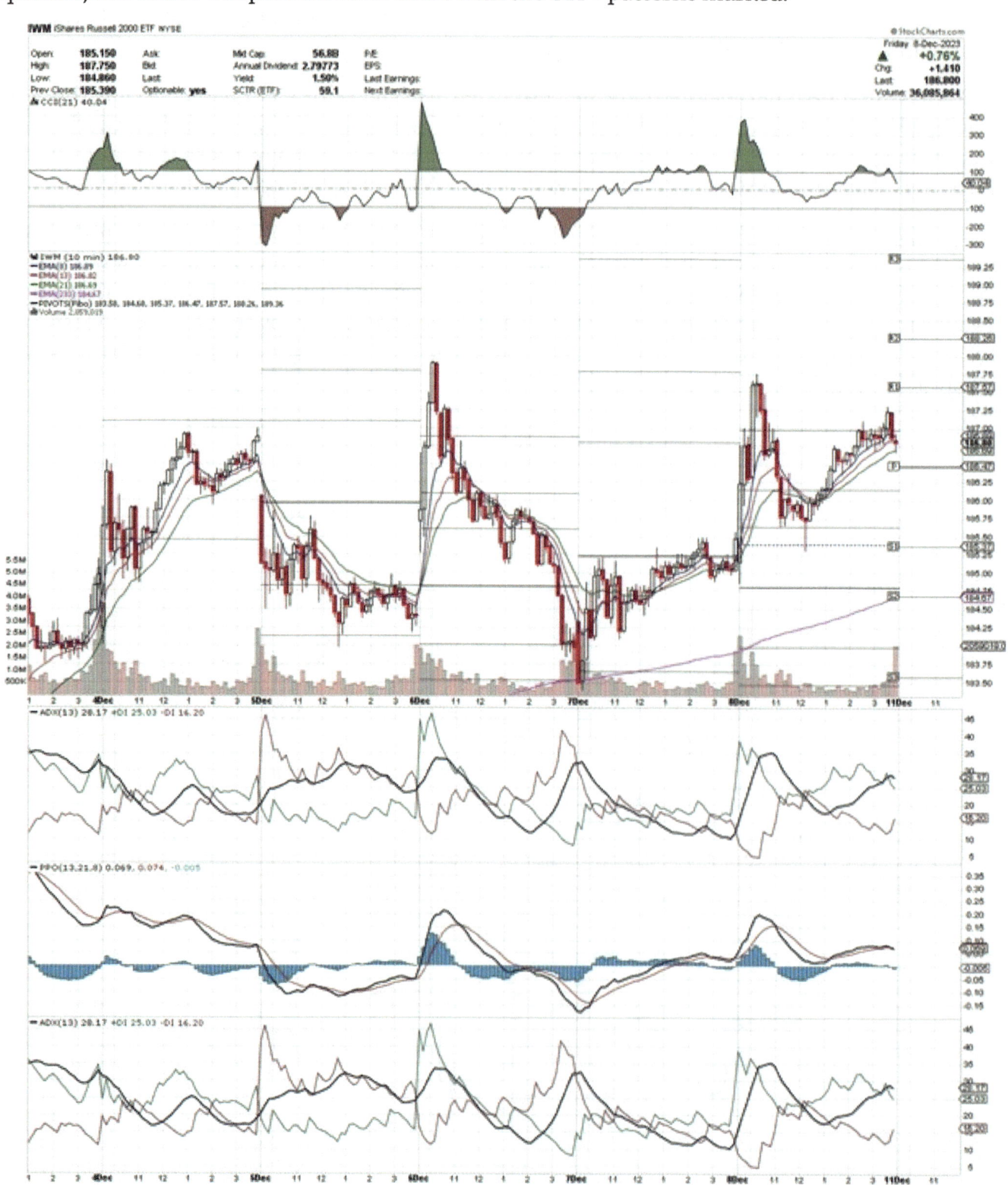

Figure 24 - Courtesy of Stockcharts.com

This will take some time to grasp. Understanding this, I have no doubt that even now you can pick these CYF+ patterns out on a chart, and you will be able to start seeing which patterns are likely to be successful as they move through their stages.

Look at the next chart It is for the (Russell) IWM Index and see if yu can spot the CYF+ patterns, the squeezes, and then I will post the same chart with the CYF+ patterns marked.

Figure 25 - Courtesy of Stockcharts.com

Here is the chart with the areas marked.

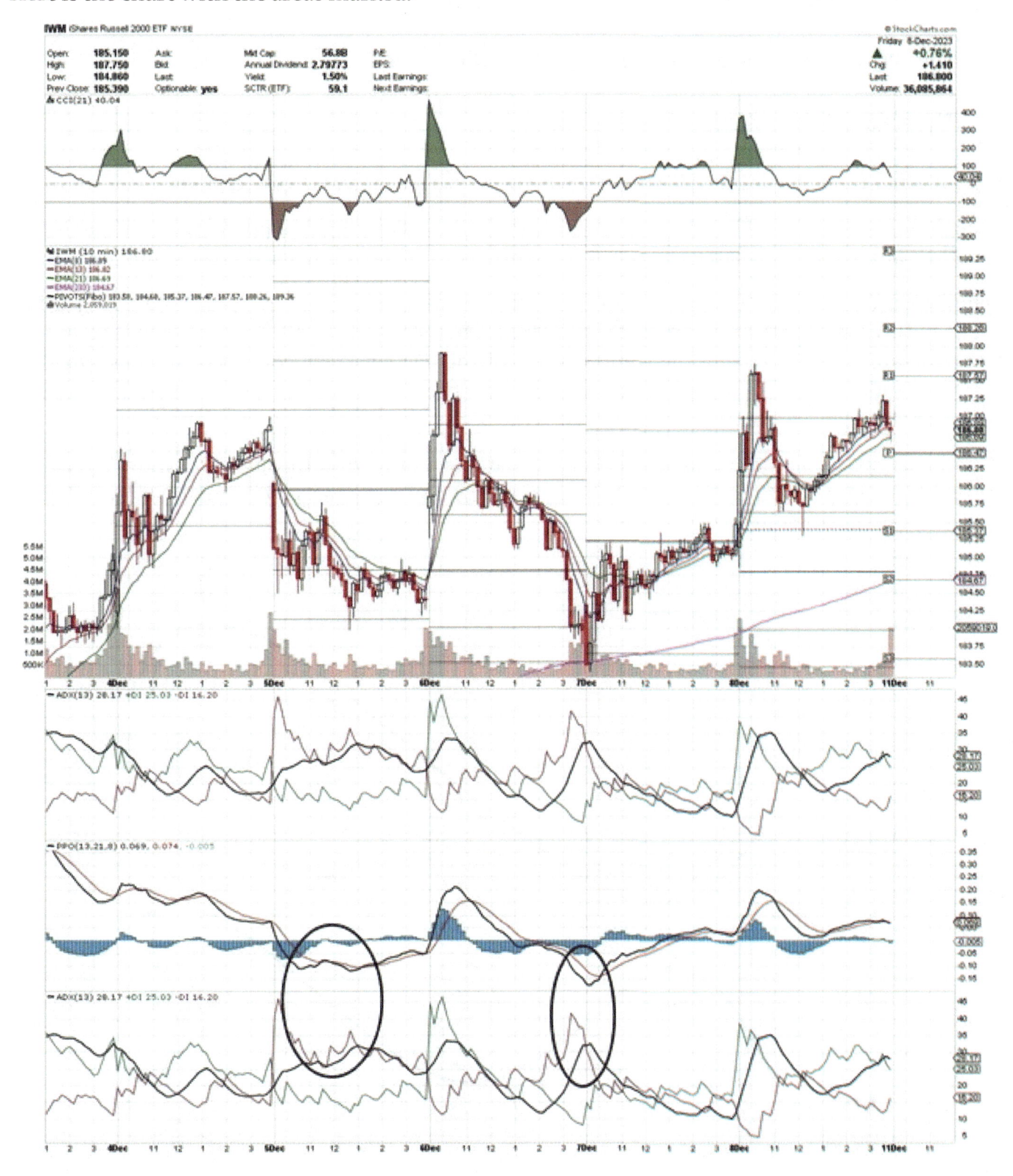

Figure 26 - Courtesy of Stockcharts.com

There were 3 PPO crosses down on the 3rd, 4th and 8th and these PPO crosses failed. The -DI (red)

ADX lines were weak.

Each of the CYF+ patterns have three elements in common.

1) The PPO black line has crossed up and is above the red signal line.

2) The green +DI is in charge (above the red -DI).

3) ADX has risen, meaning a rise in price with strength since the +DI is in charge.

The three elements must be taking place at the same time. One might happen a few minutes before another, but for there to be a CYF+ pattern, all three must have taken place at the same time.

The earlier drop in price is what creates the next CYF+ pattern for the equity. I am jumping ahead, but the three elements listed above are the Sweet Spot stage of the CYF+ that we will go over in more detail. The Sweet Spot or strength stage of the CYF+ pattern conceives (creates) the CYF- pattern, and the CYF- Sweet Spot conceives (creates) the CYF+ pattern. More on this as you move through the next few pages.

The image below is a drawing of the stages that the CYF+ flows through if it moves perfectly through the stages. On the chart above, the patterns on December 5th-6th and 7th-8th are close to looking like the drawing.

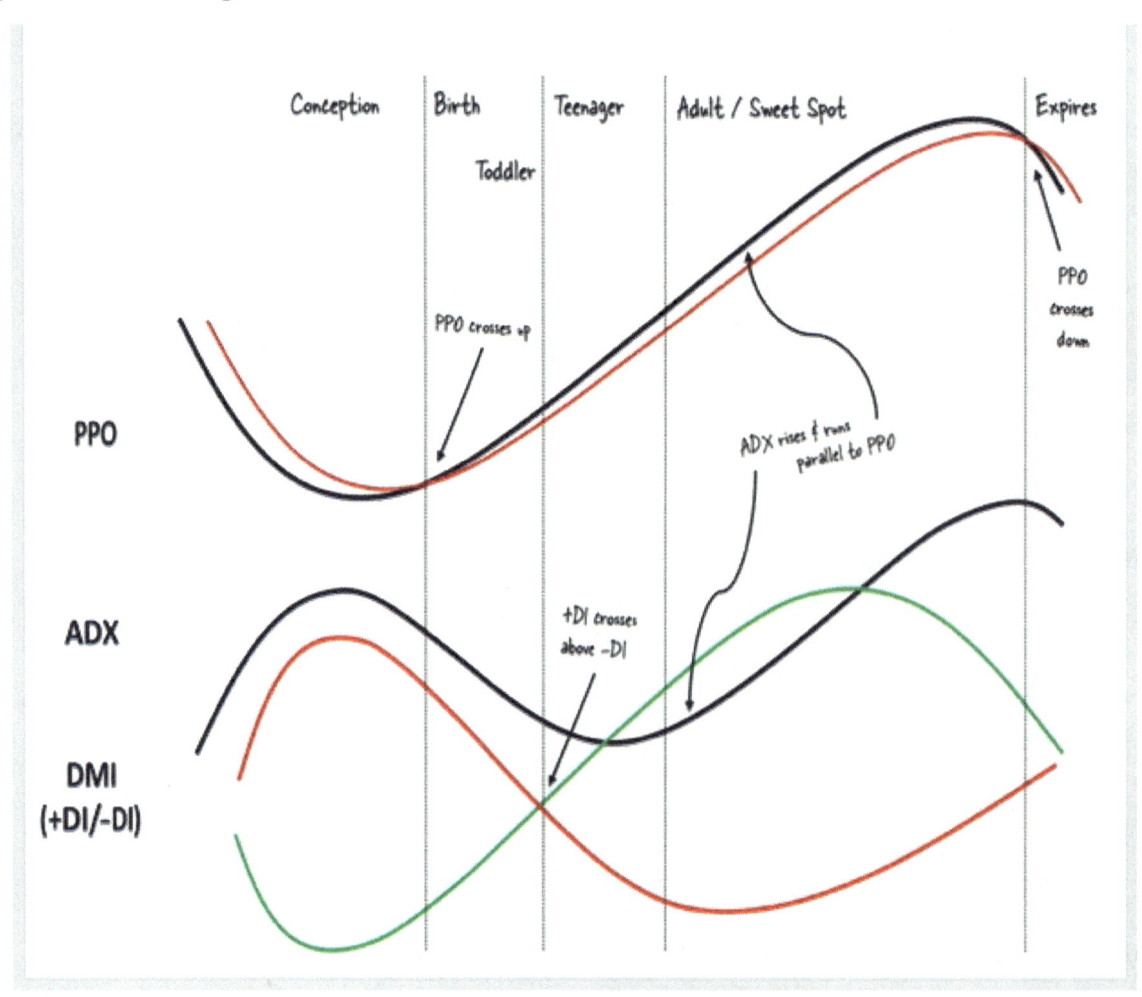

Figure 27 - Courtesy of Wendy Kirkland

The picture above shows the patterns we have been looking at on the charts when we look at the PPO in the middle and the ADX on the bottom for the CYF+ pattern for Call trades.

Earlier I mentioned that the CYF+ and CYF- pattern move through a life cycle from birth to expiration (death). I will restate again, every stock chart you look at, in any timeframe, will be in one of the life-cycle stages pictured above for CYF+ or in similar life-cycle stage (birth to death) of the CYF- pattern. These are the stages you will learn to recognize so you can anticipate what will happen next.

The CYF+ pattern is formed by a large drop in price, and this is the conception stage. When the PPO line crosses up and over the signal line again, the pattern is born. During the "toddler" stage, the +DI starts working its way up and over the -DI and eventually the ADX line itself. As this toddler pattern is gaining strength and learning to walk, it can take a tumble to the floor (testing levels of support). This is what I refer to as a wobble. The toddler can wobble on its legs until it gains enough strength to continue its trek with confidence.

Eventually, it moves into the "adult" or Sweet Spot stage where the PPO line is heading in an upward direction, and the ADX strength line turns up to add momentum and drive to the trade. This stage is the crux of the CYF+ pattern. You will learn to notice the new CYF+ as it is conceived and is born, and then you will observe casually its movements until it begins the Sweet Spot stage. You will consider an exit just as it rolls over into the downward plunge.

You will see your belief in your own success fulfilled here. You see, observe, and put your plan in place, while holding a positive expectation and preparing yourself for the joy of riding the wave.

Let's look at a few more charts where I will mark the stages. See if you can recognize them. Skim through the charts above and note the CYF+ patterns that had profitable moves and those that didn't. Note where the CYF+ was only a shallow advance and then reformed. Did it play out the next time?

It doesn't matter if the underlying equity is a major index, an ETF, or a stock, the CYF+ pattern reacts the same as it begins to unfold and plays out, or it reforms and tries again.

Let's put all the CYF+ pieces together before we move on to the CYF- Put pattern. By then maybe you will understand my terms and references for what is taking place, making it easier to apply the terminology to the CYF- Put pattern.

This is a description of what has been taking place on the charts so you will more easily recognize the actions. During this learning process, it might be helpful to write these stages down on a sticky note as a cheat sheet. You will soon have the stages memorized and will easily recognize the stages.

CYF+ PATTERN

1. The PPO and ADX black (thick) lines come close together to form the CYF+ pattern with the -DI in charge. (Conception). A down move is taking place to conceive the new CYF+ pattern.

2. The PPO line crosses up over its signal line, and the ADX black (thick) line pushes in the opposite direction from the PPO line as if it is repulsed by it. (Birth)

3. As the CYF+ pattern continues to unfold, the PPO and ADX lines will move further and further away from each other. (Toddler)

4. It is only when the +DI line turns up and eventually crosses over the –DI line that the price will "really" move upwards. The PPO line cross itself can only take the price so far. If the +DI falters and doesn't continue by taking control, the CYF+ pattern is likely to fail and need to reform because the price will go flat or head back down. A PPO cross down over the signal line is the stop or exit for the trade. Exit quickly and loses will be cut short. You can always reenter when you are given the confirmation signals again. (Teenager)

5. Quite often, as the PPO line is moving upward, it will weaken for a period of time, drop back and test the PPO signal line. The signal line will then act as a trampoline, and the PPO line will bounce up from there. There are times that it will do this twice during the climb up. I call this a wobble. The lines/direction are weak as if on wobbly legs and can fall before picking itself up again to proceed. In actuality, these are tests of support (floors). (This can happen anywhere along the lifespan but most often, it occurs while being a wobbly Toddler or moody Teenager.)

6. While the PPO line advances upward, and the +DI line has crossed up and over the –DI line, the ADX Strength line will turn up to support the new uptrend. I call this the Sweet Spot, Strength Stage, or it is called the "adult" stage of the CYF+ pattern. It is our Sweet Spot.

In this stage of the pattern, the PPO and ADX thick lines run up parallel to each other. They almost look like railroad tracks. As long as the lines remain in this formation, the price will continue up. (Adult)

7. The last stage and exit is when the PPO and ADX line turn and start heading down, or the PPO rolls over the signal line. This is a final signal to exit if you are not using some other signal like a drop of CCI as an earlier exit. (Expiration-Death)

8. This is a new stage that was added well after I began teaching these patterns. Stage 8 is an add-on Sweet Spot stage. This has come about in the last few years because of the strength of the overall market as it reached highs prior to the Pandemic. The Stage 6 Sweet Spot would form, and eventually the PPO would rollover, and the CYF+ would expire. The trade closed. But shortly thereafter, the Sweet Spot would be resurrected and would form again as if it had rested and then experienced a renewed burst of strength.

On the next few charts, I will annotate the chart with numbers that tie in to the descriptions above so that you begin to recognize each stage.

Create a cheat-sheet and keep it close to help you recognize the stages. Before you know it, you will have them memorized and the stages will easily reveal themselves to you.

Again, remember KYO+/KYO- is the same as CYF+/CYF-.

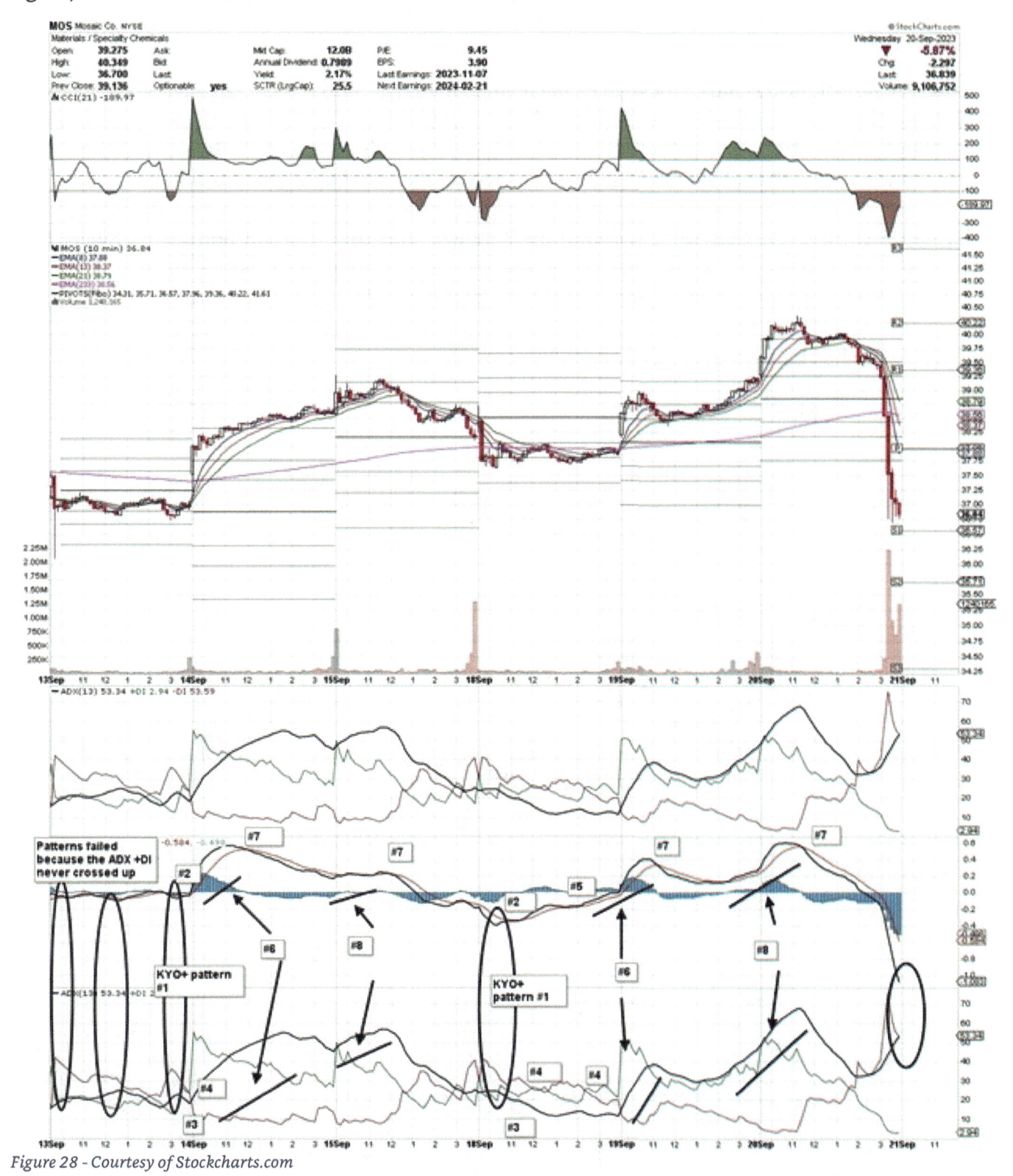

Figure 28 - Courtesy of Stockcharts.com

Mosaic's (MOS) chart is a great example of a CYF+ pattern that went through all the stages in an orderly fashion twice. This chart is offered here as an example of a CYF+ pattern with several repeat stages. There were two Stage 6s, where the PPO and ADX rose, running parallel to each other early on September 14th and 18th and then again on 15th and 19th. This is when the PPO crossed down suggesting the trade was over and expired, and then it rose again, where the PPO crossed back up, and an add-on Sweet Spot was formed (#8). A key element to these add-on Sweet Spots on this chart was the strength of the +DI line.

On the left side of MOS's chart, a new CYF+ pattern formed (#1), and it went through stage #3 twice, each time the pattern failed when then the PPO crossed down #7. There was no #4 through #6 Sweet Spot. As mentioned earlier, there must be a Sweet Spot because it is the Sweet Spot that forms the alternate CYF- pattern. The CYF+ pattern fizzled out before the Sweet Spot formed.

MOS had a third CYF+ that went through all 7 stages, and then had an add-on #8 Sweet Spot patterns (Strength Stage). It did this twice, each time adding an extra stage #8 strength stage where the ADX line rose. Stage 7s are then end of a pattern and happen after a #6 and an #8.

The KYO+ on the chart note is the same as CYF+.

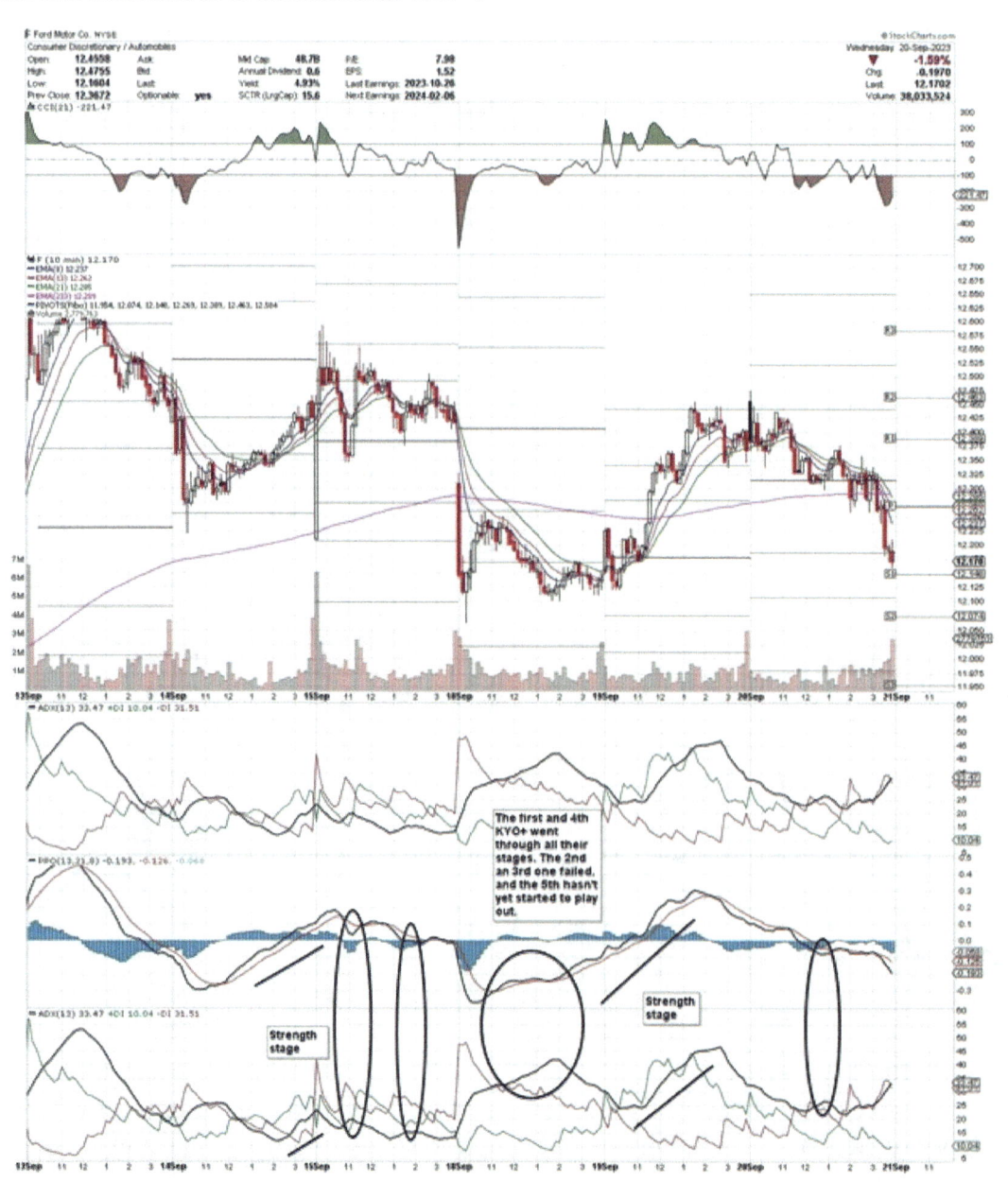

Figure 29 - Courtesy of Stockcharts.com

On Ford's (F) chart, its CYF+ went through all 7 stages, and then the PPO crossed down twice, forming new CYF+ patterns that soon failed. In the second and third CYF-, the bearish (15th and 18th) patterns formed and went into quick strength stages forming new CYF+s, which soon failed, never having the ADX rise while the +DI (green) line was on top. The PPO crossed down again and formed the last or 4th CYF+ on the right side of chart. It took a while for this pattern to really get going, and then rose most of the 19th. Now a new CYF- formed and is playing out forming a new CYF+.

Take an extra minute to go back and study the importance of the DI lines and ADX. The PPO cross tells us overall direction, but the ADX shows us strength while the DI lines tell direction of that strength.

As you study and review charts, the subtle nuances will become easier to spot as you recognize the stages.

Again, here is a condensed version of the cheat-sheet.

1. The PPO and ADX lines come close together with -DI in charge.

2. PPO lines cross up, and ADX line starts to push away from PPO.

3. The lines move further away from each other.

4. +DI crosses –DI line, and then the ADX line itself

5. PPO line wobbles - maybe once, maybe twice. If PPO fails and crosses back down, this is a stop exit.

6. PPO and ADX move into the Sweet Spot/Strength Stage – like railroad tracks where lines run up parallel to each other.

7. Time to exit with PPO drop below its signal line.

8. Add-on Sweet Spot stage

I cannot stress strongly enough how important the +DI is to the CYF+ pattern. Especially in these shorter time frame charts, it is the key. It truly reflects the direction of the trend and whether the price has a chance of moving up into a new uptrend, or if it will drop back to then have to try to break out again.

As mentioned earlier, we are going to focus on the CYF+ pattern, but we are adding the CCI indicator as one of our entry signals as trend moves from overbought to oversold and back again. We will work through several examples of this. The CYF+ pattern will help us determine what stage the pattern is in and what is likely to happen next with price's direction.

I will get into the specifics of exact entry and exits as we proceed, but, for now, I want you to focus on these stages of the CYF+ pattern.

On the next few charts, I will mark the conception of the CYF+ pattern with an oval, and then mark a possible entry with a square on the CCI that assumes all the other guidelines as to premium, etc. are met. In addition, I will insert parallel lines for the Sweet Spots. Stage 6 will be part of the original pattern while the +DI is in charge and Stage 8's will be after there has been a cross of -DI and then back to +DI.

Oracle's (ORCL) had a couple CYF+ patterns that went through all the stages, two added Sweet Spots or Strength Stages after a quick PPO cross down where the -DI didn't stay in control long before the +DI took over again and PPO and ADX rose again.

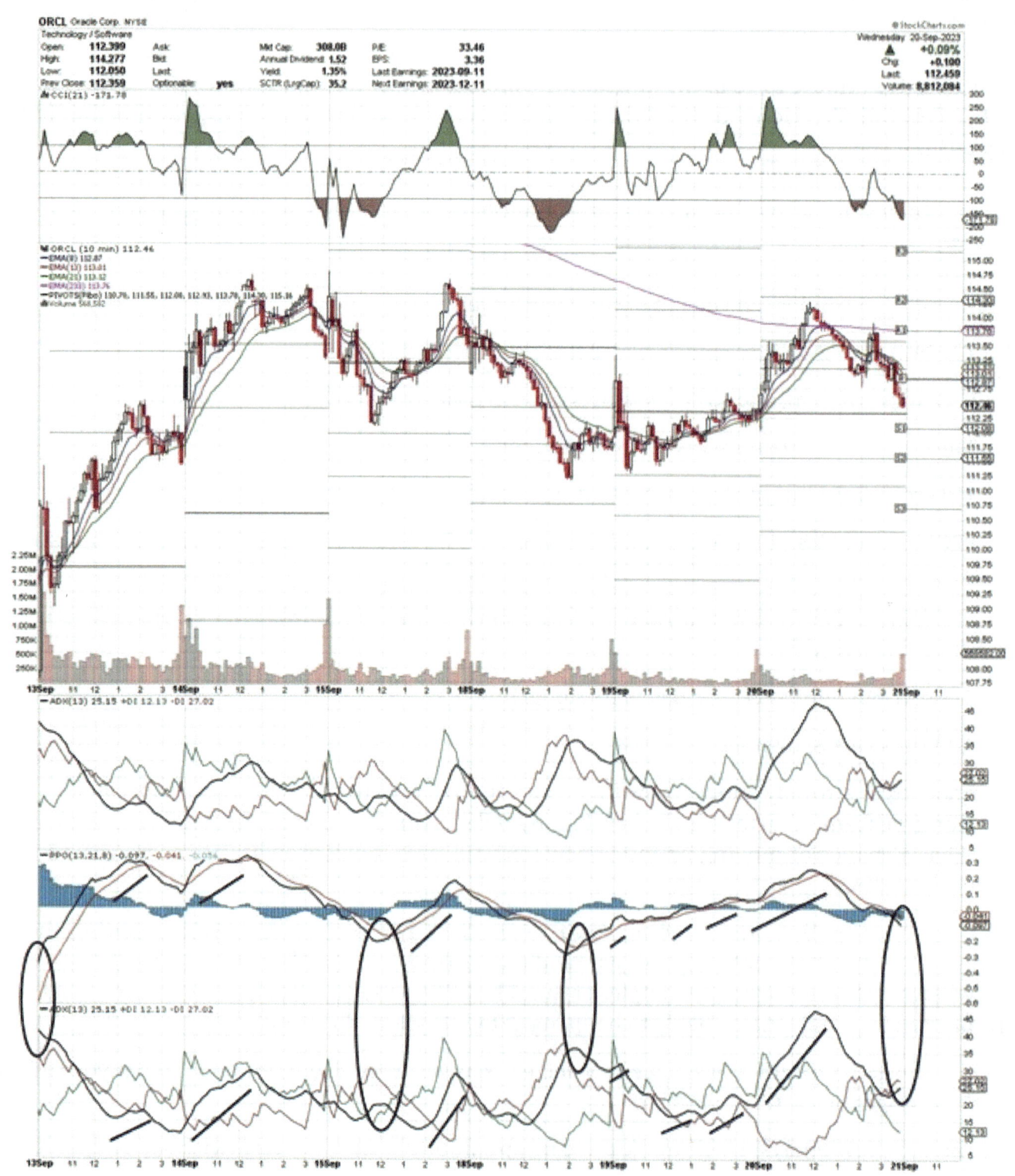

Figure 30 - Courtesy of Stockcharts.com

There is usually a clear entry pattern as a CYF+ pattern forms. It should also have had a CCI cross into the oversold area (See the circles), where it rises both above the -100 and zero line of the CCI indicator. You will stick with the trade until you hit a profit target or when the CYF+ pattern goes through its stages to a +DI cross-down below ADX (first sign of weakness) or a Stage 7 PPO cross-down.

The CYF+ early on Sept 13th flowed through stages to a Sweet Spot in orderly fashion. There are times (like this chart) where the Stage 6 Sweet Spot might not seem to be enough. Holding until the next morning (from Sept. 13th to 14th) would have paid off with the move up that started again on the 14th. Notice the -DI (red line cross) was weak.

Additional crosses above the zero line on the CCI mark either other possible entries at the beginning of an add-on Sweet Spot leg or the start of another CYF+ pattern. The ADX and +DI lines are key to these additional entry opportunities.

It doesn't always happen this way, but often, if the first Sweet Spot stage isn't impressive, or let's call it wimpy, then the second Sweet Spot can be the more impressive of the two. So, if you have experienced a sluggish, wimpy original Sweet Spot (the one most closely connected to the CYF+'s birth), then watch and look for a second stronger, more impressive Sweet Spot or Strength Stage.

If there happens to be a 3rd or 4th add-on Sweet Spot pattern, don't look for them to be "super" profitable unless there is a sizeable pullback from which they are recovering, but in short-term day-trading small moves can still be very profitable trades.

CYF+ patterns work in three ways.

1. Sometimes, a CYF+ pattern will reform several times, but, eventually, it will unfold completely. All CYF+ patterns will "finally" go through all the stages, and this then ends that original pattern.

2. It can also get right down to business as it forms. It goes through the stages and then goes into a CYF- pattern, which will form another new CYF+ pattern.

3. The third option is for the CYF+ to form, go through the stages, weaken, and have several add-on Sweet Spot stages as if it is clawing its way higher and higher. At some point, the original CYF+ pattern will expire, and eventually another one will form.

Understanding this CYF+ forming process and the stages will help you analyze where the pattern is along the way. You will be able to spot if the pattern is weakening and likely to reform, or if it is showing strength and is apt to move through stages #1-7 and perhaps, stage 8.

From here on out, as you spot a CYF+ pattern on a chart, follow the stages and analyze where it is in the unfolding process. Use your cheat sheet until you have the stages memorized. The more you do this, the faster you will train your eyes and mind to digest the information, recognize the stage, and interpret its message.

As I mentioned, I made a little cheat sheet on a yellow-sticky note and kept it near my computer with the stages numbered and a short description. This helped me to keep things straight and is a quick reference as you are starting out.

FedEx's (FDX) chart below shows several CYF+ patterns. Entering when the CCI crosses the zero line helps to bring you into the trade when price is ready to move in an upward direction and can keep you out of a trade while price goes flat or consolidates.

The first CYF+ failed and second had a nice long Sweet Spot, and you will note that the +DI remained in control during those Sweet Spots and then after the PPO crossed down there was a CYF- that went into very quick Swet Spot forming a new CYF+ pattern that when the PPO crossed up, it went right into a Sweet Spot with a huge gap up. There was a second Sweet Spot that recovered a portion of the quick sell-off.

In the fourth CYF+ on the right side of the chart, the pattern was well formed and got right down to business and moved through all the stages, and +DI remained in control throughout.

I used to use an indicator called Bid/Ask Middle that was only available on one charting service and not Stockcharts.com. I relied on it to help with entries. Eventually, I discovered that CCI's zero line gave me the same line-cross confirmation. I relied on this information because it helped to keep me out of some of the oversold CCI/CYF+ patterns that weren't "really" ready to get started yet. The CCI zero cross added the needed protective confirmation.

CCI with a parameter set to 21 matched Bid/Ask Mid exactly, but Bid/Ask Mid would often have little tests (support/resistance) soon after it crossed, and sometimes these tests would throw me out of a trade with a quick little fake cross up or down.

I tweaked the parameter to 34, and this helped to avoid those false cross tests of support and resistance. If the CCI 34 happened to cross back down/up, it was likely to be a real breach of support and resistance and a legit reason to close the trade.

CCI 34 crosses the zero line a half-step behind where CCI 21 would have crossed, but I would rather have the extra assurance as to new direction than a little extra profit on the trade. Overall, the winnings outweighed the losses in a trade that turned and failed soon after entry.

I will add a second chart of FDX with the CCI 34 and you will see it cut out the false crosses on September 21st and 22nd.

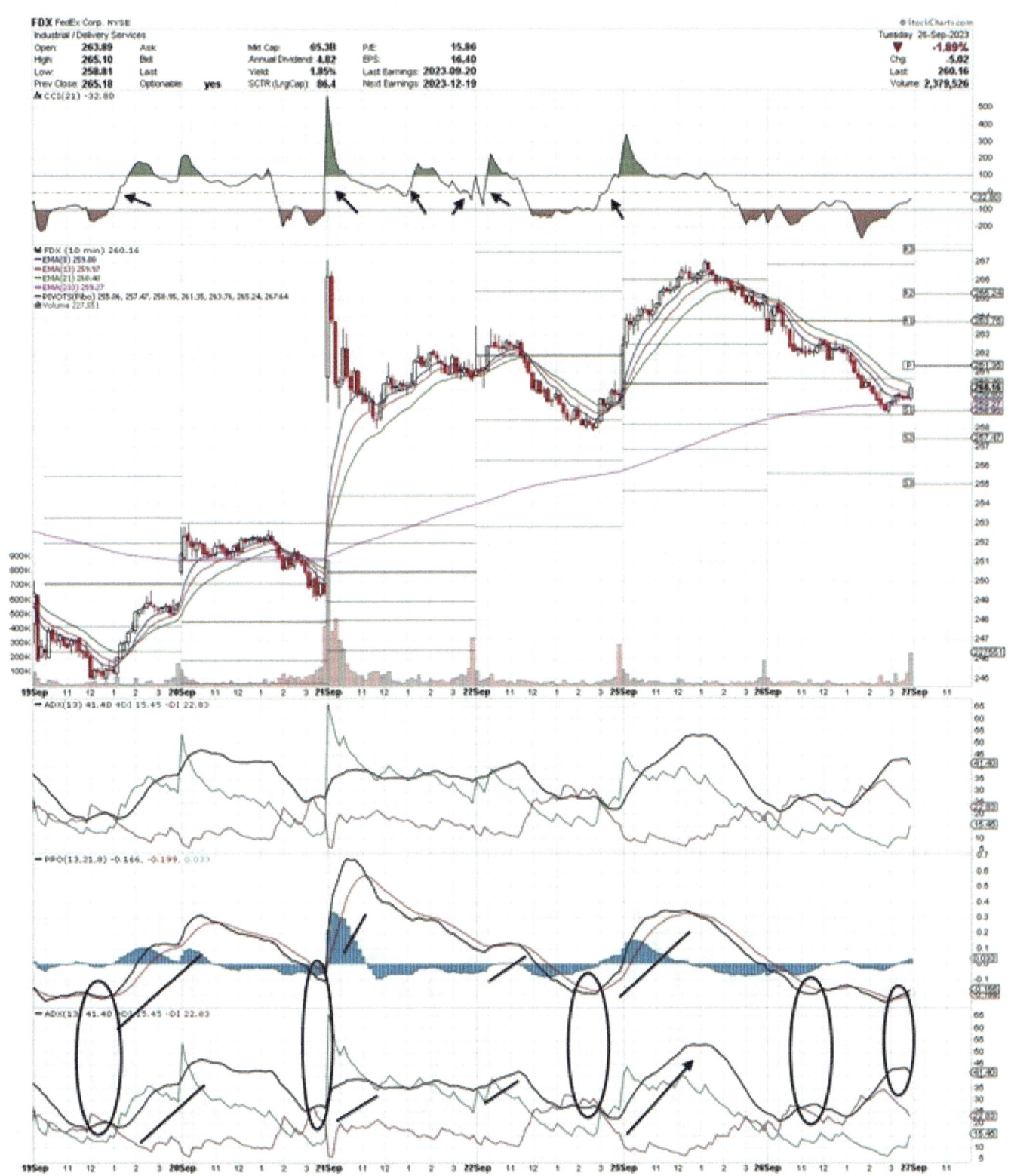

Figure 31 - Courtesy of Stockcharts.com

Figure 32 - Courtesy of Stockcharts.com

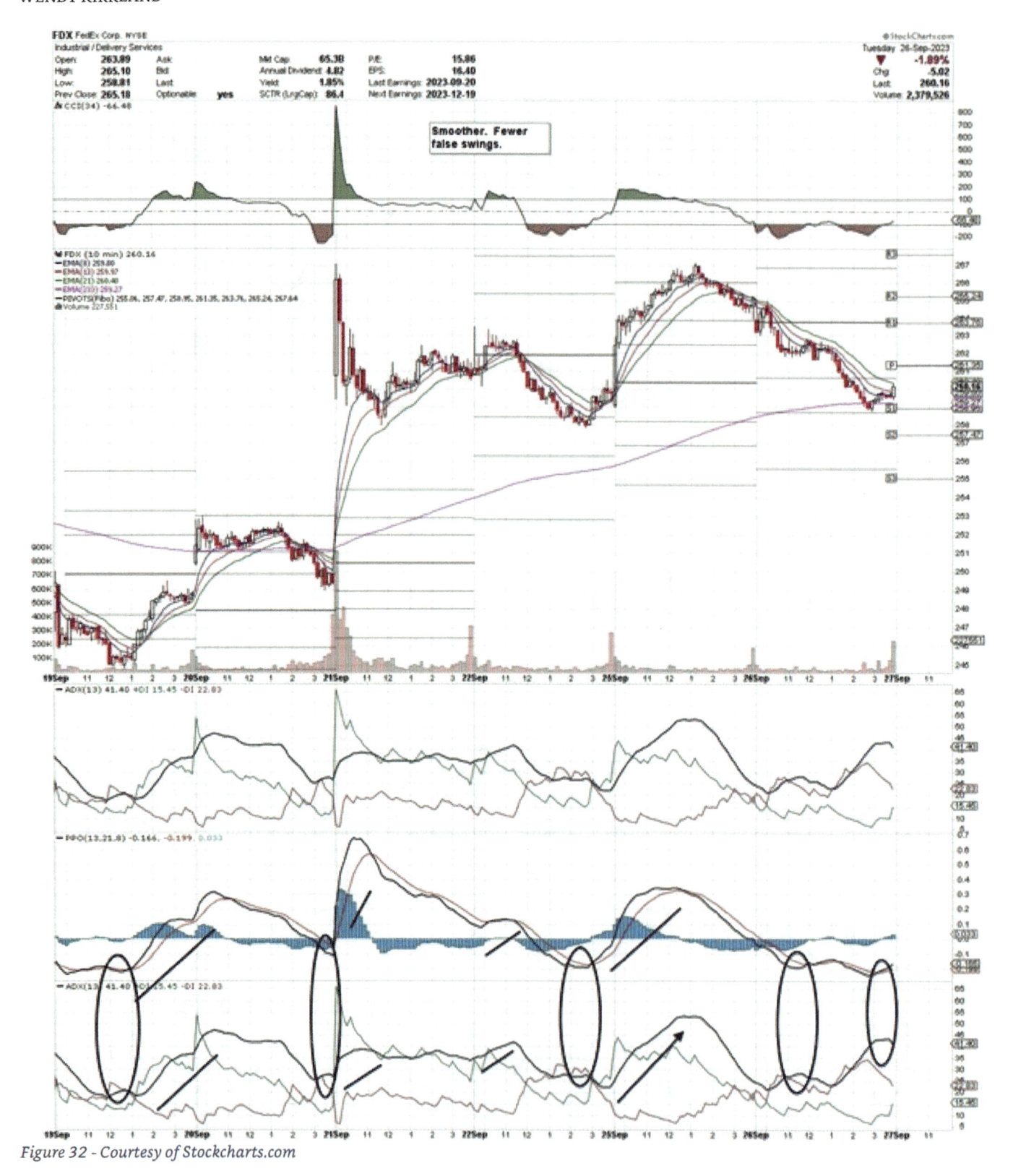

On Visa's (V) chart below, seven CYF+ patterns formed, and yet there was only one false CCI cross, meaning that, though price went up, it may not have been enough to profit. Waiting for the CCI zero cross adds a level of protection.

During volatile periods, when there seems to be swings rather than a solid direction, I often tweak the CCI to 34 rather than 21. CCI 21 matches the B/A Mid I used to use, but CCI 34 smooths it out and avoids a few of the false crosses (like those seen on Visa's chart below) as the line tests support and resistance.

If the day seems to be strong with movements heading in one direction on the indexes, I want an early or "right-on-time" entry and will switch it back to CCI at 21. If the day seems volatile with several morning or afternoon swings, I tweak the CCI to 34. This is just an effort to fine tune to match what the day is dishing out.

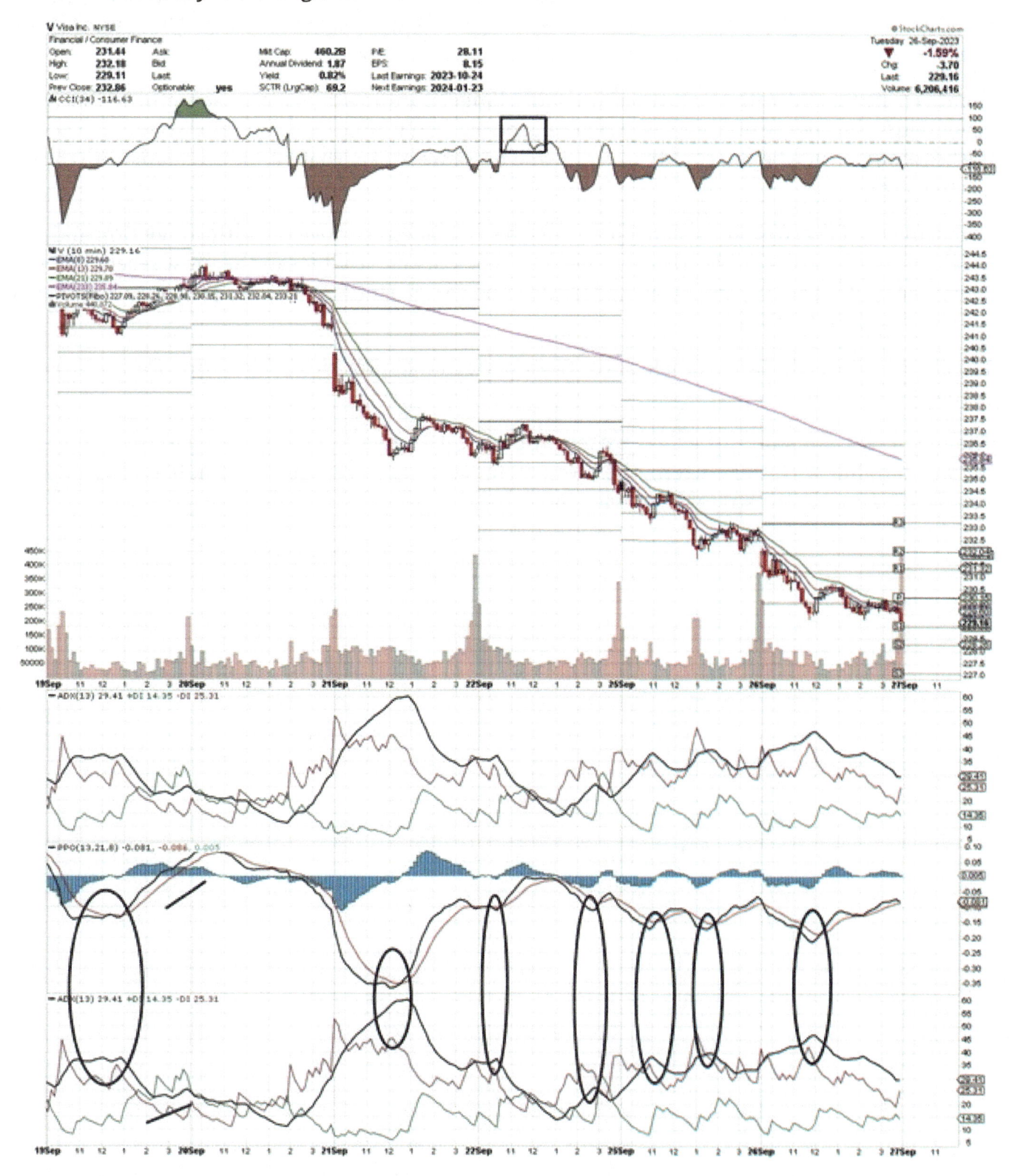

Figure 33 - Courtesy of Stockcharts.com

As wonderful as the CYF+ pattern is, there are times (few) that trading it can be tough. Visa's chart is an example of those challenging patterns.

It formed and reformed numerous times and never did create a pattern that went through all the stages with a Sweet Spot. Each time the PPO crossed up, the price went up, but the +DI lagged, and then PPO quickly failed, and the price dropped. It stayed down only a short time, short enough that it became hard to spot the areas where the PPO and ADX lines came together. There were short-lived CYF+'s throughout the whole chart after the quick CYF+ on September 19th.

Whatever happened with the fast patterns and longer forming one, it was something that went beyond just the energy of the CYF+. Maybe all the pattern formations and reformation pushed all the bears out, or maybe you could think of it as a pressure cooker that builds up steam until the top has to fly off.

Each time the PPO crossed its signal line, and the +DI failed to move up with conviction and stay up, the possibility of a viable trade was negated. Look at the +DI lines in the most recent CYF+ on September 22nd. The DI lines have braided back and forth. Until the -DI declares its strength, and the CYF+ trade is apt to fail.

The chart below is the last example of the CYF+ pattern that provides information for trades going to the upside – Calls.

Then next, we will look at the CYF- pattern for Puts. It's a tweak on the CYF+ pattern. Once you become familiar with this pattern, then we will move on to the charts as a whole and apply what you have learned to the strategy – entries and exits.

Figure 34 - Courtesy of Stockcharts.com

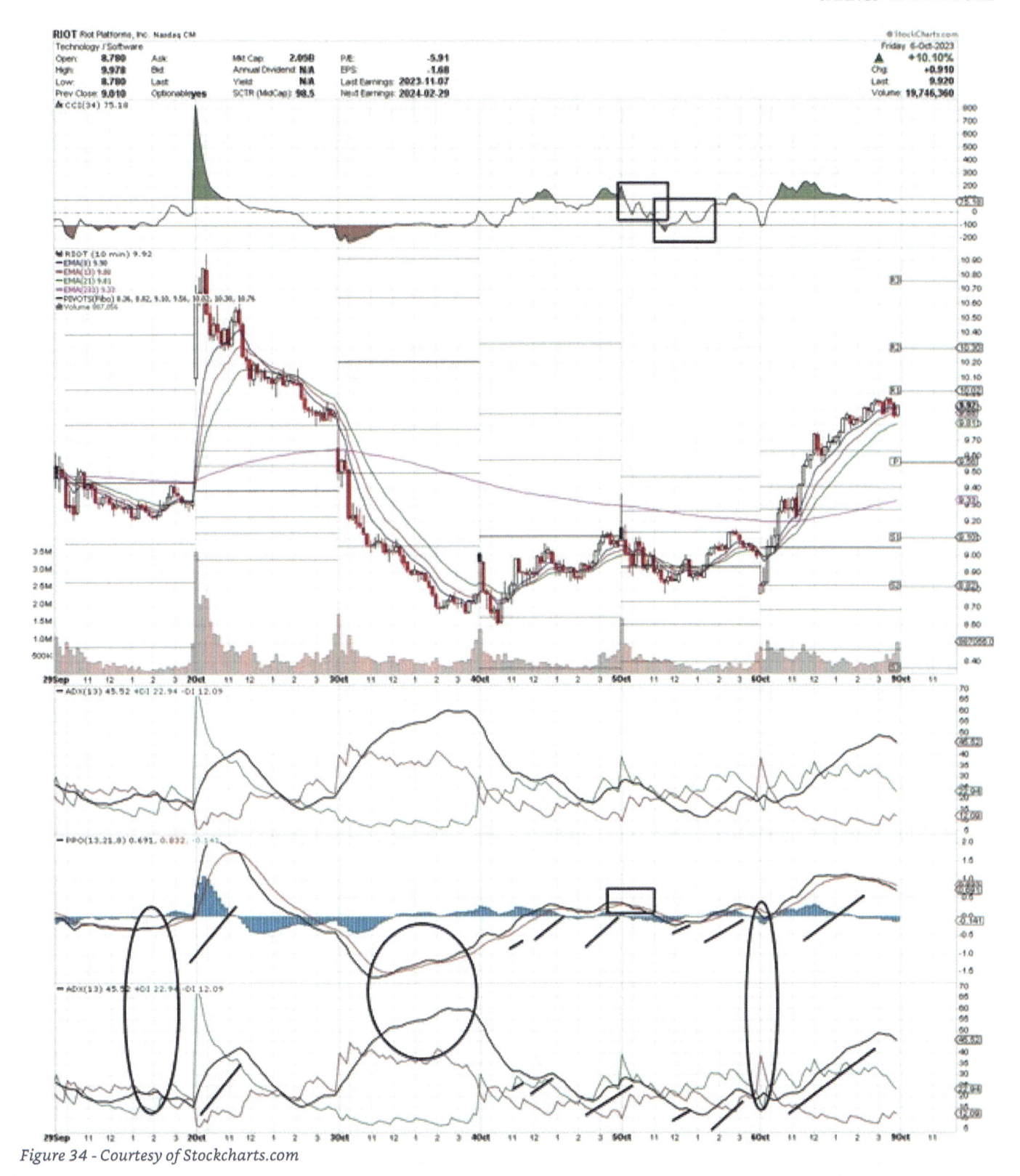

I am including this last chart as further proof or illustration of the importance of the DI lines along with the ADX line as well as CCI. Again, the squares note CCI crossover points, I want you to note they are not far off from the PPO cross down.

Notice the strength of the +DI on the CYF+ pattern on October 6th on the chart. The +DI crossed up over the -DI with conviction. There were 5 Sweet Spots (stage 6) where the PPO and ADX headed up

109

running parallel to each other after the CYF- and -DI and dropping CCI failed.

An aspect discussed earlier and that needs to be included is the EMA lines - the 8, 13, and 21-EMA. Notice how the 21-EMA supported the 8-EMA and kept it from dropping further each time the -DI rose and tried to flex its muscles. There are numerous aspects to consider, but, before long, your eyes will soon start to recognize these nuances.

Hang in there. You can do this! Decide on success.

Joy Reminder:

Laughter is healthy medicine, and we all have this healing essence available to us whenever we recall a funny story, tell a joke, or act in a silly way. We magnify the effects of this healing when we share it with the people in our lives. If we're lucky, they will have something awesome to share with us as well, and the life-loving sound of laughter will continue to spring out of our mouths and into the world.

CYF- PATTERN FOR PUTS

For the CYF- adapted pattern for Puts, we will be using the PPO indicator on the bottom and the ADX that is on top of the PPO. This pattern has been described in other materials as P3.5 pattern and has developed into the CYF- pattern

In some ways, the conception stage of the CYF- pattern is less obvious than the CYF+, but you can train your eyes to pick it out. More obvious is the CYF-'s Sweet Spot. During this stage, the equity's price drop is a certainty, and this will be our focus for the Put trades.

To identify the conception stage of the CYF-, look back at the CYF+ pattern and its stages. It is the CYF+ Sweet Spot stage that creates the conception (formation) stage of the CYF-.

And now I'll let you in on the secret - it is the CYF- Sweet Spot stage that formed all the CYF+ patterns that we looked at earlier. The patterns flow back and forth from one to another with a few occasional wobbles along the way. Those wobbles on both sides are the Stage 8 Add-on Sweet Spot stages.

Both patterns, CYF+ and CYF-, can expire with a Stage 7 PPO rollover and then have this renewed burst of energy (Stage 8) and move further along in the previous direction before it eventually fails, and the opposite pattern is conceived.

Remember that CYF+ Sweet Spots form new CYF- patterns, and the CYF- moves through the same stages as the CYF+, except they are the reverse. The CYF+ has a PPO cross up, and the CYF- has a cross down. The CYF+ has the PPO and ADX lines push away from each other for a Stage 3, and the CYF- has the lines heading down and running parallel.

Let me make a list of the stages for the CYF- and mark a few charts, so that you can tie in this information. Below is a cheat sheet of the stages. Let's use the same charts posted above with the close areas circled.

Stages of CYF- Put Pattern:

1. ADX and PPO come close together as they mimic each other.

2. –DI Rising

3. PPO crosses down and over its signal line.

4. –DI crosses +DI and eventually the ADX line.

5. PPO wobbles against the signal line.

6. The spread apart of PPO and ADX lines creates the Sweet Spot.

7. Exit - Rollover of PPO line and drop of –DI.
8. Add-on Sweet Spot stage.

To help you conceptualize the relationship between these indicators, let me provide you with a drawing that illustrates these stages without the particulars of a given chart. Again, notice the life-cycle stages of birth to expires (death).

The conception stage of a CYF- is the Sweet Spot stage of the CYF+ pattern where the lines head up running parallel to each other. It then runs through birth, toddler, teenager, and adult stages until it finally expires.

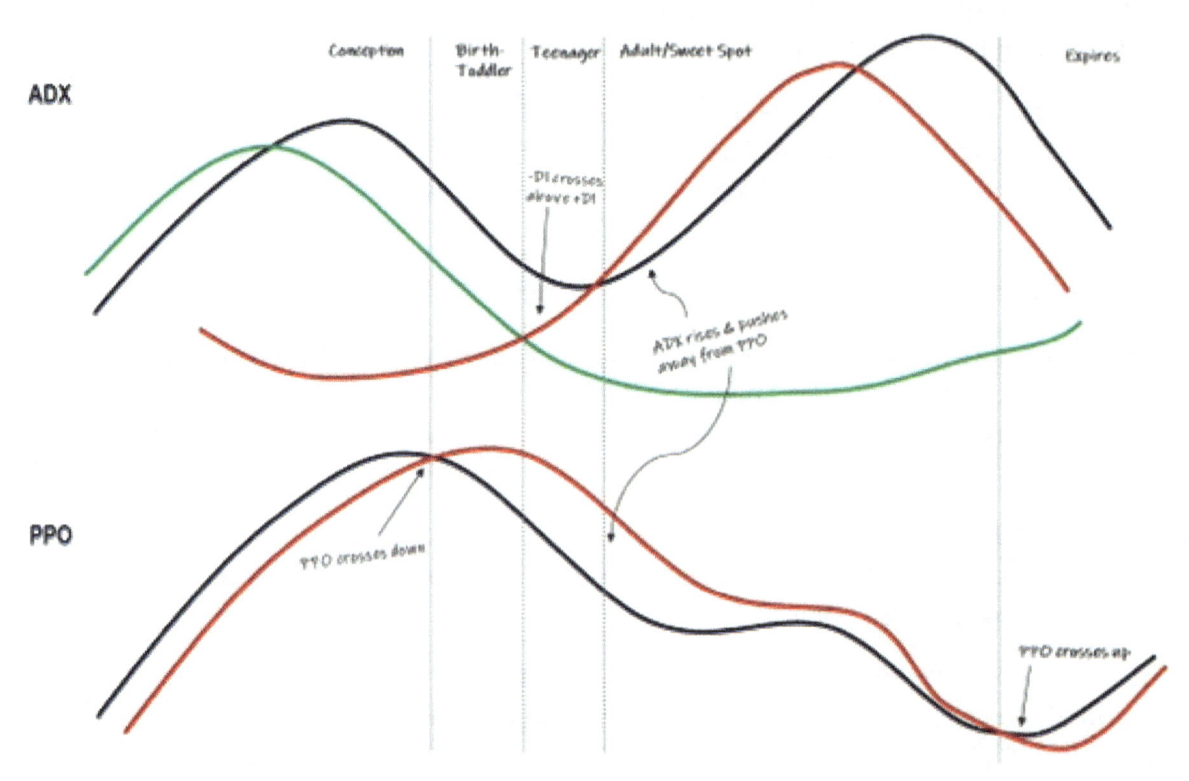

Figure 35 - Courtesy of Stockcharts.com

You will notice in the next few charts I will draw your attention to the 233 EMA. Price and the other EMAs being above the 233 EMA is overall bullish. The price and EMAs being below is overall bearish. Often the 233 will act as support or resistance.

On the NFLX's chart below, you will see that there was a CYF+ Sweet Spot stage on November 29th at about 12:30, where the PPO and ADX were both heading up and running parallel. This is the conception stage of the CYF-. This pattern will then run through all the same stages as the CYF+ pattern "if" it has the -DI crosses and ADX strength to do so. Otherwise, it will fail and reform in the same way as the CYF+ can fail.

The CYF+ Sweet Spot that formed this pattern, the uptrend, weakened to the point that the PPO line crossed down and over its signal line. At the same time, the –DI of the ADX is beginning to show strength by heading up to cross over the +DI line.

Remember the KYO+/KYO- symbols on the chart below match CYF+/CYF- exactly.

Figure 36 - Courtesy of Stockcharts.com

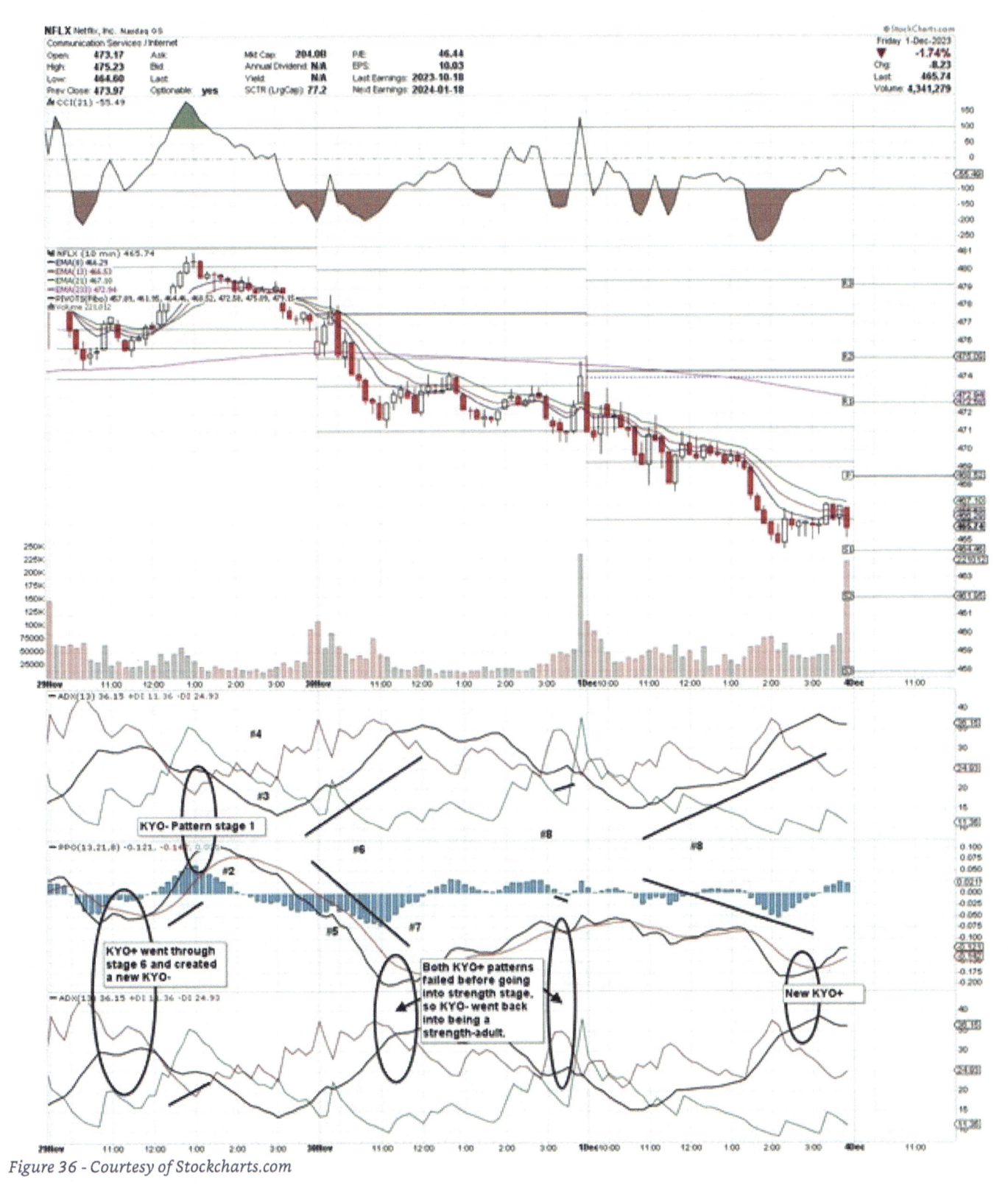

The CYF- went through all its stages and when it was an adult in stage 6, it conceived a new CYF +. The CYF+ pattern failed it never became an adult. It did this twice. When a pattern fails, the previous pattern, in this case, the CYF- became an adult again, stage 8, so it would then conceive another CYF+.

We are getting closer to having all the elements for our patterns in place. Let's look at a few CYF-charts where the stages are marked, and then we will move on to tie everything together.

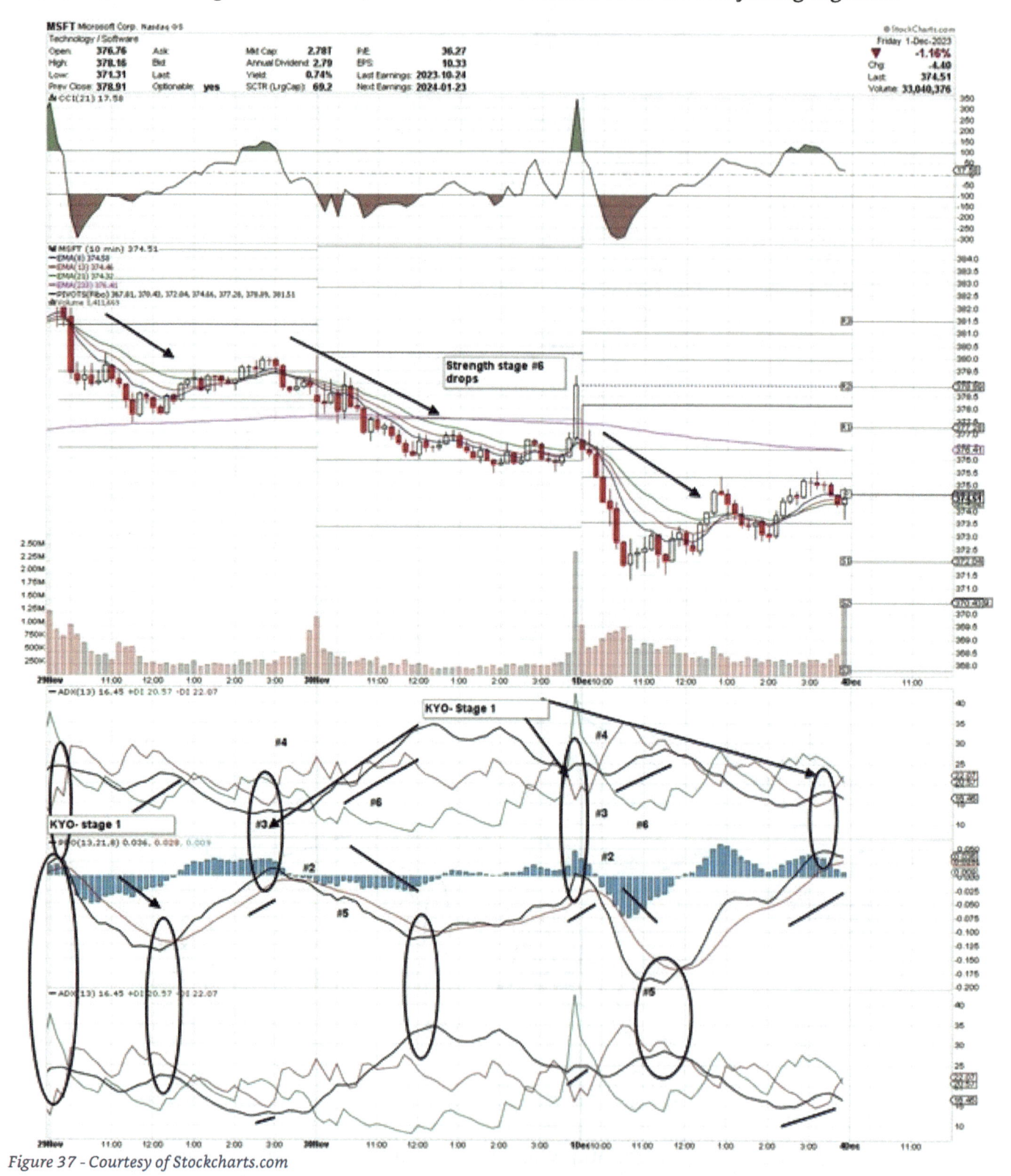

Figure 37 - Courtesy of Stockcharts.com

MSFT's chart above illustrates how a CYF+ Sweet Spot stage forms new CYF- patterns and how the CYF- Sweet Spot stages form new CYF+s.

My very best suggestion is to review and study lots of charts. Place one symbol in after another when you have your chart template set up. Allow your eyes to circle around the chart and to first pick out the conception stages for both the CYF+ (lines drawing together) and CYF- (upward parallel lines) patterns and then locate the Sweet Spots for both patterns. For the CYF+ look for upward parallel lines and, for CYF-, look for the lines pushing away from each other.

Reminder - for CYF+ patterns, use the PPO with ADX beneath it and, for the CYF-, use the PPO with the ADX above it.

Remember as you move through the patterns and their stages, glance up at the volume bars underneath the candlesticks.

Notice how as one pattern wraps up, the volume bars may be slightly larger and swing between selling and buying. And, then as a new pattern gets started again, volume may be higher. During periods of consolidation (flat areas), the volume bars are likely to be very small.

Volume bars that are way out of proportion from candlesticks should be warning signs. Often these funky bars are the first or last bar of the day, showing that a combination of selling and buying are taking place at the same time.

I will post a few more charts with circles around the beginning of the CYF+ patterns and the stages marked for both CYF+ and CYF-. Then the patterns will move through the 7 or perhaps 8 stages until it then forms the alternate pattern.

KYO+/KYO- on the chart stand for CYF+/CYO-.

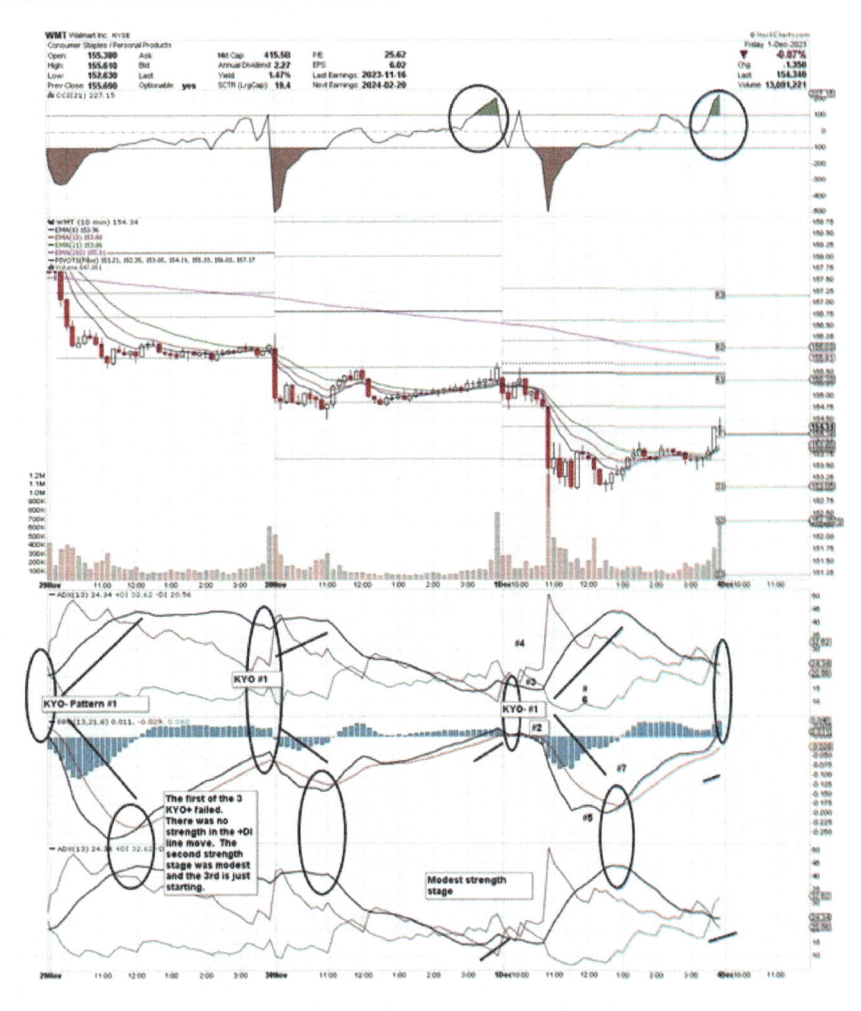

WENDY KIRKLAND

Figure 38 - Courtesy of Stockcharts.com

Meta Platform's (META) chart is shown below.

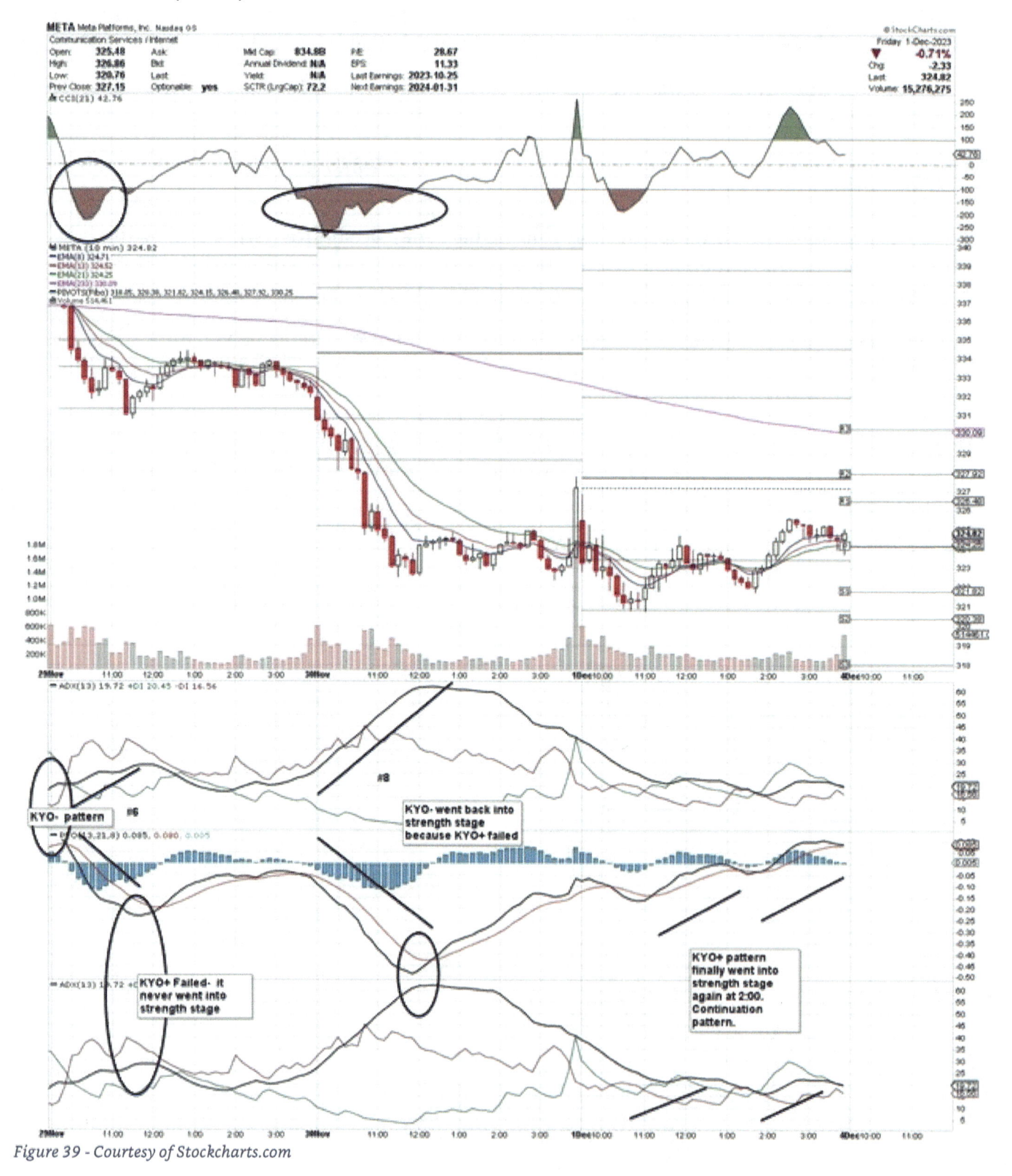

Figure 39 - Courtesy of Stockcharts.com

Shown below is Occidental Petroleum (OXY) chart. It shows an CYF+ that just didn't have the energy to move for an extended period of time to make it to the strength stage and it finally failed.

Figure 40 - Courtesy of Stockcharts.com

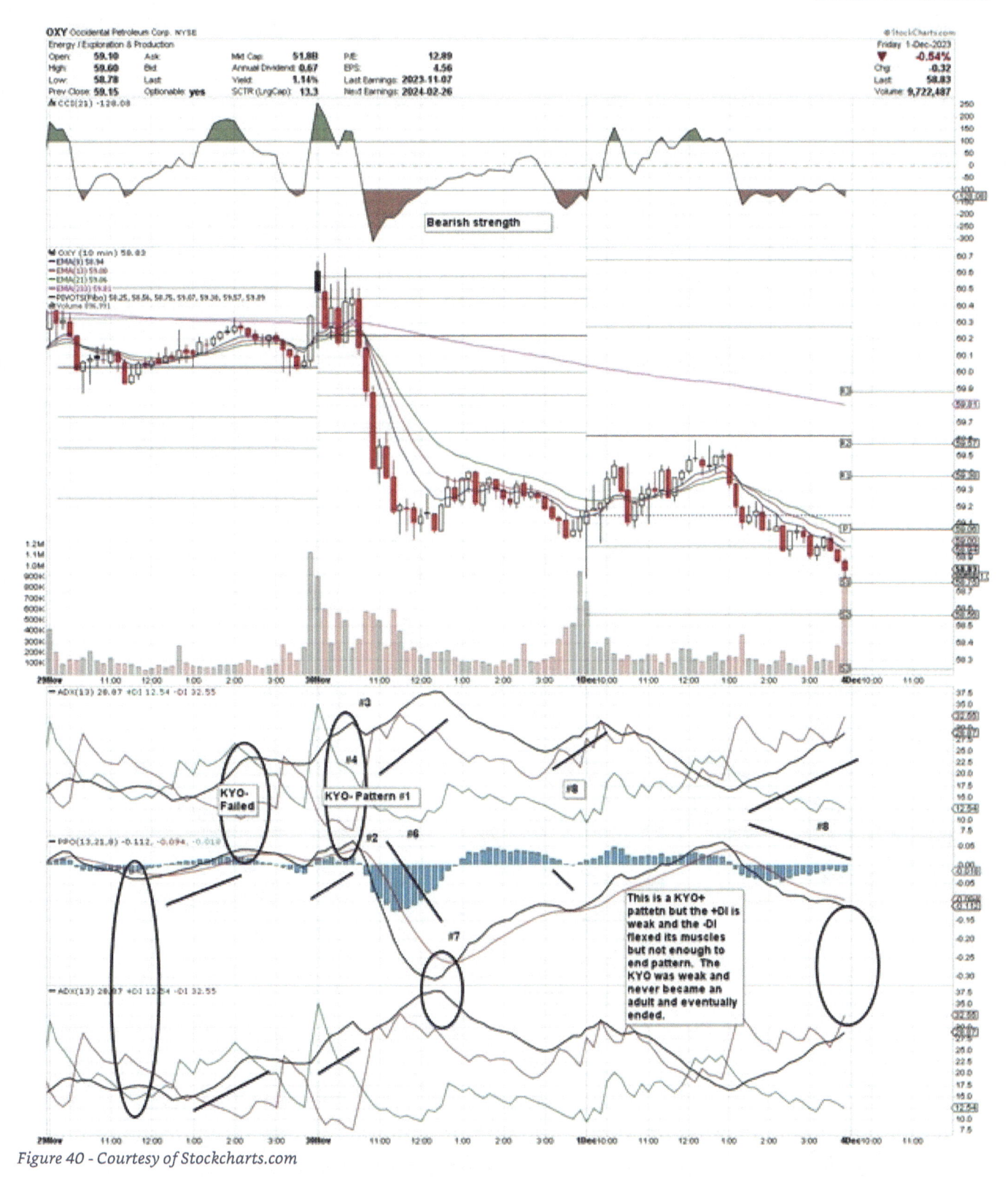

On OXY's chart above, there was a questionable CYF+ pattern in the middle of the chart. The pattern formed and moved through the stages until stage #6 Sweet Spot stage. Did the ADX ever rise? Technically, the PPO stayed up, but the +DI didn't cross. It finally did about 2:00, but the ADX never rose, and the pattern failed. In the end, the PPO crossed down, meaning the CYF+ filed so, it went into a stage #8 of the CYF- or bearish strength stage.

KYO+ or KYO- are the same as CYF+ and CYF-. The important aspect is + or -.

117

Figure 41 - Courtesy of Stockcharts.com

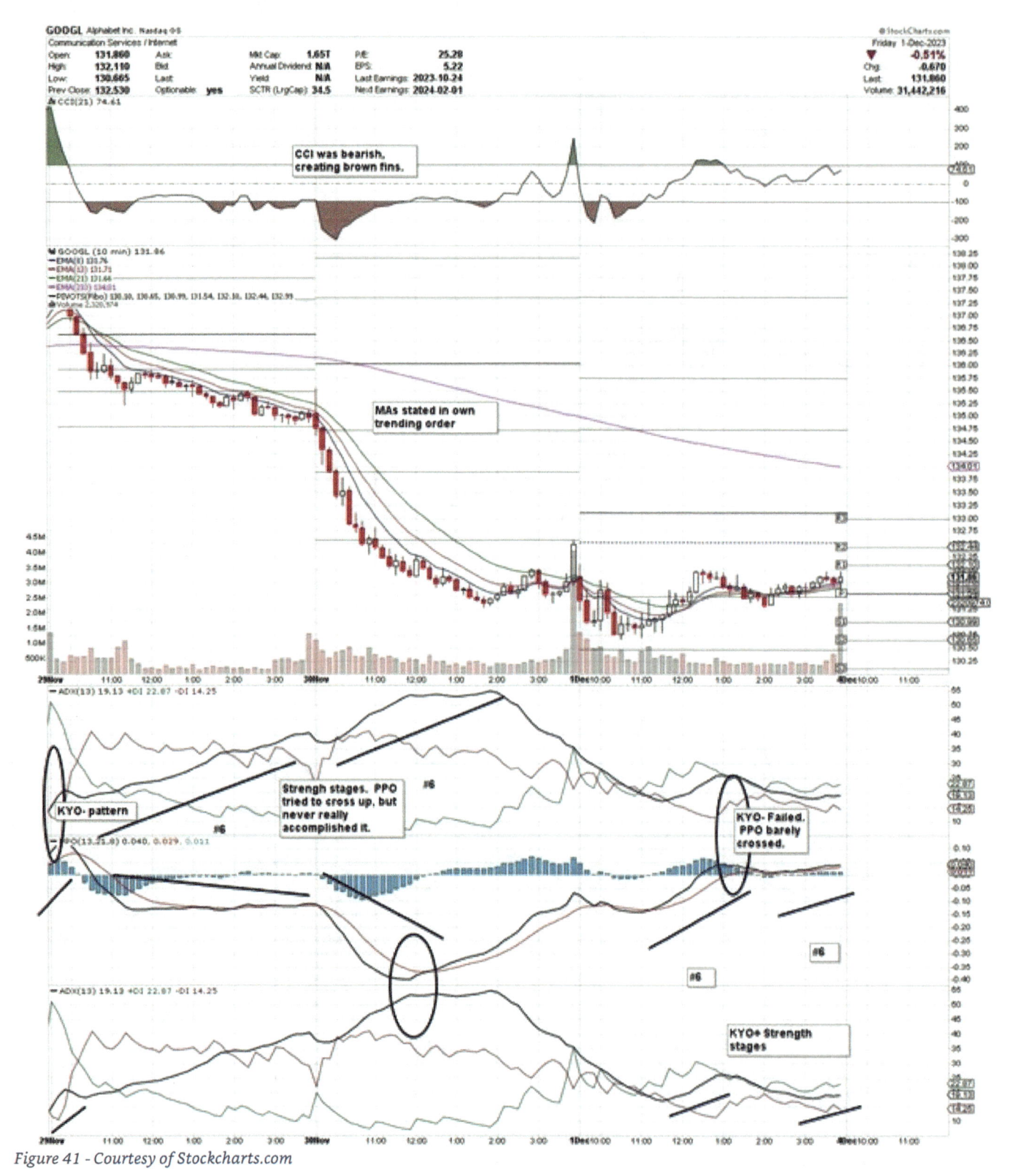

Google's (GOOGL) chart above is a good illustration of the strength of the -DI line. After opening on November 30th, the CYF+ pattern started to play out, yet the +DI was only able rise a little. The -DI stayed in control position until the very end of the day. This messed up the CYF+ pattern until the next day.

To condense this information, the Sweet Spot that is the strength stage is also the stage that creates the reverse pattern, for that to happen, you must have:

CYF+ = PPO cross up, +DI in control, and ADX rising

CYF- = PPO cross down, -DI in control, and ADX rising

When you have these three elements in either direction, you have the needed elements for conceiving the reverse or opposite pattern.

I am going to post another image. This diagram looks complicated at first glance, but its symmetry is beautiful. It shows the directions of each of the indicators needed for each stage of the pattern. It also illustrates that it is the Sweet Spot of the patterns that forms the opposite pattern. The upper red highlights the CYF- and the lower green, the CYF+.

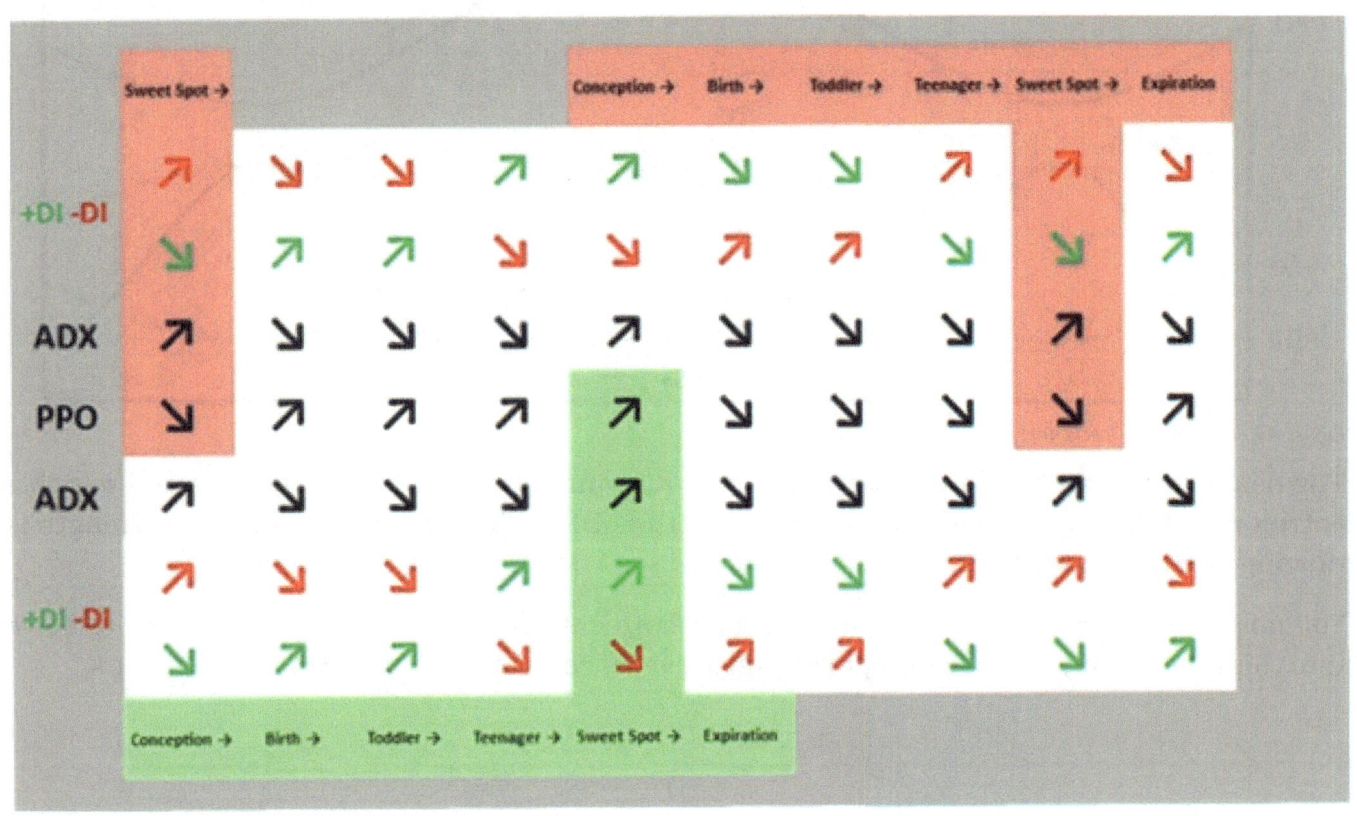

Figure 42 - Courtesy of Wendy Kirkland

The next image takes this information and applies it to a line graph depicting the indicators and showing the directions of the lines for each. Of course, these lines represent a perfect pattern flowing from one stage to another without any wobbles or support/resistance tests along the way. The minor little signs of weakness or pullbacks, whether it is attributed to tests or profit taking, are a natural part of the unfolding process. I have described this as being like a toddler learning to walk. The toddler is apt to stumble and fall a couple times during the process of gaining strength and confidence in its ability to move into new territory.

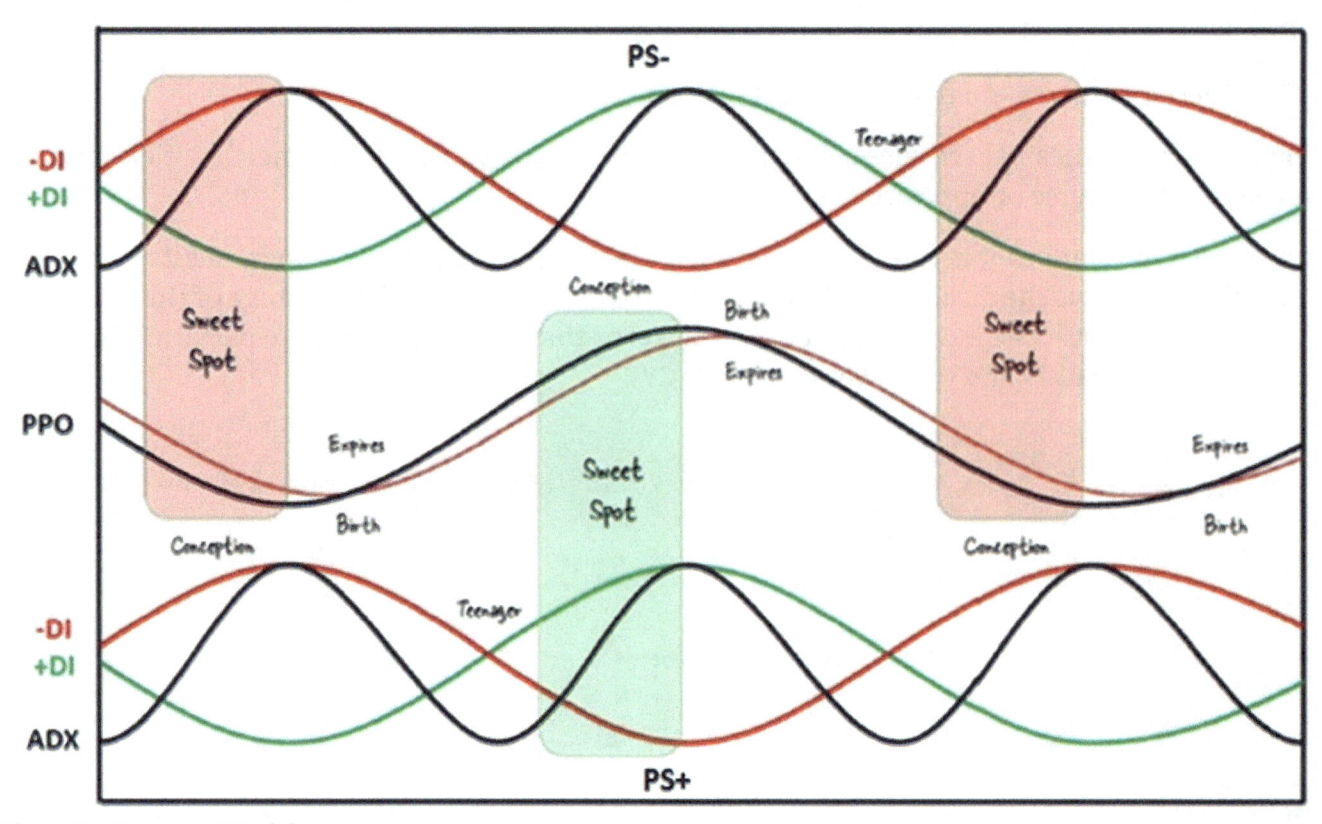

Figure 43 - Courtesy of Stockcharts.com

The next chart is our last in this section. Again, it is annotated with pattern stages and possible entries noted by squares marking the area when the ADX indicator turns up, showing strength is moving into the trade's direction.

You now have the chart information needed for both entries and exits and we are going to delve into this more deeply so you can begin to gain a level of confidence in your trading decisions.

Figure 44 - Courtesy of Stockcharts.com

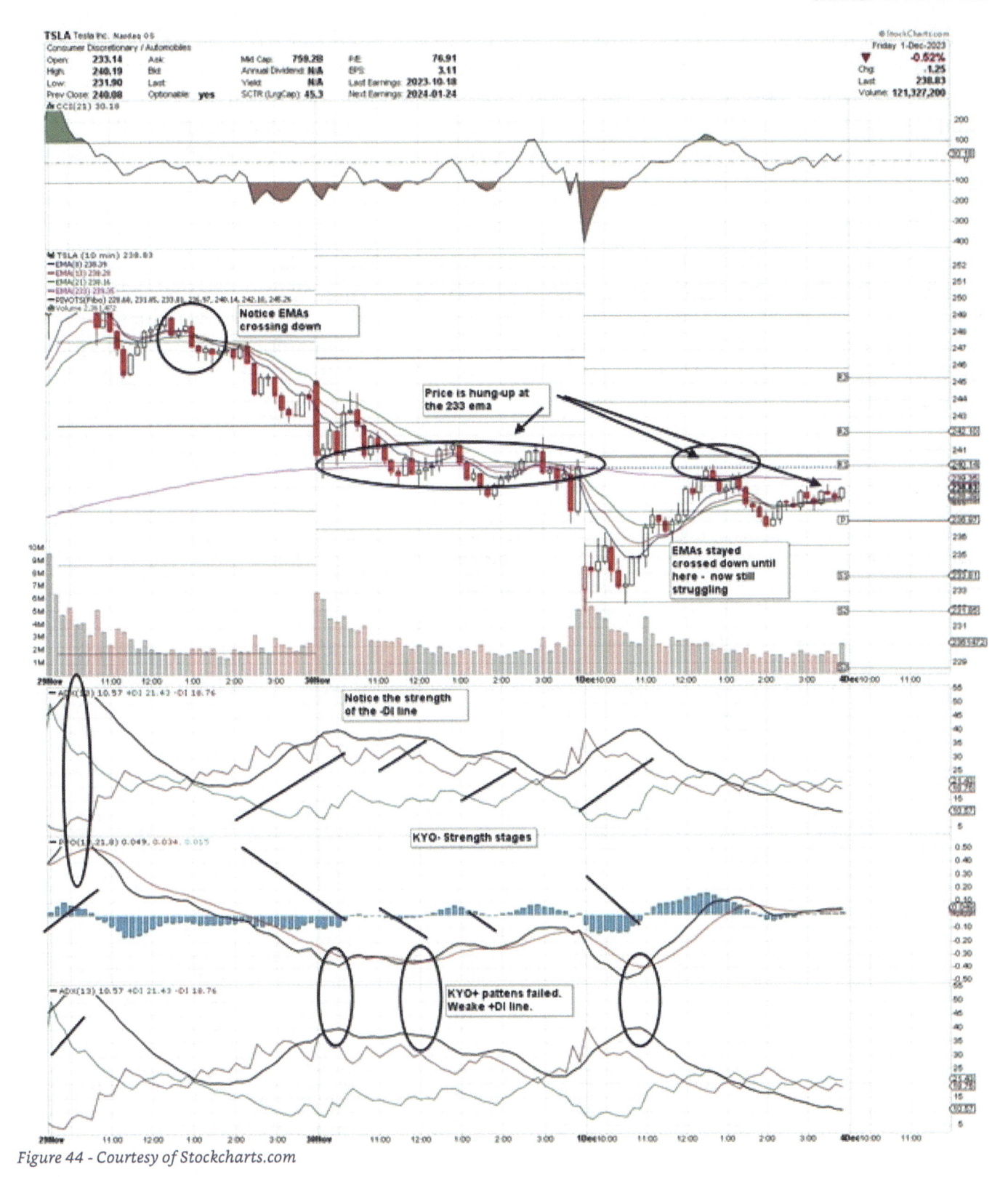

Tesla's (TSLA) chart is above.

The beauty of the two patterns is that one pattern flows into the other. As the CYF- pattern unfolds and plays out going into the Sweet Spot, the chart starts to form the CYF+ Squeeze pattern. As the CYF+ Squeeze pattern forms and plays out going into the Sweet Spot, the CYF- pattern is forming.

Another point that should again be stressed relating to sweet spots or strength stages is that they are the crux of the pattern, "the strength stage". If a pattern gets started and fails to have a stage 6 sweet spot and its PPO crosses up or down, depending on whether it is in a CYF- or CYF+, that failure instantly triggers a sweet spot or strength stage in the previous pattern. Logically, it makes sense. If a pattern fails by not having the power to have a strength stage and fails by having a PPO cross, it makes sense that it failed because of the more powerful strength of the other pattern.

The failure of one pattern can bring about an exit of a trade for little profit or perhaps, even the stop-loss close that brings a small loss to a trade, but it can also, bring you a certainty that there will be a strength stage move in the opposite direction. Since it isn't an original pattern sweet spot, the add-on sweet spot may not last for an extended period, but sometimes it does, especially if there have been several in a row. The point is, it is as close to a guarantee of price direction and movement as you can get and is an opportunity to trade if you are able to monitor the chart and the ADX indicator.

Joy Reminder:

At our most essential level, we have a core where our sense of who we truly are resides. At times, we forget it is there. We ought to regularly remind ourselves. Visit often. We can cling to these core beliefs when things around us are falling apart, knowing that a light shines from within ourselves that can never be put out. Difficult times can be a gift in that they provide an opportunity to remember this inner light that shines regardless of the circumstances of our lives.

When life settles down, we find ourselves to be more self-reliant, knowing that our strength comes from this light that shines at our core. We also find that we no longer need to lean on outside support. Knowing and relying on this strength brings a sense of confidence and joy in all aspects of our life.

ENTRY SIGNAL AND HOLD CONFIRMATIONS

I will now add a few more charts, so you can tie in the other indicators as either an entry signal or trade confirmations to hold until weakness develops.

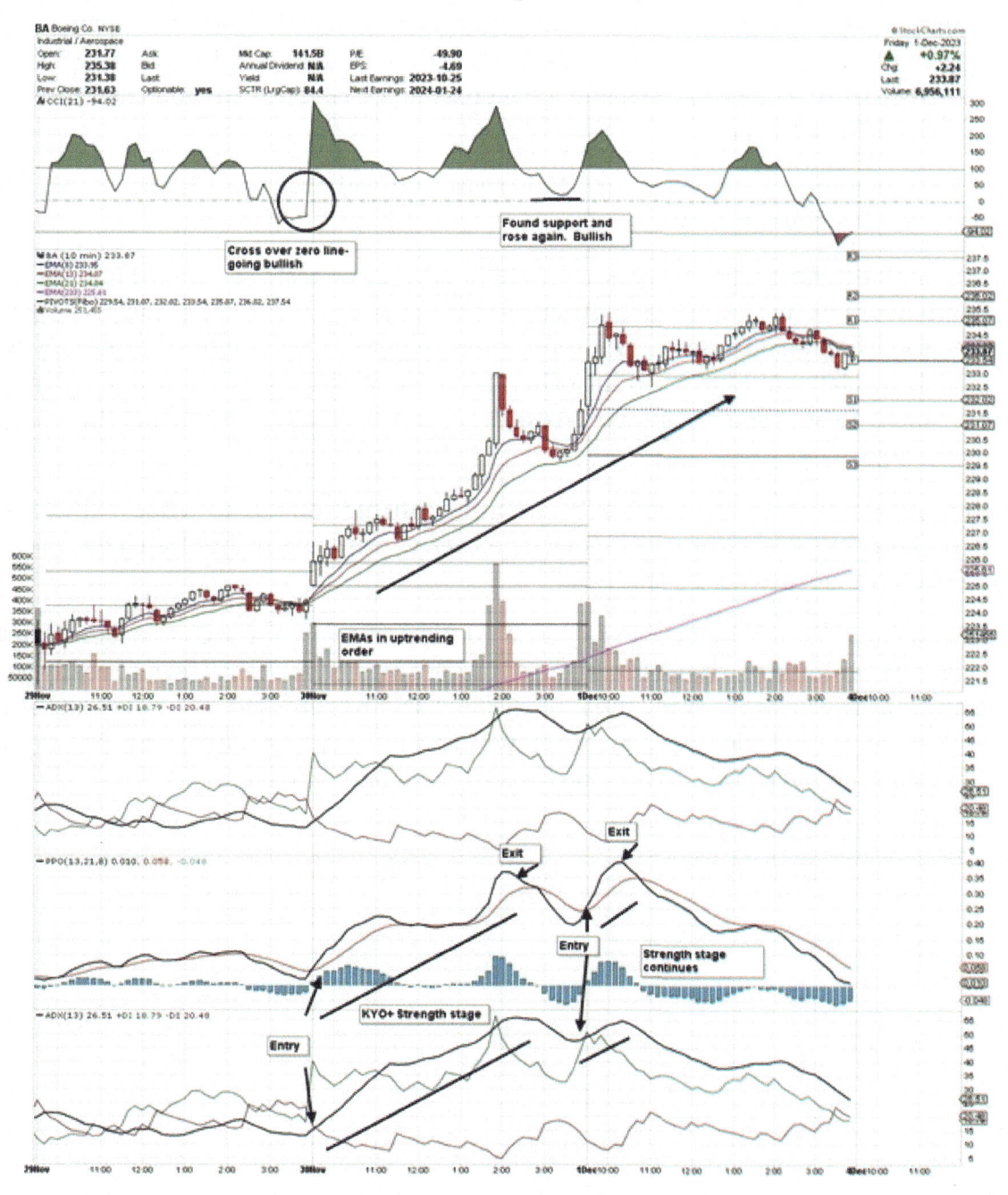

Figure 45 - Courtesy of Stockcharts.com

The ADX and CCI indicator gives us our trade entry signal. First, we visibly see the conception of a CYF+ or CYF- pattern. Note that the CCI points to the equity being oversold in a CYF+ pattern and overbought in a CYF- patterns.

When the CCI crosses up and over the zero line for a CYF+ pattern or down below the zero line for a CYF- pattern, adds confirmation to an ADX rising confirmed entry signal. This isn't jumping the start signal like in a race, or entry at the very first sign of a new trend direction but is waiting for confirmation of the zero-line cross of CCI and ADX rising.

Admittedly, there are traders who have a great appetite for risk, who will enter a trade when the CCI crosses either the -100 or 100 lines, but, as you can see on BA's chart above on the 29th, there were lots of ups and downs. This is the CYF+ that finally played out on the 30th and 1st.

Once you have entered a trade, there are further confirmations that will take place as the trade continues to play out. The CYF+ and CYF- patterns will flow through their stages. Primarily, you will have a +DI cross in a CYF+ pattern and a -DI cross in a CYF- pattern, and then those lines will cross up and over the ADX line.

The EMAs are likely to cross where the 8-EMA crosses up and over the 13, and 21-EMA in a CYF+ pattern or the 8-EMA down and over the 13, and 21-EMA in a CYF- pattern.

As there are wobbles, short areas of weakness, profit-taking and tests of support and resistance, the EMAs will dip down or up toward each other without crossing. As these areas of weakness start, they can be used as a signal to close a trade and capture profit. This might be especially wise if the CYF+ pattern is in a late #6 stage. If on the other hand, the wobble is happening shortly after stage #4, it is more likely to be a test, and support/resistance is more likely to hold, and the trade will flow into the later stages.

The patterns and indicators can provide clues and confirmations as to what is likely to happen next, which can bring a level of confidence in either continuing to hold a trade, take profit by closing the trade, or close to keep a loss small.

In Home Depot's (HD) chart below, there was a confirmed entry for a CYF+ trade. After the CCI crosses above the zero line on the CYF+ pattern. It took a while for the pattern to really get started. It seemed stuck at the Pivot Point for most of the 30th. DI lines crossed up or over the alternate DI line, EMAs crossed up, and the CYF+ pattern flowed through its stages until the PPO crossed down to say the pattern was over, and a new trend direction was ready to begin.

Figure 46 - Courtesy of Stockcharts.com

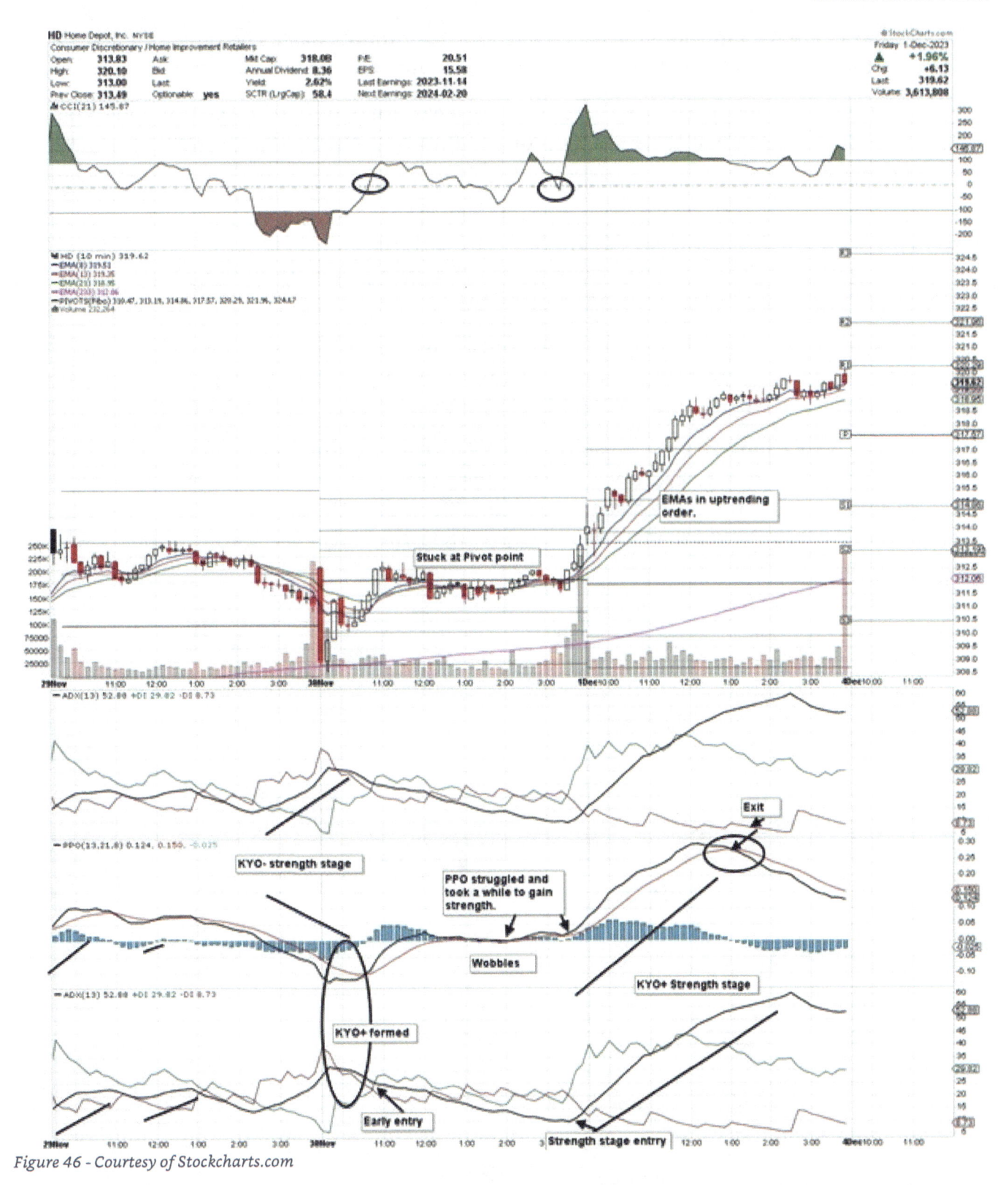

I want to make an important point. Thus far in this book, we have looked at charts and the CYF+ and CYF- patterns as they relate to a 10-minute chart as a probable day-trade. This trade could have lasted two days. Please understand that what you have learned as it relates to chart set-up, patterns and their stages, and indicators can be applied to any time-frame chart.

On a daily or 30-minute chart set-up, the CYF+ and CYF- patterns go through the same stages. The

CYF- indicators are read in the same exact way as a 10-minute chart. The only difference is the length of time it takes for the patterns and indicators to move and do their "thing".

A 10-minute chart might take two or three hours for a pattern to unfold and go through the stages, and a daily might take two or three weeks, while a 30-minute chart might move from stage #1 to #7 in 1 or 2 days.

I will re-address this topic later when we discuss the fact that the strategy you are learning can be applied to swing-trading as well as day-trading. The patterns and chart set-up are flexible. There are apt to be periods of time that day-trading doesn't fit into your current life circumstances, and trading in different time frames would be a better fit.

We will discuss the specific differences, strike and expiration adjustments needed to hold a trade for a longer period in an upcoming section, but, for the moment, let me post a daily and 30-minute chart so that you can see the same CYF+/CYF- patterns as they move through the stages.

On DE's chart below, I marked the stages of the CYF- patterns with squares and the CYF+ Squeeze patterns with circles and placed lines on the Sweet Spots. You will notice that the stages are identical as those on a 10-minute chart. The main difference is the length of time it takes to flow through those stages. Rather than a few hours per trade, the daily chart patterns took weeks to a month or more.

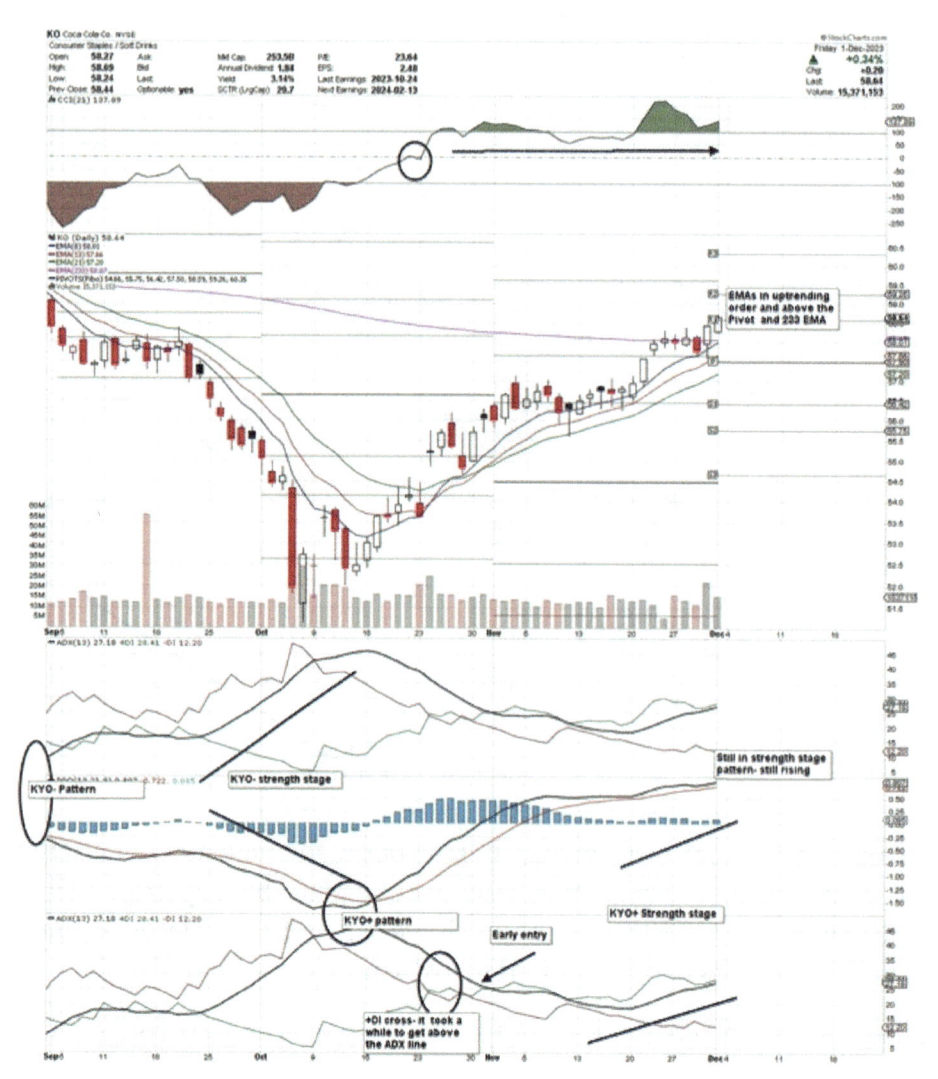

Figure 47 - Courtesy of Stockcharts.com

On the following daily chart for Coca Cola (KO), you will note that the patterns lasted a month and a half to flow through all the stages and it hasn't finished yet.

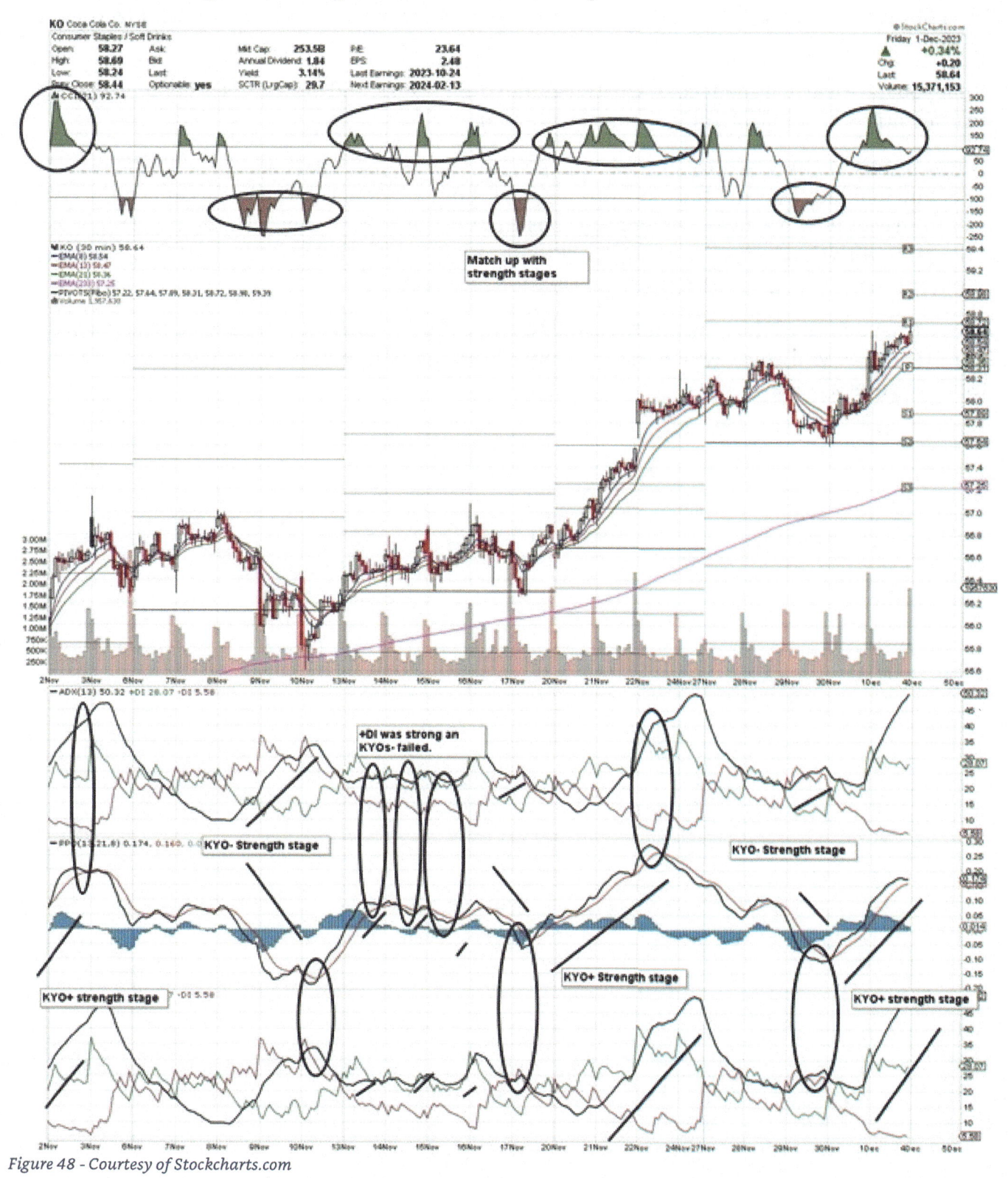

Figure 48 - Courtesy of Stockcharts.com

The stages #1 through #7 are the same on all charts. A CYF+ Squeeze #2 is a PPO cross up on all time frame charts. CYF+ stage #6 is the Sweet Spot on all charts. The stage just takes longer to develop and go through the stage. That is the only difference.

An oversold CCI on all time charts is the same pattern on the indicator, a brown lower fin.

The EMA crosses react the same way and impart specific information that relates to that time frame.

What you have learned about charts, patterns and their stages, and indicators is not only useful but very versatile and will work on any time frame chart.

I suggest during this learning process that you do a lot of chart-gazing. Like walking outside at night and looking skyward, the more often you pick out and identify the Little Dipper and Orion's Belt, the easier it is to zero in and identify those patterns no matter how cluttered the night sky. It is the same with the charts. The more you skim through charts and locate the patterns, the easier it is to spot them amongst all the other information on the chart.

Now, we have covered the indicators, including entry signals and confirmations. Let's look at exits. From there, we will cover which options, expiration and strike price to consider buying as you decide to enter a trade.

EXIT INDICATIONS

For exits, it is logical to decide that, if a pattern is in a stage #6 Sweet Spot of a CYF+ pattern, it would be beneficial to pay close attention for weakness since the next stage -stage #7 - the PPO cross down is the end of the CYF+ pattern when it expires or dies. It might not make sense to wait for that cross and give back some of your profit, so you can watch for other earlier signs of weakness.

On a CYF+ pattern, a +DI cross down below the ADX is likely to be a first sign of weakness or that a change taking place. Is the -DI heading up as if it is gaining strength?

When the ADX line that was previously heading up, showing strength, turns, flattens out and heads down can be a sign that the strength has weakened, and it is time to close the trade. If the ADX's trip up seems overly short, then a flattening or turn down can be just a pause, a wobble and it could head up again. So, look to see what other indicators are saying.

Is the CCI overbought and creating a peak or perhaps, crossing down below the 100-line on the CYF+ pattern?

In an uptrend and a CYF+ pattern, candlesticks are often lined up above the 8-EMA. If they drop below the 8-EMA, heading toward or below the 13-EMA, this is a sign of weakness. In a CYF- candlesticks are often lined up below the 8-EMA, if they cross up over the 8-EMA, heading toward or above the 13-EMA, this is a sign of weakness.

What are the 8, 13-EMA and 21-EMA doing? Is the 8-EMA heading down toward 13-EMA? Has it crossed down?

If you haven't decided to exit and take profit for any of the signals above, a CCI cross below/above the zero line would be a line-in-the-sand closing sign, as would a stage #7 PPO cross down telling you the CYF+ is over, or a cross up for CYF- pattern saying the pattern is complete and over.

Exits can be difficult for some traders. Either they get so excited that they have made a little money, they quickly close the trade taking profit, which, don't get me wrong, there is nothing wrong with taking profit. However, it can be beneficial to close a trade based on a specific reason or indicator suggesting change and a weakness.

I just listed specific chart indicators that suggest a change is taking place. Another way to decide to close a trade can be because it hits your profit target.

You could decide to close a trade based on a percentage. If the trade gains 50% of the premium you paid, you will close the trade and be happy. Or 20% or 75%. You can have that set amount as part of your trade plan or set the amount as a limit sell order at the time you enter the trade.

Another exit target could be a Pivot Point or a support and resistance level. Again, this level becomes part of your trade plan. Perhaps, if you decide when price reaches the R1 pivot point, you will close the trade.

Often, you will have several indicators pointing toward weakness at the same time. One signal or indicator can act as confirmation for another.

It is advisable to have an exit plan and to stick to it, otherwise you start second guessing and then, if the premium rises and then starts to drop, you can become wishy-washy with no plan of action to rely on.

You want to have two exit plans. One is when you will close the trade to take profit, and the other is when you will close the trade if it goes against you, and you have a loss. What is an acceptable loss? Again, this can be a percentage. Are you okay with a 20% loss? A 50% loss?

In trading, there is only one aspect that you are truly in control of and that is loss. Determine your comfort level and stick to it.

You can also have line-in-the-sand loss exit. A PPO cross? Perhaps, a cross down below yesterday's low? A cross of the zero line on the CCI indicator?

Let's look at a couple charts, noting the various exit opportunities. Note which were early and cut profit short and price would have gone higher, or which zeroed in on exact time or were late where profit slipped away.

The charts below are different time frames, again, note how the patterns and their stages are the same. The only difference is the time it takes to flow through the stages.

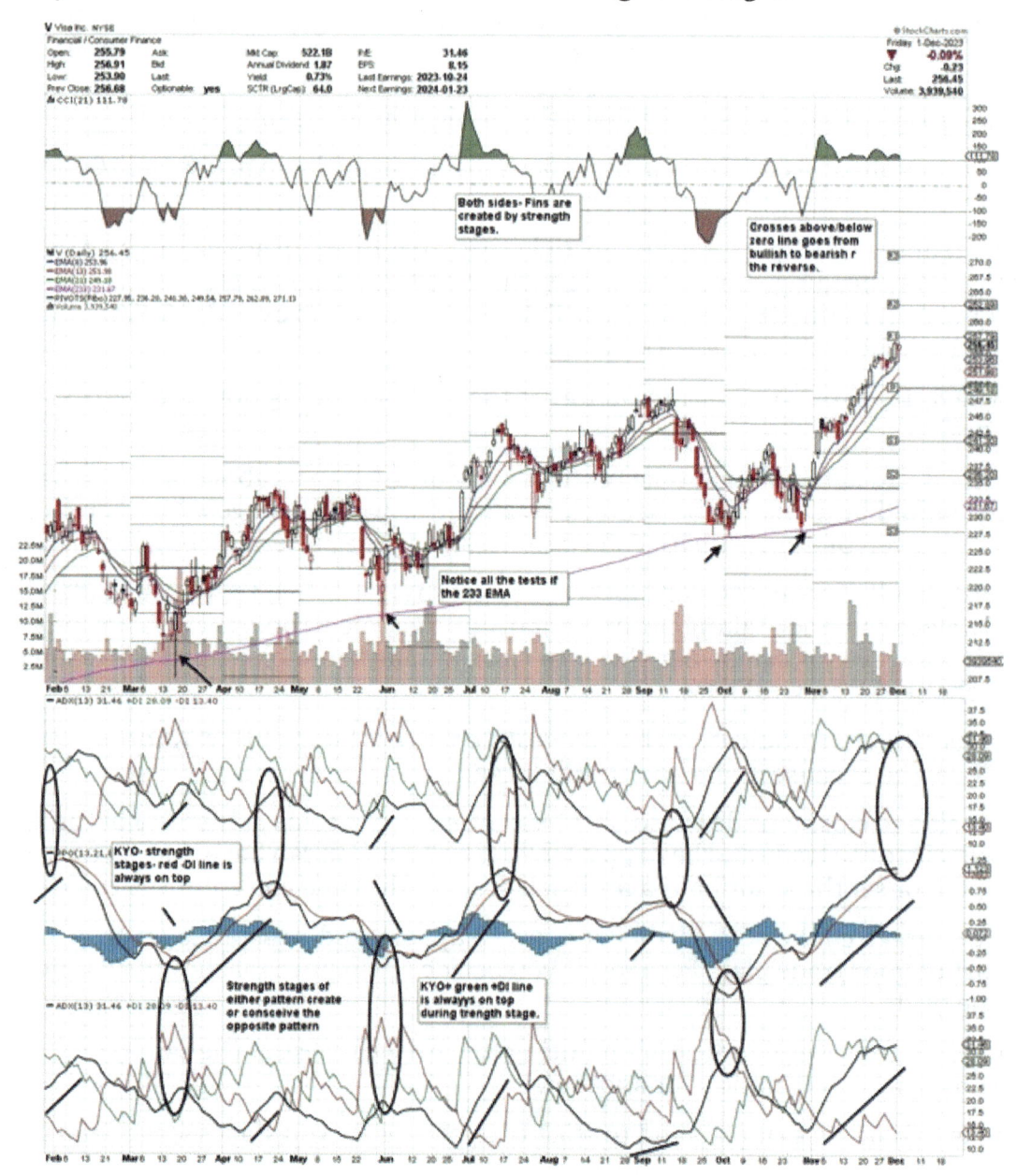

Figure 49 - Courtesy of StockCharts.com

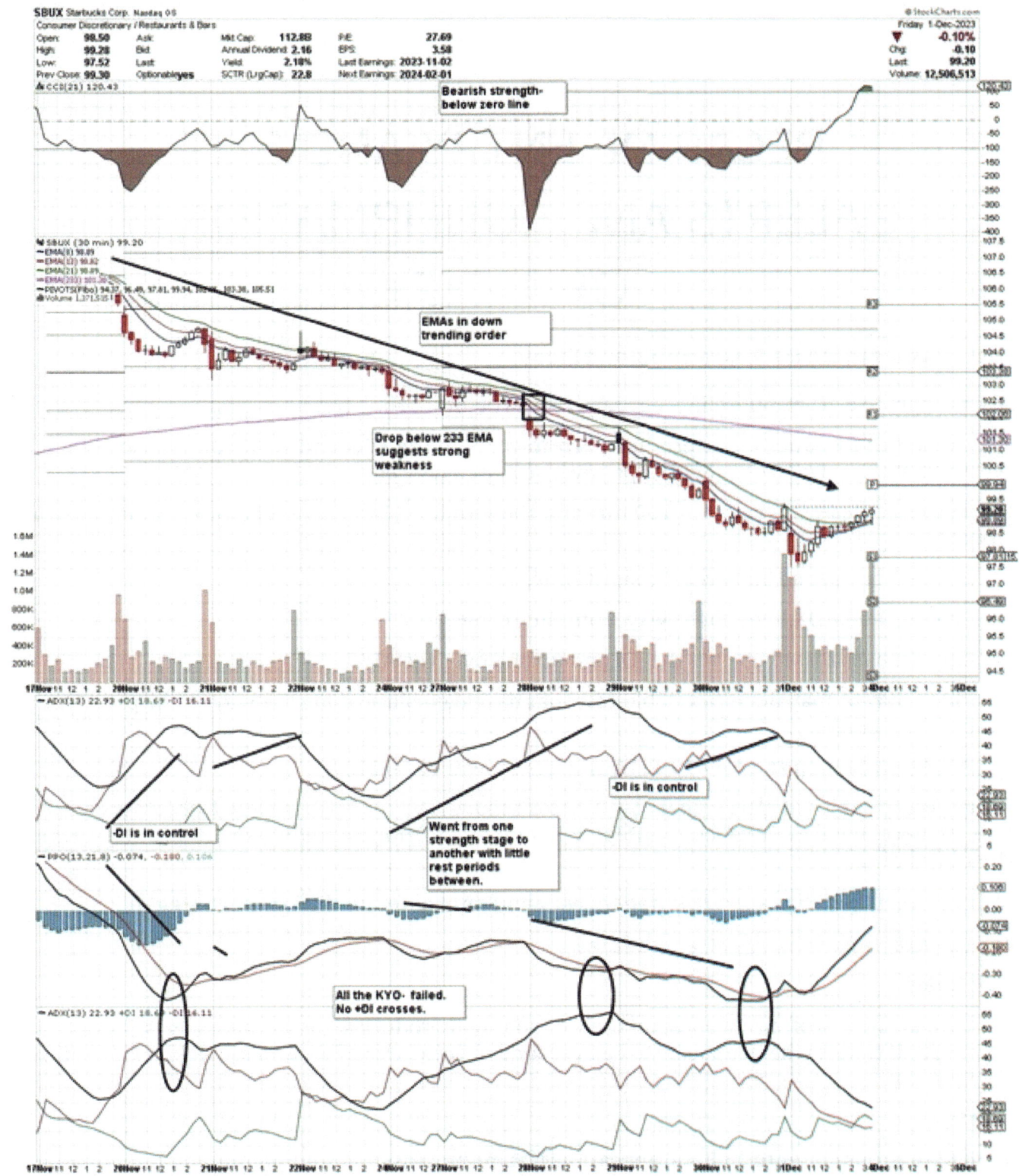

Figure 50 - Courtesy of StockCharts.com

RECAP OF ENTRY AND EXIT ALERTS AND CONFIRMATIONS OF A CYF+

Alert Signals that a trade is forming and Entry:

Alerts apply to a 10-minute chart but can be used on other time frame charts.

1. A new CYF+ Squeeze pattern has been formed by the PPO and ADX coming close together. (Verify that there was a CYF- Sweet Spot overhead that conceived it).

2. The CCI crosses up over the -100 line and the zero line (Can happen before or after other alert signals.)

3. The PPO crosses up and over the signal line.

4. The PPO and ADX lines push away from each other.

5. The +DI has crossed up over the -DI and up and over the ADX.

6. There may or may not be a wobble-test that has taken place along the way at any place through the previous stages.

7. 8-EMA crosses up and over 13-EMA and head toward 21-EMA

Entry- Entry can be at alert signal #5 (+DI cross above ADX) or at alert signal #2 (cross of CCI zero line) or alert signal #7 (EMA cross). Depending on risk tolerance, traders select an entry that suits their level of risk.

Entry- Sweet Spot Signal: (A few traders wait and only enter on the strength stage)

1. The ADX line turns up – Strength stage.

Exit Rules:

Remember there is often a wobble on the PPO that will produce some of these alerts, so look at the PPO to see if that is what it appears to be. A second or third area of weakness (wobble) is likely to be the true exit.

Alerts:

1. 8 EMA drops closer to 13 EMA, appears as if it might cross.

2. Negative candles (in conjunction with other alert indicators).

3. +DI starts to head down or crosses below the ADX.

4. PPO histogram blocks begin to narrow downward.

5. The PPO starts to curl or flatten out.

Confirmation Sell Signals:

These signals can happen one at a time or in conjunction with another signal. Many times, it is better to take a profit once your trade reaches its target at the top of the Sweet Spot rather than to wait for more than one signal and give back a portion of your profit. The signals below are the "line-in-the-sand" exit signals, beyond the price hitting your stop-loss, or hitting your profit target where you have chosen to close the trade.

1. CCI line crosses down from being overbought- below 100-line.
2. CCI crosses down below zero-line.
3. The PPO crosses down over its signal line (unless the +DI remains super high above the ADX).
4. Cross of the 8-EMA over the 13-EMA.

RECAP OF ENTRY AND EXIT ALERTS AND CONFIRMATIONS OF A CYF-

Alert Signals that a trade is forming and entry:

Alerts apply to a 10-minute chart for day-trading, but remember, the alerts are the same for the patterns on any time frame chart you may choose to use for swing trading too.

1. A new CYF+ Squeeze pattern has been formed by the PPO and ADX coming close together. (Verify that there was a CYF- Sweet Spot overhead that conceived it).

2. The CCI crosses up over the -100 line and the zero line (Can happen before or after other alert signals.)

3. The PPO crosses up and over the signal line.

4. The PPO and ADX lines push away from each other.

5. The +DI has crossed up over the -DI and up and over the ADX.

6. There may or may not be a wobble-test that has taken place along the way at any place through the previous stages.

7. 8-EMA crosses up and over 13-EMA and head toward 21-EMA

Entry- Entry can be at alert signal #5 (-DI cross above ADX) or at alert signal #2 (cross of CCI zero line) or alert signal #7 (EMA cross). Depending on risk tolerance, traders select an entry that suits their level of risk.

Entry- Sweet Spot Confirmation Signal: (Some traders choose to just trade strength sweet spots).

1. The ADX line turns up – Strength stage.

Exit Rules:

Remember there is often a wobble under the PPO signal line that will produce some of these alerts, so look at the PPO to see if that is what it appears to be. A second or third area of weakness (wobble) is likely to be the true exit.

Alerts:

1. 8 EMA drops closer to 13 EMA, appears as if it might cross.

2. Negative candles (in conjunction with other alert indicators).

3. +DI starts to head down or crosses below the ADX.

4. PPO histogram blocks begin to narrow downward.
5. The PPO starts to curl or flatten out.

Confirmation Sell Signals:

These signals can happen one at a time or in conjunction with another signal. Many times, it is better to take profit once your trade reaches its target at the top of the Sweet Spot, rather than wait for more than one signal and give back a portion of your profit. The signals below are the "line-in-the-sand" exit signals, beyond the price hitting your stop-loss or hitting your profit target where you have chosen to close the trade.

1. CCI line crosses down from being overbought- below 100-line.
2. CCI crosses down below zero-line.
3. The PPO crosses down over its signal line (unless the +DI remains super high above the ADX).
4. Cross of the 8-EMA over the 13-EMA.

Now that you know the signals for entry and exit. We will look at the option chain, so you'll know how to locate the expiration and strike to select for the day-trading strategy.

TRADE PLAN

Now that you have started the process of identifying recognizable chart patterns, perhaps, have created a list of high ATR equity candidates to focus on, and are aware of the entry and exit alerts and signals, it is wise to come up with a trade plan that suits your personality and appetite as a trader. Do you want consistent profit? Or do you want every penny a trade has to offer? Do you have low risk tolerance? Are you more of a risk taker? Weigh your comfort levels and establish the guidelines you will follow for entry and exits.

Will you enter at the first possible confirmation, or will you wait to make sure there won't be a test as the pattern gets started?

Write it down.... I will use this as an entry signal. I will the this as an exit confirmation. Or I will take profit at this area or percentage. I will close the trade if it goes through this area or creates this amount or percentage loss.

We are going to establish rules for which option strike and expiration to select but start now by beginning to establish your trade plan and then stick to it. Sure, you can adapt and change the plan as you gain more experience, but make those changes intentionally for sound reasons, not being fickle by changing willy-nilly with every trade.

Joy Reminder-

By implementing a mind-set of joy and enthusiasm and sharing it with others, we can engage more deeply in each experience and bring a sense of enrichment to our lives. While we can spontaneously experience many moments of joy and humor during our daily routine, we can also choose to look for and appreciate these qualities "consciously" with intention. By choosing to apply a mind-set of joy in all our activities, we can enjoy each experience on a more meaningful level.

When we share our cheeriness with others, we can contribute to the higher purpose of joy and gratitude that benefits everyone. Bring that sense of joy to each experience today by sharing your lighthearted mood with others.

OPTION CHAIN

Option chains are the place where you as a trader will find specific information about the options that are available for each equity.

As discussed earlier, there are two types of options. Call options are selected when you expect the price of the equity to go up, and Put options are selected when you expect the price of the equity to go down.

On the option chain pictured below, the Call option information is listed on the left side of the chain, and Put options are on the right with the strike prices running down the middle.

Options are available for different time-period expirations. There are weekly options that expire on the 1st, 2nd, 4^{th,} and 5th Friday in a month. The 3rd Friday is when all monthly options expire. There are also quarterly expirations, which expire at the end of each yearly quarter, and LEAPS options, which expire on the last day of each trading year.

With the popularity of option trading, the market continues to add more and more expiration dates. The QQQ, IWM, SPY, and DIA now have daily expirations that appeal to day-traders.

The image below is a chart for the various option expirations, and then the next chart is an expanded version of one of the expiration periods. Some equities offer all the option expiration types, and others just offer monthly expirations. Much depends on the popularity of the equity. SPY, the ETF for the S&P, which is the ETF with the highest volume, offers options that expire every day of the week, plus monthlys, quarterlys, and LEAPS (yearly) expirations.

Show all Expirations
Show all w/o weekly's
DecWk2
Dec '23
Dec '23
Dec '23
DecWk4
DecWk4
Dec '23Q
JanWk1
JanWk2
Jan '24
JanWk4
Feb '24
Mar '24
MarWk5
Apr '24
May '24
Jun '24
Jun '24Q
Sep '24
Sep '24Q
Dec '24
Jan '25
Jun '25
Dec '25

Figure 51 - Courtesy of TC2000

On the chart above, most of the available expiration dates are listed.

Let's open December expirations, below for Apple (AAPL). Notice the columns on both sides of the strike price column are labeled OI and Volume.

Volume is the number of option contracts that have been bought and sold over the course of the current day. OI, or open interest, is the accumulative number of contracts that remain open at this point for that expiration's strike price.

Symbol	Name	Implied Vol	Historical Vol	Price	Change
AAPL	APPLE INC	0.157	0.210	191.24	1.33

2023-12-01 - Calls

Symbol	Bid	Ask	Price	TPrice	Volume	OI	NS	Strike
AAPL	5.70	6.65	6.22	0.00	4253	14829	W	185
AAPL	3.30	3.80	3.70	0.00	5946	6951	W	187.5
AAPL	1.09	1.50	1.16	0.00	59605	22662	W	190
AAPL	0.00	0.01	0.01	0.00	71221	41698	W	192.5
AAPL	0.00	0.01	0.01	0.00	1766	29524	W	195
AAPL	0.00	0.01	0.01	0.00	444	22484	W	197.5

2023-12-01 - Puts

Symbol	Bid	Ask	Price	TPrice	Volume	OI	NS
AAPL	0.00	0.01	0.01	0.00	12668	53422	W
AAPL	0.00	0.01	0.01	0.00	20116	22569	W
AAPL	0.00	0.01	0.01	0.00	65371	16799	W
AAPL	0.86	1.58	1.35	0.00	5632	12382	W
AAPL	3.35	4.25	3.70	0.00	429	187	W
AAPL	5.90	6.80	5.95	0.00	148	141	W

2023-12-08 - Calls

Symbol	Bid	Ask	Price	TPrice	Volume	OI	NS	Strike
AAPL	6.45	6.75	6.56	6.75	1652	11738	W	185
AAPL	4.25	4.40	4.31	4.64	3289	1823	W	187.5
AAPL	2.40	2.45	2.40	2.89	18532	10723	W	190
AAPL	1.02	1.06	1.05	1.61	26309	5788	W	192.5
AAPL	0.33	0.35	0.33	0.78	15969	14220	W	195
AAPL	0.10	0.11	0.11	0.33	5299	3420	W	197.5

2023-12-08 - Puts

Symbol	Bid	Ask	Price	TPrice	Volume	OI	NS
AAPL	0.15	0.18	0.18	0.24	13267	12373	W
AAPL	0.39	0.40	0.40	0.63	15092	7313	W
AAPL	0.96	1.00	1.00	1.38	22743	11830	W
AAPL	2.10	2.16	2.23	2.59	6659	1954	W
AAPL	3.90	4.10	4.05	4.26	515	1661	W
AAPL	6.00	6.55	6.35	6.31	124	6	W

2023-12-15 - Calls

Symbol	Bid	Ask	Price	TPrice	Volume	OI	NS	Strike
AAPL	7.10	7.30	7.15	8.10	2467	31537	S	185
AAPL	5.05	5.20	5.22	6.13	940	12027	S	187.5
AAPL	3.30	3.40	3.30	4.43	5482	72408	S	190
AAPL	1.90	1.94	1.89	3.05	7506	13112	S	192.5
AAPL	0.96	0.99	0.96	1.98	9326	42812	S	195
AAPL	0.43	0.45	0.43	1.21	2652	6385	S	197.5

2023-12-15 - Puts

Symbol	Bid	Ask	Price	TPrice	Volume	OI	NS
AAPL	0.56	0.58	0.56	0.61	6792	34945	S
AAPL	0.98	1.01	1.03	1.13	4753	13774	S
AAPL	1.68	1.73	1.74	1.91	15818	23186	S
AAPL	2.78	2.84	2.89	3.01	2455	5233	S
AAPL	4.35	4.50	4.30	4.43	351	11485	S
AAPL	6.30	6.60	6.40	6.14	15	172	S

2023-12-22 - Calls

Symbol	Bid	Ask	Price	TPrice	Volume	OI	NS	Strike
AAPL	7.60	7.75	7.60	9.94	311	6653	W	185
AAPL	3.90	4.00	3.85	6.22	1388	12848	W	190
AAPL	1.42	1.47	1.43	3.44	1847	15148	W	195

2023-12-22 - Puts

Symbol	Bid	Ask	Price	TPrice	Volume	OI	NS
AAPL	0.82	0.85	0.84	0.77	3375	17307	W
AAPL	2.07	2.14	2.13	1.97	2073	1454	W
AAPL	4.55	4.80	4.73	4.10	237	775	W

Figure 52 - Courtesy of Optionistics.com

New weekly options are born or created on Thursdays and can go out five weeks in time. As the current week is nearing expiration on Friday of the week, the new weekly option is created five weeks further out in time.

On the table above, the strike prices for the expiration period runs through the middle of the Calls and Put columns. The Strike price is the guaranteed price of your option. This is the price that is promised to be paid for that life-raft no matter the condition.

For Call options, the prices that are higher on the chain (a lesser amount) are said to be in-the-money (those in the light shaded areas), and those lower on the chain (a greater amount) are said to be out-of-the money (those below the light shaded areas).

For Put options, it is the reverse, the strikes in the lower light shaded areas are said to be in-the-money, and those above the light shaded areas are out-of-the-money.

I will go deeper into the meaning of these terms, but for the moment, I just want you to become familiar with the chain. Your broker's option chain may look a little different, but in general terms, it will cover the same information.

The break between the shaded area and the unshaded is the strike that will be close to the current price. The closest strikes above or below are apt to either be a small amount above or below the current price.

Greeks are the components used in the calculations of the option's premium, and I often put importance on them when I write about a strategy.

2023-12-08 - Puts

Strike	Symbol	Bid	Ask	Price	TPrice	Volume	OI	NS	IVol	Delta	Theta	Gamma	Vega	Rho	Strike
185	AAPL	0.15	0.18	0.18	0.24	13267	12373	W	0.1716	-0.0795	-0.0480	0.0325	0.0392	-0.0029	185

2023-12-08 - Calls

Strike	Symbol	Bid	Ask	Price	TPrice	Volume	OI	NS	IVol	Delta	Theta	Gamma	Vega	Rho	Strike
185	AAPL	6.45	6.75	6.56	6.75	1652	11738	W	0.2045	0.8822	-0.0769	0.0364	0.0523	0.0311	185
187.5	AAPL	4.25	4.40	4.31	4.64	3289	1823	W	0.1790	0.7911	-0.0978	0.0606	0.0761	0.0282	187.5
187.5	AAPL	0.39	0.40	0.40	0.63	15092	7313	W	0.1553	-0.1762	-0.0761	0.0629	0.0686	-0.0065	187.5
190	AAPL	0.96	1.00	1.00	1.38	22743	11830	W	0.1445	-0.3684	-0.1029	0.0985	0.0999	-0.0137	190
190	AAPL	2.40	2.45	2.40	2.89	18532	10723	W	0.1645	0.6171	-0.1191	0.0876	0.1011	0.0222	190
192.5	AAPL	2.10	2.16	2.23	2.59	6659	1954	W	0.1334	-0.6350	-0.0945	0.1064	0.0995	-0.0237	192.5
192.5	AAPL	1.02	1.06	1.05	1.61	26309	5788	W	0.1510	0.3811	-0.1090	0.0953	0.1009	0.0138	192.5
195	AAPL	3.90	4.10	4.05	4.26	515	1661	W	0.1375	-0.8443	-0.0617	0.0657	0.0633	-0.0317	195
195	AAPL	0.33	0.35	0.33	0.78	15969	14220	W	0.1446	0.1682	-0.0688	0.0656	0.0666	0.0061	195
197.5	AAPL	0.10	0.11	0.11	0.33	5299	3420	W	0.1498	0.0617	-0.0345	0.0307	0.0322	0.0022	197.5
197.5	AAPL	6.00	6.55	6.35	6.31	124	6	W	0.1463	-0.9428	-0.0312	0.0296	0.0304	-0.0358	197.5

Figure 53 - Courtesy of Optionistics.com

The element of the Greeks that I often stress is the Delta. Delta is the amount that the strike's premium will increase in value for each dollar move in the equity's price. (The darker shaded strikes are Puts and the light shaded are Calls.) If the strike's Delta is .53, the Ask premium will increase .53 cents for each dollar move in the equity's price.

I am going to insert a different company's option chain because in Optionistics, you must mentally deduct the -% amount from 100 to know the Delta percentage. All service chains look a little different. The information is the same, it is just presented with variations.

For the day-trading strategy, the Delta is less important than it might be with other strategies. We are going to zero in on out-of-the-money (OTM) strike prices that are at or below a premium of .30 cents, and they are apt to have a very low Delta. Focusing on these lower priced premiums will allow us to purchase more contracts for the same total investment per trade, which means a small, quick move in price will give us a great level of profit.

We will cover the importance of this element as we move into the guidelines for the strategy.

The Ask premium changes as the equity's price goes up and down throughout the day. The Ask amount is what you are likely to pay when you buy-to-open your trade. The Bid premium is what you are apt to receive when you close your trade or sell-to-close. The difference between the two is the commission the Exchange receives for handling the trade.

On the chain below, let's zero in on the OTM option in the .30 range.

I had to select OTM strikes to get far enough OTM to select a premium below .30.

The 202.50-strike had a premium of .16, so it is within our .30 limit. There were several below 202.50-strike that fit, but I selected 202.50 which is .16 which fits our criteria.

Each contract you purchased at the 202.50-strike will cost $16. Therefore, buying 20 contracts will be a $320 total investment, which controls 2000 shares of Apple (AAPL) until the option's expiration on December 15th, five trading days from the current date.

2023-12-15 - Calls								2023-12-15 - Puts							
Symbol	Bid	Ask	Price	TPrice	Volume	OI	NS	Strike	Symbol	Bid	Ask	Price	TPrice	Volume	OI	NS
AAPL	6.15	6.35	6.30	6.30	4170	75194	S	190	AAPL	0.29	0.30	0.29	0.32	27421	40451	S
AAPL	4.00	4.10	4.15	4.27	7851	15123	S	192.5	AAPL	0.63	0.64	0.63	0.78	31269	12378	S
AAPL	2.25	2.28	2.29	2.62	36806	41496	S	195	AAPL	1.35	1.37	1.35	1.63	24777	23855	S
AAPL	1.02	1.05	1.05	1.43	34895	11921	S	197.5	AAPL	2.60	2.69	2.64	2.94	8014	3111	S
AAPL	0.40	0.41	0.40	0.69	29172	66521	S	200	AAPL	4.45	4.55	4.50	4.69	2047	1298	S
AAPL	0.14	0.16	0.16	0.29	6375	4200	S	202.5	AAPL	6.70	7.10	6.80	6.79	302	1777	S

Figure 54 - Courtesy of Schwab.com

Let's put this information all together.

This is an option chain for AAPL. You are analyzing information for the expiration date of December 15th. Since it is for a Friday's expiration, we know it is a weekly expiration. The Ask premium is $0.16 for the 202.50 strike. As AAPL's price goes up, the strike moves deeper toward being in-the-money. The Bid is .13, and this is the likely amount you would receive when you close the trade if this is the current Bid premium when the Exchange receives your order form to close the trade.

The .02 difference between the Bid and Ask is the commission the Exchange receives for handling the trade.

Again, we will delve into the specifics for expiration, strike, Delta, volume, and OI guidelines for this strategy in the next section. For the moment, skim over the option chain so that you are familiar with the overall set up of the chain and how you locate the important elements of information.

Joy-reminder-

Taking time to consider the ways we can best achieve our goals opens us to new possibilities and boosts our potential for success. Taking any form of action toward our goals is beneficial, but we can increase the effectiveness of our actions if we take time to carefully consider and plan first. By consciously opening our minds to new ideas, we hone mental clarity and increase the likelihood that we will receive insights, intuition or gut-feelings that could aid us on our journey. If we then use our new ideas and insights to form a detailed plan of action, we can focus our energy to efficiently achieve our goals. By combining optimism with intentional planning, you can make the achievement of your goals a joyful reality.

CHANGE YOUR FUTURE DAY-TRADING OPTION GUIDELINES

In the Day-Trading strategy, we will be selecting both Call and Put options from an option chain, considering the following criteria:

First Requirement: The first consideration will be open interest. Open interest is the number of open contracts at the current moment, whether they are long or short positions. You want "Some" open interest, if you purchase an option with no open interest, you may have trouble selling the option when you are ready if there aren't enough interested traders wanting to buy it from you.

To fine tune this even further, make sure there is at least some amount of volume. "Some" is a rather ambiguous term, but since there is not a set number requirement for volume, "some" will have to do. The point is that you want to see daily activity.

Volume is the number of contracts bought and sold for the day, while open interest is an accumulated total for all the contracts on that strike option.

If there is no volume on the strike price you are interested in, it may be that you are looking at a Call option chain when the market is heading down, so there might not be interested buyers, and this may explain the lack of volume.

This is a general trading rule, no matter what equity you are trading, and it is almost a moot point with many of the higher volume ETFs because of the huge amount of open interest in most of the strike prices. But, on occasion and especially with the new weekly options, there can be strikes where there is not enough open interest or volume.

This can also take place on options that are deep out-of-the-money, which are the type of options you will likely be buying or very deep in-the-money, too deep for traders to be interested.

On Thursdays when new weekly options are created or born, there will be no open interest because it is the first day that they are being traded. The volume accrued during the first day of trade will become open interest tomorrow. So, on that first trading day rather than looking for open interest, you would want to see some volume or more before taking a position at that strike.

In one of the next guidelines, I will discuss the other aspects found on an option chain, but for now let's just note the open interest and volume mentioned in this requirement.

Second Requirement: The second consideration is option expiration. In the Day-Trading strategy, it is suggested that you purchase an expiration that is in the current week's expiration.

You will likely want to sell and close your trade as soon as the pattern gives an exit signal to avoid accelerating time decay. In a sense, it is like a snowball rolling downhill. As you near the expiration date, the time decay escalates as the date nears, and this is especially true when you are trading this week's option as expiration closes in.

The more time you buy, the higher the premium will be. Time has value. But remember, no matter how far out your expiration date is, you can sell and close the trade anywhere along the line. In the Day-Trading strategy, you are likely to only be holding the trade for a few hours at most.

An easy way to think of time decay is to liken it to a use-by date on a gallon of milk. On the first day of the use-by time frame, you have 5 days to consume the milk. As each day passes, there is less time value, a shorter time to utilize the product, until on the last couple days when you better drink quickly before it is poured down the drain.

Expiration erodes much more quickly as time approaches the expiration date.

The Day-Trading strategy focuses on both upward and downward equity movement. Quite often, but not always, a Put trade, as opposed to a Call trade, has a more rapid descent. It often takes more time for an equity to paddle up stream and less for the stream to thrust the equity down. You want enough expiration time to take full advantage of the move if there is a delay or if the move lasts longer than expected, but you don't want to be paying for an extra week or two when the plan is to only hold the trade for an hour or two.

These guidelines relate to the Day-Trading strategy and the 10-minute charts we've been studying. If you were to decide to trade 30-minute, 60-minute or daily charts, you, of course, would need to follow the same guidelines but adjust the specifics so they relate to those time frames. You would want to buy more time, so the pattern has time to unfold.

Another over-shadowing consideration is the environment of the stock market. Think of this as the mood of the market. Is it turbulent? High volatility, low volatility? Is it in a solid uptrend? Is it going into a correction? Is there a sector rotation taking place? The answer to any of these questions could influence the amount of time that it could take your trade to develop. It would be a shame to only plan for a one-hour Call trade, while the indices are pulling back and selling off.

Depending on the market atmosphere, you will be participating in a variety of trade lengths, so it pays to be aware of the trading weather conditions.

The overall objective of the Day-Trading strategy is to get into a trade at the beginning of the move and exit quickly at the end of the trade before giving back any profits.

Third Requirement: A third, yet major, consideration must be available funds. Since extra time or expirations that are further out in time will be available at an increased premium, you can only work with the funds you have on hand to invest. Don't be tempted to cut the expiration period short because of a shortage of funds! Find another equity, one that has a lower premium.

For our Day-Trade option trades, set an average total investment for each trade – which on average should be no more than 10% of your account balance. That might be an investment amount between $100 and $500. Decide on an amount that fits your trade account. This is the total amount at risk for the trade. You can't lose more than the $100 to $500 you invest, and you know the full amount that is at risk before you ever enter the trade.

A good rule to consider is to invest no more than 10% of your account balance in any one trade and have only half your account invested at any one time.

The main reason for setting a $100 to $500 limit is that trading fees or commissions need to be considered when trading multiple contracts. One broker might charge $6.95 for 1 to 10 contracts and $1.25 for each contract thereafter. Other brokers may have slightly higher or lower commission fees. Lately, many brokers have been lowering fees or setting a low base fee.

By limiting each trade to an average of $100 to $500, you are limiting the risk on each trade and controlling the costs to place the trade and being consistent.

Again, good risk management suggests placing no more than 10% of your account balance into any one trade and only having about half of your account working at any one time. This protects your account should the worst of the worst happen within the market.

If you are starting with a small account, say $1,000 and investing no more than $100 in each trade, it will take a little while to build the account up, but it does happen. Let's say you did 2 trades investing $100 each and made a 30% profit or $33 or $66 for the two contracts and the trade fee was $7.50 for each trade or $15 for the two trades. That gives you a profit of $51 that is added to your account. Perhaps, on your next trades you can invest $110. This amount will continue to increase. Follow your rules and guidelines.

I do not give personal investment advice. Deciding on an amount to invest is a personal choice and should be decided on by the guidance of your licensed broker.

This brings up the importance of finding an online broker with reasonable fees.

It is also advisable that, once you decide on an option trade limit total, stick with that total. Don't trade $100 on one trade and $350 on another and $500 when you feel flush. Come up with a trade amount that feels comfortable and maintain the trade range until you make a conscious choice to change to another amount as your trade limit.

Consistency is part of the plan and helps set in place certain expectations. Remember, you are reinforcing and sending out a message to the universe that you expect consistent returns on your trades as you follow your trade plan. My dad's saying of, expect the unexpected and expect it to be great, comes into play here. You are expecting awesome results each time you put your plan in place. You are taking the same consistent steps expecting the same terrific outcome. Remember, these are planned day-trades. Believe in them! Know they will be profitable.

Fourth Requirement: The next option for consideration is strike-price. The strike price we select should be out-of-the-money with a premium less than .30, and this will depend on the equity you choose to trade. Remember, we defined these terms earlier as we discussed the strike prices.

Let's say you want to purchase a Call option to benefit from a specific equity's stock. Its current price is $68.25 a share. You can agree to buy shares of the stock for $65, or you can agree to buy the stock for $80. If both options cost the same, which one would you choose to buy? The options with the $65 strike price. That's a no-brainer.

Now let's assume the stock increases in value to $75. If you had the right to buy the stock for $65, you could "exercise" your right, purchase the stock for the strike price of $65, and then sell it for the stock price of $75, thus earning a profit of $10 per share, or $1,000 for your 100-share option contract.

You would not "exercise" your right to buy if you owned the $80 strike option, but the stock price was $75. You would choose to do nothing because there would be no profit in it. You'd be paying $5 more than its current price.

The example of buying and selling stock is used for illustration in our example. The process of buying and selling the stock happens silently behind the scenes through the broker's website and at the Exchange. You are not involved in this process and all you see is the end profit/loss result.

The fact that there would be a $1,000 profit on the option with a $65 strike price, and no profit on an option with an $80 strike price illustrates how an option's value increases or decreases, depending upon the agreed-upon price at which the stock can be purchased.

The $10 per share you earned if you exercised your option is the "intrinsic value" of the option. You want the intrinsic value to accrue quickly as the stock value increases for Calls or drops in the case of a Put option. Therefore, you want to buy your options out of the money for the Day-Trading strategy. For the strategy covered in this book, I recommend buying "deep" out-of-the-money (OTM) with a low ask premium of .30 or less, but a strike that has a good bit of open interest. You want other traders to also be in the trade.

The option chain below is for Coca Cola (KO). Again, the Call options are on the left side, strikes through the middle, and Put options on the left.

Sometimes new traders have trouble understanding the concept of Puts or the essential difference between Calls and Puts.

The arrows are pointing to the open interest of that strike price.

Trade	Select	ⓘ	93	3,083	4.47	+1.47	2.30	5.00	45.00	0.20	0.25	0.25	-0.19	100	1,234	ⓘ	Select	Trade
Trade	Select	ⓘ	47	686	3.50	+0.98	2.14	3.65	46.00	0.28	0.40	0.33	-0.29	45	386	ⓘ	Select	Trade
Trade	Select	ⓘ	118	382	2.97	+0.86	2.17	3.05	46.50	0.35	0.87	0.40	-0.34	83	99	ⓘ	Select	Trade
Trade	Select	ⓘ	99	338	2.66	+0.94	2.06	2.60	47.00	0.48	0.55	0.50	-0.42	198	181	ⓘ	Select	Trade
Trade	Select	ⓘ	102	2,795	2.11	+0.77	1.62	2.25	47.50	0.52	0.66	0.61	-0.42	139	2,184	ⓘ	Select	Trade
Trade	Select	ⓘ	76	467	1.85	+0.80	1.50	2.06	48.00	0.58	0.80	0.77	-0.43	447	158	ⓘ	Select	Trade
Trade	Select	ⓘ	117	131	1.54	+0.77	1.21	1.47	48.50	0.41	0.98	0.90	-0.55	59	478	ⓘ	Select	Trade
Trade	Select	ⓘ	477	172	1.12	+0.52	0.73	1.17	49.00	1.01	1.17	1.13	-0.65	690	66	ⓘ	Select	Trade
Trade	Select	ⓘ	944	3,299	0.66	0.36	0.63	0.70	50.00	1.23	1.73	1.60	-1.02	214	1,772	ⓘ	Select	Trade
Trade	Select	ⓘ	997	367	0.4	+0.29	0.35	0.50	51.00	0.01	4.75	1.82	-1.98	2	17	ⓘ	Select	Trade
Trade	Select	ⓘ	289	0	0.28	0	0.17	0.32	51.50	2.60	2.84	2.60	0	163	0	ⓘ	Select	Trade
Trade	Select	ⓘ	177	143	0.20	+0.13	0.14	0.25	52.00	3.05	4.40	2.84	0	3	0	ⓘ	Select	Trade
Trade	Select	ⓘ	538	2,865	0.16	+0.10	0.10	0.15	52.50	2.63	3.75	3.33	-2.06	5	1,511	ⓘ	Select	Trade
Trade	Select	ⓘ	54	0	0.10	0	0.07	0.13	53.00	2.20	6.60	0.00	0	0	0	ⓘ	Select	Trade
Trade	Select	ⓘ	33	0	0.06	0	0.00	0.07	54.00	2.60	7.00	4.65	0	2	0	ⓘ	Select	Trade

Figure 55 - Courtesy of Charles Schwab

Calls give the option trader the opportunity, but not the obligation, to buy the stock for the strike price and sell it for (hopefully) the stock's current higher price.

The example below is fictitious and partially based on the option chain information above.

Example: You've bought the Call Strike price of 52 for the $0.25 Ask premium as the stock's price increases so too will the Ask premium. Open interest of 143 is an okay amount but check out the 52.50 strike with 2,865.

If you paid the $0.25 Ask premium, your total investment is $25 for the 100-share option contract. As price increases, say up $1.25, your Ask premium may increase to $0.45.

Bid price is a little lower by the spread (cost of handling the transaction). In our example, let's use a $0.02 spread, so you could expect the Bid, or the amount you would receive when the option was sold to be about $.36 per share, or $36 for the option contract of 100 shares.

Pretty good trade. You paid $0.25 and received $0.36 per share or a gain of $0.11 (44%) or $11 for the 100-share contract. Had you purchased 20 contracts for a total of $500 and sold for $720, you'd reap a profit of $220.

Puts give the option trader the opportunity, but not the obligation, to buy the stock for the current stock price and sell it (hopefully) for the higher strike price.

The example below is fictitious and partially based on the option chain information above.

Example: You've bought a Put Strike price of $45 for $0.25 Ask premium, or a $25 total investment per option contract. Let's say the and price drops to $48.50.

The Ask might now be $0.49 ($0.25 +$0.24) and the Bid is a little lower by the spread (cost of handling the transaction) In our example, let's use $0.08, so you could expect the Bid, or the amount you would receive, to be about $0.41 per share, or $41 profit for the option contract of 100 shares.

Another nice trade! You paid $0.25 or $25 per contract and received $0.41 per share or $41 per contract, or a gain of $0.16 (64%) or $16 for the 100-share contract.

Had you purchased 20 contracts for a total of $500, you would have sold for $820 and profited by $320 ($16 x 20).

Fifth Requirement: The cost of purchasing an option is another consideration. The difference between the Bid price and the Ask price on an option chain listing is the amount that goes to the market-makers. You might think of it as a commission paid for handling the in and out transactions of the sale.

For example, if the Bid is $0.25 and the Ask is $0.30 at the time you purchase your option, you would most likely pay $30 for the 100-share option. If, at the time you wanted to exercise or sell to close the option, the Bid was $0.25, and the Ask was $0.30, you would receive $25 for each of your 100-share options or $25 per contract. The market-maker or the person on the other buying/selling end of the transaction receives $0.05 per share or $5, which is the difference between the Bid and the Ask, for the 100-share contract as their commission for handling the transaction.

This explains why when you purchase an option contract your account starts off with a deficit. You are down the amount of the spread.

You don't want to pay a fee that is too high. If the spread is greater than $0.10, don't purchase that option, or place a limit purchase order for a price that is between the Bid and the Ask price, bringing the spread into range. Market-makers will sometimes trim their commission if they are interested in taking part in the trade. Also, the various exchanges don't always maintain the same Bid and Ask premiums, so what seems to be a low commission for market-makers at one exchange might be within range at another exchange. The broker will check the various exchanges in their effort to fill your limit order.

Ten cents is the maximum spread and that is high. Your account will be down by a 1/3 before the price has a chance to recover. It is better if the spread is pennies or a nickel at most. The only exception to this would be if you were trading super expensive equities like Amazon (AMZN).

A second cost is the brokerage fee. This is what the broker charges to handle the trade. Each brokerage has a fee structure, and it is worth comparing these fees in relation to the bells and whistles you want from the broker. I seldom use the charts at my broker, so that is not a super important feature for me, but I do want a quick, easy-to-use trading platform that is known for fast executions.

This said, there is a trading platform called TC2000 that is very popular with day-traders because you can place your trade to buy and sell right from the price chart. As you watch the patterns unfold and see weakness setting in, you click sell right on the chart, and your order is placed there and then. TC2000 charges a monthly fee for their chart and scanning services. If you get deeply involved in day-trading, their service might be worth the expense.

The charts I have posted in the book are created through a company called stockcharts.com and they are associated with a broker, so you can also trade within their charting software. It is worth checking out.

Speaking of brokerage costs, after a few months of trading, contact your broker (especially online brokers) and ask if you are getting their best deal. You can mention that you want to make sure you are paying a fee commensurate to other brokerage firms. Often, you will find they will drop you from $9.95 per side of a trade to $6.95, then to $4.95 the next time you call, etc. Eventually, you will hit a limit, but it still doesn't hurt to ask.

Lately, there have been some newcomers with super low fees, and this is causing some of the long-time brokers to reconsider their fee structure.

DAY-TRADING REQUIREMENT RECAP

Let's recap the basic option considerations before we move on to discuss brokerage accounts.

Recap – Option Requirements – the first six aspects of the Change Your Future strategy:

#1 - Strike Prices must have "some" open interest. Also, the strike should have "some" volume. If the volume is questionable, check the historical information on the option. You don't want to be the only one in a trade or just one of very few.

#2 – Buy the appropriate time frame option expiration, most often the current week as you will be in trades for one to three days or you are intentionally doing an overnight trade.

If your option has intrinsic money value at expiration, close the trade so it is not exercised where you need to purchase the equity. In this strategy, you are trading the options with no intent to purchase the underlying equity.

If the trade has no value at expiration, you can let it expire worthless and save the fee needed to close the trade. If it has no value, there is no need to close it.

#3 – Limit total trade investment to a consistent level of $100 to $500 per trade. The amount should fit your trade account and risk tolerance. Discuss with your broker if you have questions.

#4 – For this strategy, buy strikes that are out-of-the-money and less than .30 Ask per share and that fit your available funds. Don't be tempted to buy beyond your means. This consideration ties in with Requirement 2 and 3.

#5 – Don't enter an option where the spread between the Bid and Ask is more than $0.10 or really consider the expected move if it is a high-priced stock with wide bid/ask spread. Another option is to submit a limit option premium less the amount needed to bring it in line with the requirement to see if it is accepted and filled.

TRADE EXAMPLES

Let's examine the details of a couple trades as you apply the chart patterns, indicators, and trade guidelines.

I have marked entry and exit areas.

On the Robinhood (HOOD) chart, the CCI moved into being in strength stage on open. HOOD moved to your watch list since it has had a series of strength stages, and you noticed the buying that was happening since December 1st.

Easily your mind conjured an image of a wholesaler loading up his warehouse shelves during the previous day's flat periods. There had been a steady rise through the previous days, and then a rest period where HOOD went flat. You can imagine the stockmen loading up as price went flat during the last hour of the day.

You watch and see that the CCI has crossed up above zero line. This would have been an early entry. You continue to watch and notice the ADX started heading up. The EMA crosses up and goes into up trending order.

You consult the option chain and select the 10-strike with an Ask premium of .29 (below the .30 guideline) at and open the trade.

You watch the chart as price continues to move up, and other confirmations can be ticked off a list. +DI has crossed up over the -DI and is over the ADX. The ADX has turned up, and the new CYF+ that had formed days ago moved right into the Sweet Spot.

From noon to 1:00, there is a pullback. You consider closing for a nice profit, but then decide to hold during the lunch period because of the strength of +DI.

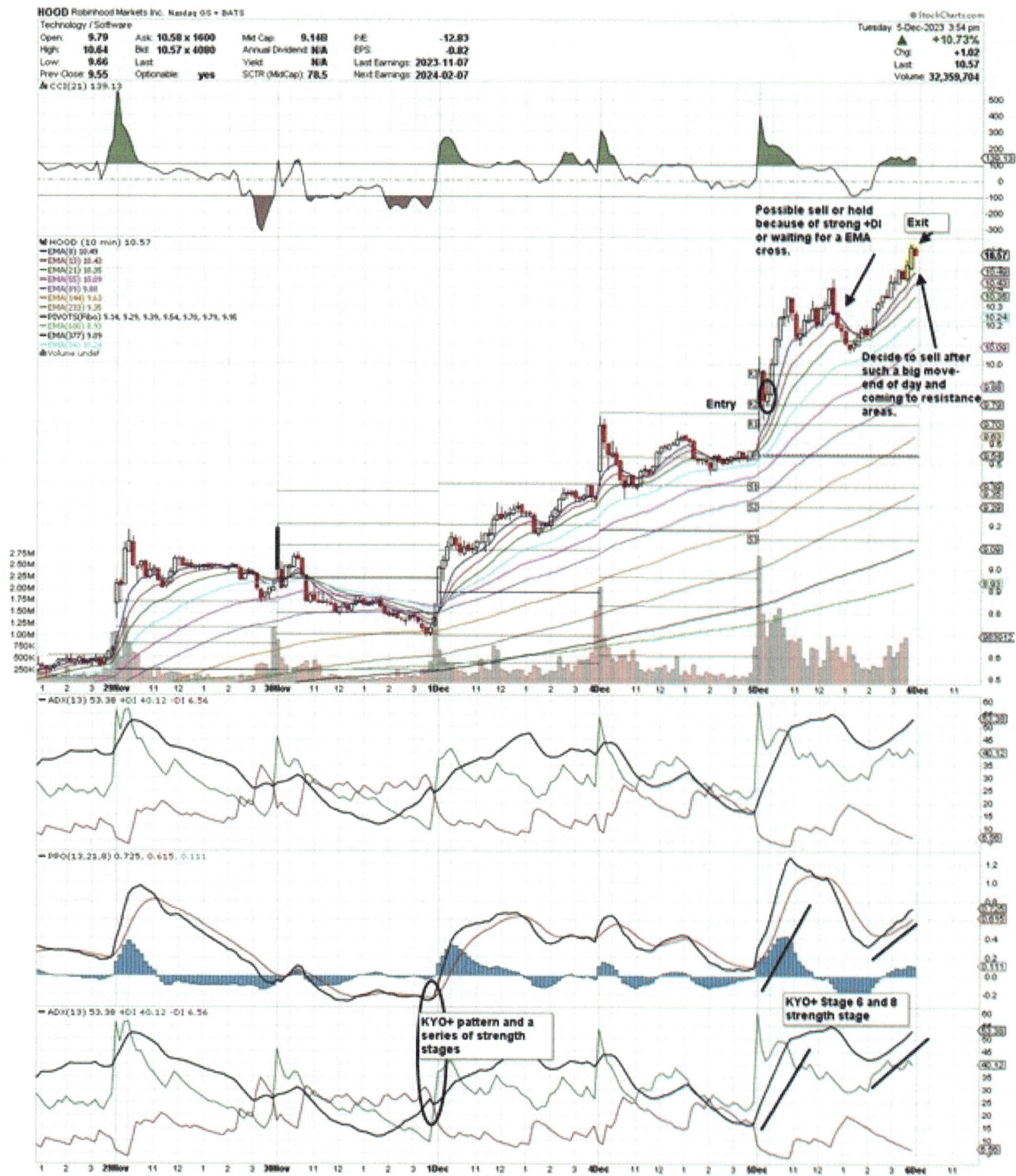

Figure 56 - Courtesy of StockCharts.com

You continue to monitor the chart after lunch. The 8-EMA is still atop the 13-EMA and then shortly after 1:00 the 8-EMA starts to rise. You notice that the -DI heads down and the ADX rises again. This is a second add-on strength stage, and you decide to sell at the end of the day rather than hold overnight.

The Bid premium at the time that you close the trade is .70. You paid .29 and sold for .70, which means you more than doubled your premium in a one-day trade.

151

It could be that HOOD will rise again tomorrow. It is hard to know, but you decide it is better to take your more than double profit, be grateful and move on to a new, fresh trade. Follow your pattern signals and guidelines and be thankful for having earned a nice profit in a short time. Our goal isn't to earn every available penny in a trade, but to expect readable, obvious patterns where we recognize entry and exit signals and then to be thankful for a profitable trade.

That was fun. Let's do another trade.

Again, on Spotify's (SPOT) chart below, I have annotated the entry and exit area.

SPOT had an opening move quite like HOOD, but you didn't see it. Then it pulled back during the lunch period. That would have been a great Put trade. Goodness, ride it up and down, but you only noticed it later after lunch. Since you decided to hold the HOOD trade during the pullback, you start looking for something else to set up.

You noticed the swings on SPOT. You saw the oversold conditions setting up around 1:00 am and then monitored as price started heading up.

You looked at the option chain and decided that, if price moved above the pivot point, you would purchase the 219-strike. At 1:45 am, the price crossed the pivot line. At that time, the Ask premium was .27. This was below your .30 limit, even though you selected a strike that was further out-of-the-money. SPOT is a more active, higher priced stock with lots of volume, so you selected a strike that other traders were also selecting.

Around 2:30 after your entry, the ADX indicator headed up into the Sweet Spot. Its strength seemed modest. You figured since this was a second sweet spot, it might not last too long or overnight, so you closed the trade at the end of the day.

Near 4:00, you closed the trade.

You purchased the 210-strike for the current week's option with 3 days until expiration for .27, and the Bid premium when you close the trade is .50. You were 3 cents shy of doubling your money, less your trading fees.

Again, another super trade that played out over about 2 hours.

Notice how price paused twice at about the 200-price level and that is close to the point where price is now heading. This was another reason to consider closing your trade. You figure it might be a ceiling that price would struggle getting through. Earning a nice profit, almost doubling your investment in a short period of time is worth just taking, being thankful, and moving on.

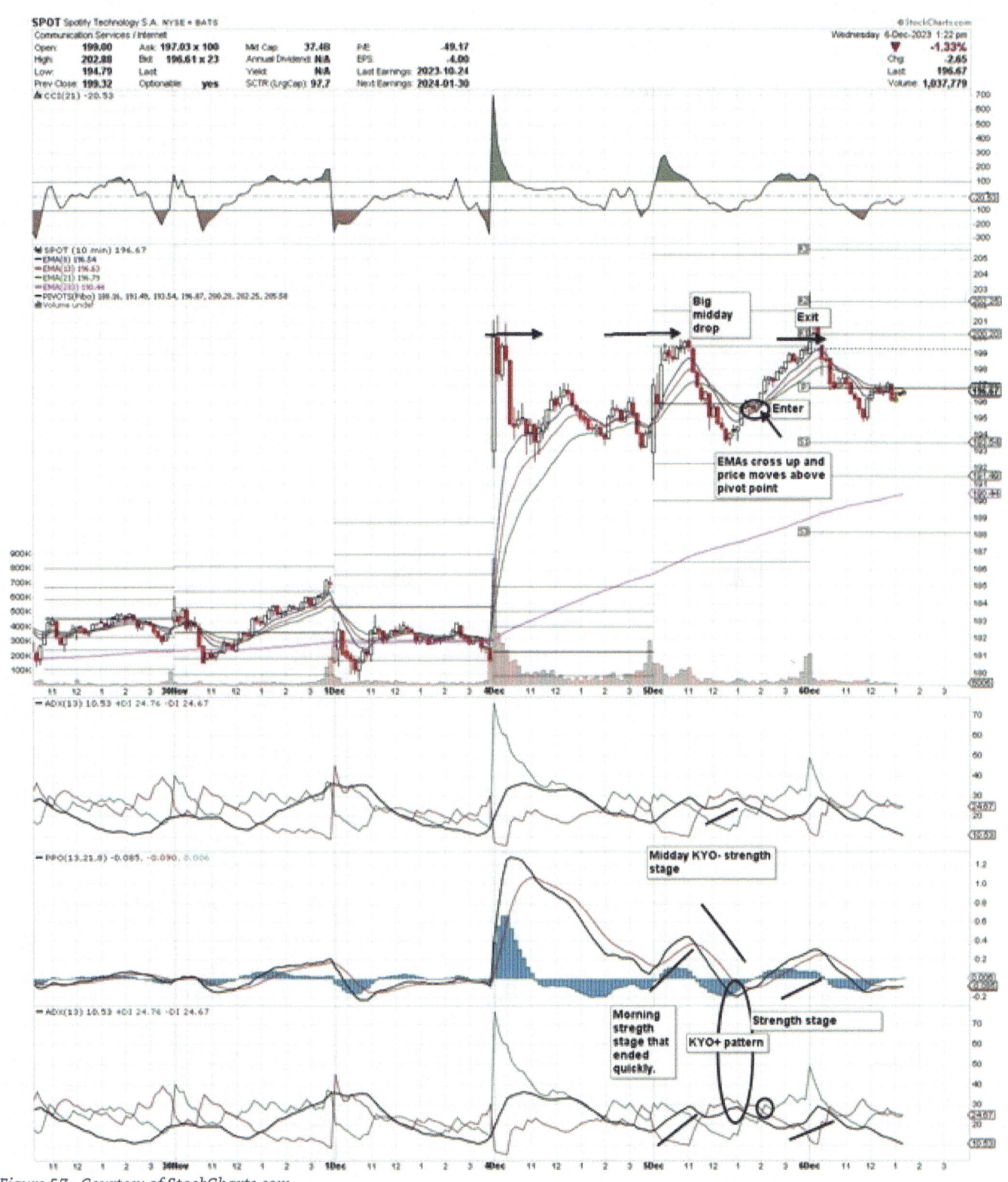

Figure 57 - Courtesy of StockCharts.com

Let's look at a bearish Put trade.

Penn National Gaming's (PENN) chart below shows that late in the day on Monday December 4th, the PPO crossed down shortly after opening and the -DI crossed up and over about 10:45. EMAs were in down-trending order showing a bearish CYF- patterns has set-up.

You could have selected Friday's expiration of the 24-strike Put for .15. Or $15 a contract and perhaps, bought 10 for $150. You could have sold at the end of the day for .27 or a gain of .12 or $1 per contract or $120 for the 10 contracts or 80% gain.

The last candle of the day was bullish and suggested a change in direction might happen in the morning.

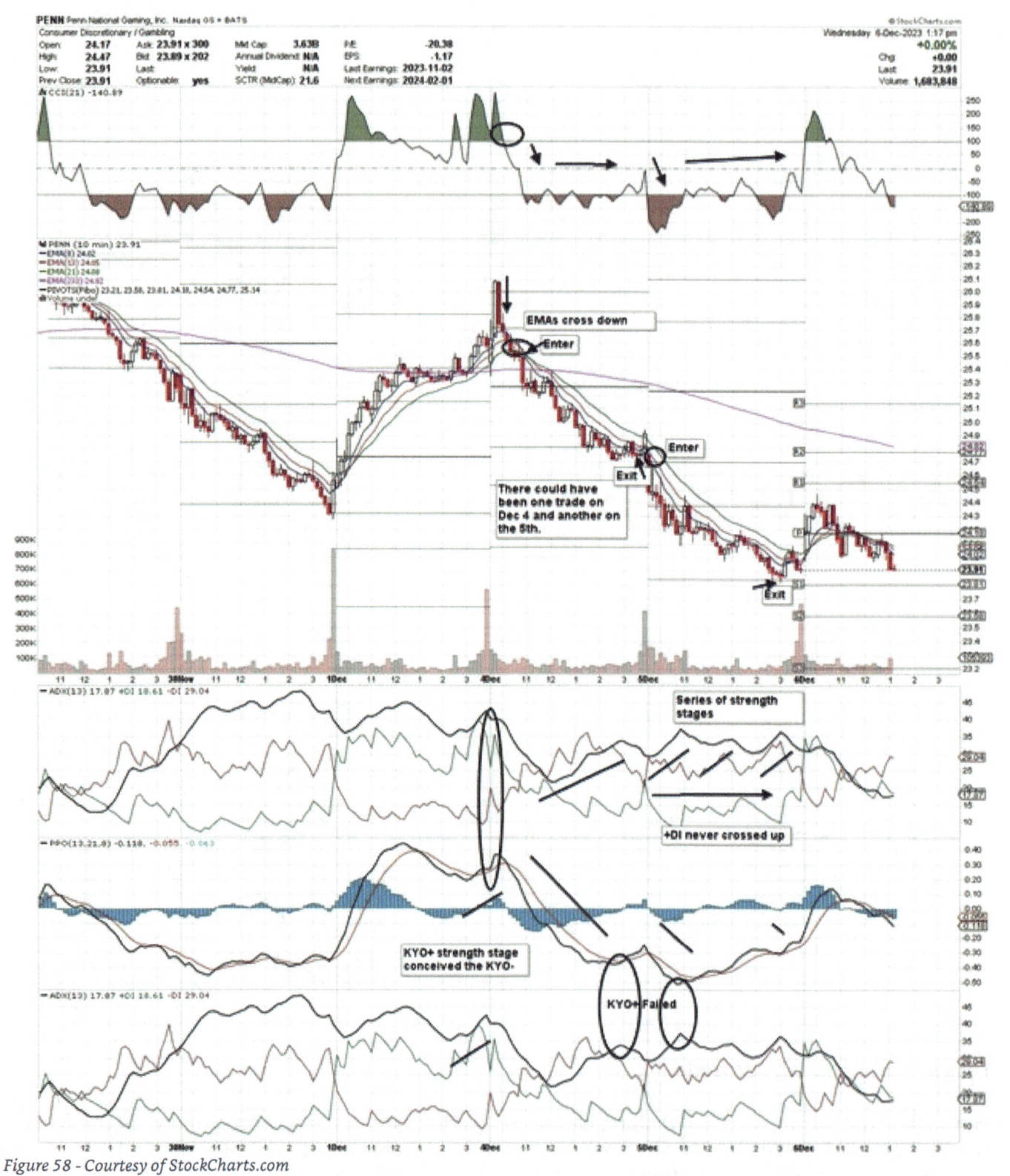

Figure 58 - Courtesy of StockCharts.com

When you check the chart the next morning, the previous day's positive move didn't carry through and the price started dropping again. You reentered. You bought the same strike and Friday's expiration for .27. PENN's price dropped throughout the day and before the close of the market-day, you sell for .52 which is a 92% gain on this second trade.

Way-to-go!

Joy-reminder-

As we delve into uncertain territory like option trading and move toward new opportunities for wealth, we often reach a crossroads where the choices seem to involve the risk of facing the unknown versus the safety and comfort of our norm and all that we have come to trust. It can feel safer, more natural, and comfortable to remain stuck in our old way of thinking rather than tentatively step out and embrace something new.

We may feel like a tightrope walker, carefully teetering along the narrow path to our goals, sometimes feeling that we are doing so without a net. Knowing we have some backup may help us work up the courage to take those first steps, until we are secure in knowing that we have the skills to work without one. That security can come in the form of a chatroom where like-minded traders are proceeding along the same path and supporting each other.

Chatroll.com is a chat service where a chat group can be formed. I am not aware of one as I write this book, but likely one or two will form as the book gets distributed or groups form.

The chatroom is a place where wealth can be achieved, friendships developed, and lots of fun experienced- all sources of joy.

OVERNIGHT STRATEGY

The concept behind the overnight strategy is to look for equities that are extremely overbought or oversold on CCI near the end of the day. Let's say between 2:30 ET and 4:00 ET before the market closes, the CCI should drop or rise to an extreme level and start giving the first appearances that it is ready to move in the opposite direction.

The CCI should rise or drop and look to be breaking through the 100/-100 line and heading toward the 0-line. There should be a new CYF+ or CYF- pattern forming and perhaps, other entry confirmations such as EMA cross, PPO cross, DI lines heading toward each other.

On IWM's chart below, the CCI was rising and neared the zero-line going into bullish territory. There were other confirmations. There was a new CYF+ forming. The +DI was near a cross and there was a crazy amount of volume. Something positive is going on.

The point of this overnight strategy is to spot a move before it happens and exor as it is just starting and expect it to pop and gap in the morning at the open. Some trades will continue for 30 minutes to an hour, and other times, soon after opening, the price will reverse so that you must be on your toes to watch for the exit.

The second chart shows you IWM's next morning's move. The exit was shortly after 10:00am when price began to pullback and reverse.

The trade resulted in about a $5.50 price move until about 1:00 ET when it started to pullback, and you closed. The Ask premium for next week's expiration of the 187-strike was .27. The Bid premium on close was 1.17. That was a .90 gain or 333% on that quick overnight/morning rise.

Figure 59 - Courtesy of StockCharts.com

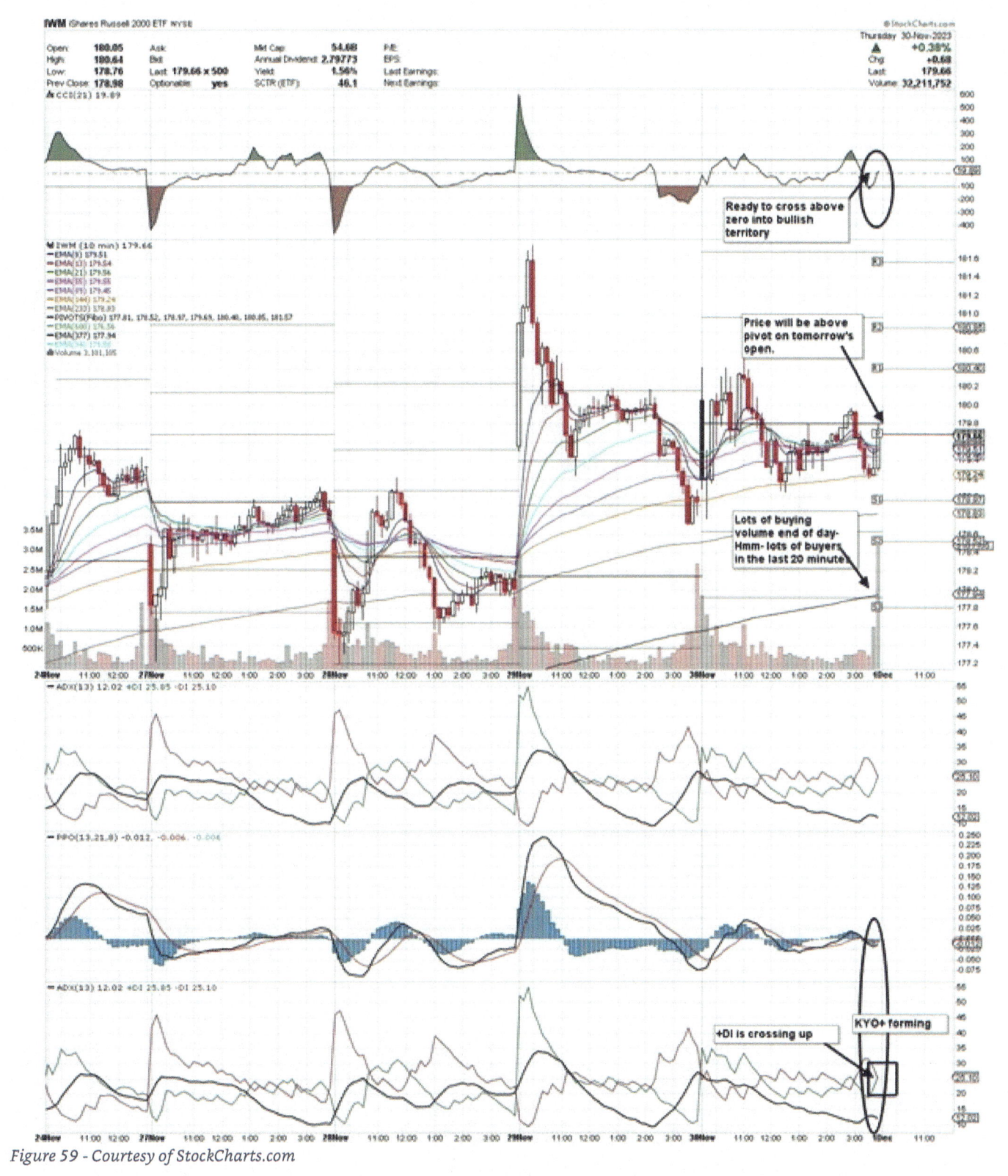

Let's check out an overnight Call trade and a chart with oversold CCI close to the end of the day on the 5th.

On Block Inc.'s (SQ) chart below, the entry area is marked at 3:00pm. There was a little pullback when price hit the pivot point. Other confirmations soon started to take place.

157

Figure 60 - Courtesy of StockCharts.com

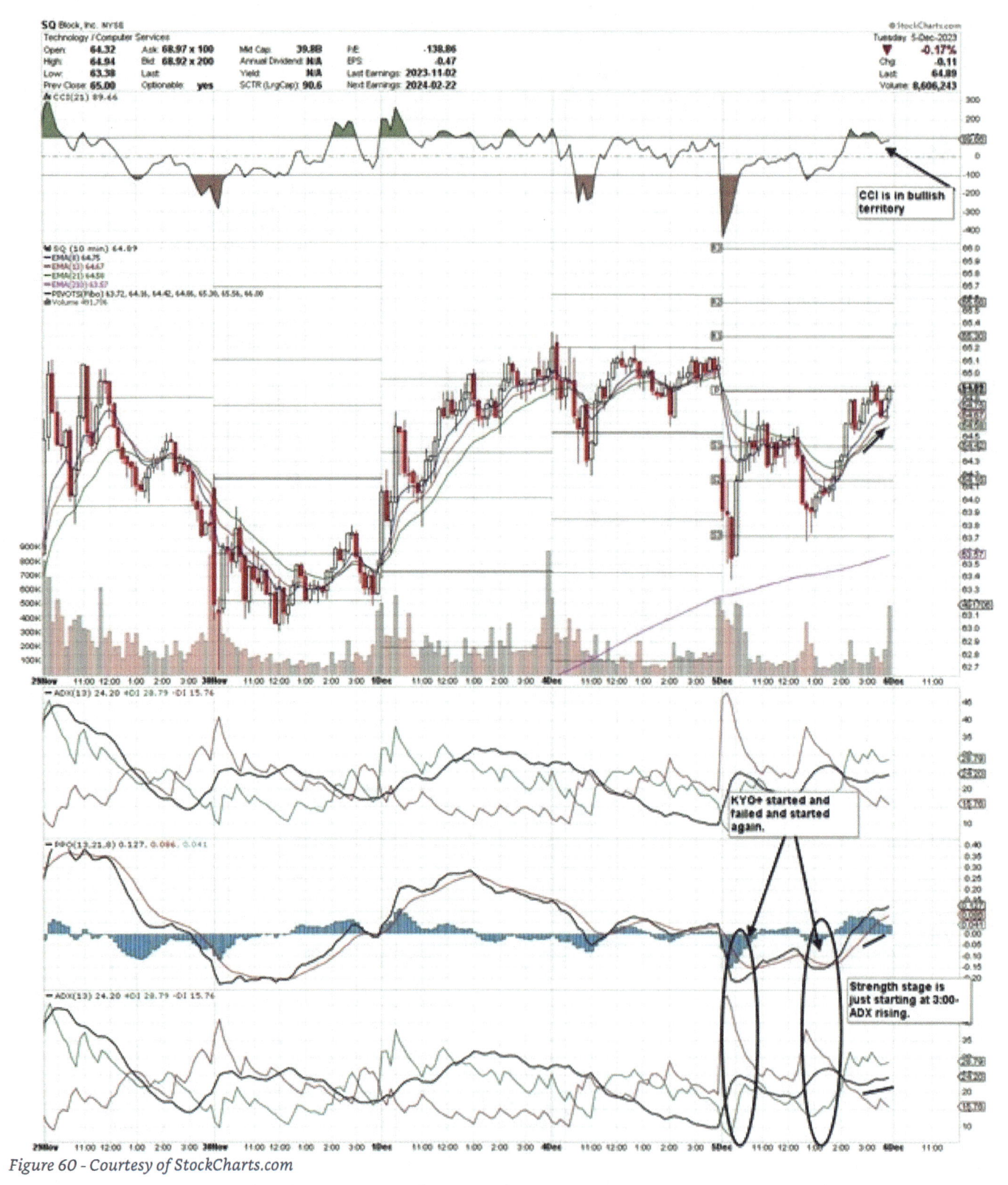

You select a Call option for the 70-strike from Friday's expiration date, 3 days away for a premium of .14. You purchase 10 contracts for $140.

The next morning there is a gap up and the price keeps rising. You are watching close and when price comes close to $70, it starts pulling back and your finger pushes the button to close.

Figure 61 - Courtesy of StockCharts.com

As mentioned, the price continued to climb after opening and about 11:00 AM it started to pullback. The PPO started to create a peak and was heading down. This was a good exit.

The point of the overnight strategy isn't to hang onto a trade throughout the day. The idea is to get in late in the day and get out the next morning and hold until the price starts to weaken. Sometimes this happens soon after opening and other times later in the day.

If price doesn't gap but slowly moves in your direction, you can continue to hold and wait for profit to come into the trade and then close when it starts to reverse.

Remember you know the stages of the CYF patterns and can predict what is apt to happen next as the stages unfold.

If the trade moves against you right from the start, it is wise to close the trade and cut the loss short. Again, you have the benefit of being able to read the patterns and their stages, but don't fool yourself into holding a trade on "hope" when it is long past its exit.

LAST MAGICAL 30 MINUTES TRADE STRATEGY

This is called the Rescue Trade.

Often when there has been a big move up or down during the day or through the afternoon session, there will often be a reversal in the last 15 minutes or so of trading. This end of day direction switch makes sense when you realize that after a big move, traders are apt to decide to bank profits.

This trade strategy works particularly well on the indices' indexes- SPY, QQQ, DIA and IWM, but also works with other highly traded equities.

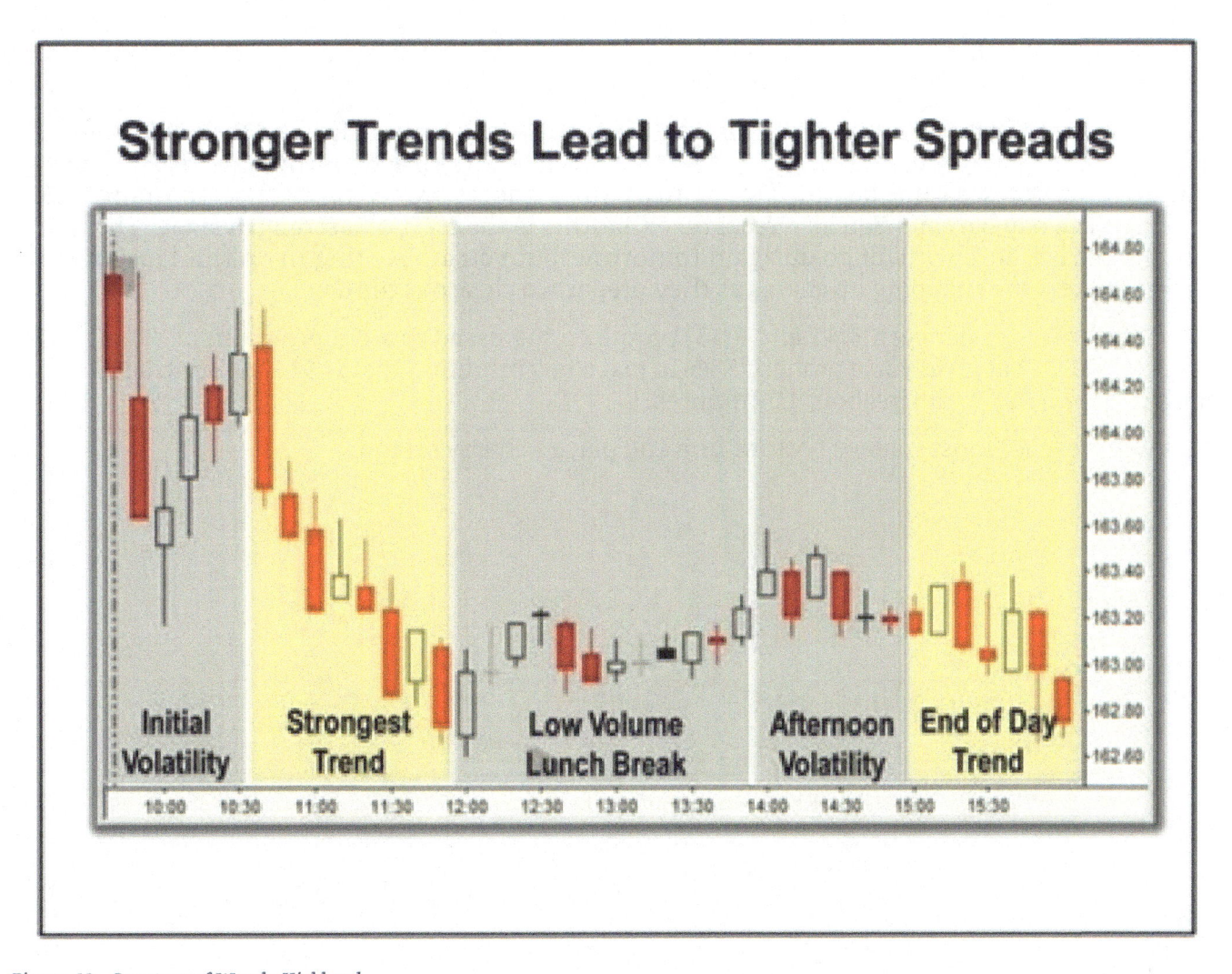

Figure 62 - Courtesy of Wendy Kirkland

In a general sense, Bid/Ask spreads can vary depending on time of day.

1) A bottleneck of overnight orders creates opening bell volatility and often wider spreads.

2) But market direction is generally established by 10:30, creating the strongest trend of the day and the tightest spreads.

3) Then, when traders break for lunch, the volume dwindles. So, spreads can become wider again.

4) And price often jumps around a bit as traders return to their desks at 2:00.

5) Then, around 3:00 volume picks up again and spreads tighten as professional and institutional traders begin placing their final trades for the day.

Around 3:45pm is Rescue Trade time. You enter a trade with a strike that is close to the current equity price at-the-money. The spreads between the Bid/Ask are often a penny or two. Selecting the current day/week's expiration is okay since you plan to close the trade within a few minutes of opening it.

Once the selling and reversal takes place between 3:45 and 3:58 or so, close the trade.

You are likely to have earned 20-50%+ in a few minutes.

Let's look at an example of a Rescue Trade.

At 3:45pm, you select the 189-strike and tomorrow's expiration for IWM since it is Thursday. You decide to buy a little further out-of-the-money because it still has a full day until expiration. You have changed the chart to a 2-minute chart so you can keep a close eye on minute-to-minute price moves. The Ask premium is .26. You purchase 20 contracts for $520.

IWM is oversold and has now risen to the zero line, and price starts rising, and the EMAs have been sitting on the 233 EMA all afternoon. The PPO also crosses up as price continues to rise for the next minute or so. You see some buying coming in as other traders are seeing the rise, thinking IWM is an end of the day bargain. You also recognize that this is the start of a strength stage. The ADX is starting to rise. Surely it will go up again tomorrow, but you are zeroing in on this closing move. Market makers are snapping up shares as they prepare to close out the day.

In the few minutes between 3:45 and 3:55, premium increased to a Bid premium of .37. (.37 less Ask .26 = .11). That gives you a profit of 38% in just a few minutes. That is $11 per contract, and you bought 20 or a $220 gain in about 10-minutes.

That will "rescue" most trader's bottom-line and place a cherry on top.

Figure 63 - Courtesy of Stockcharts.com

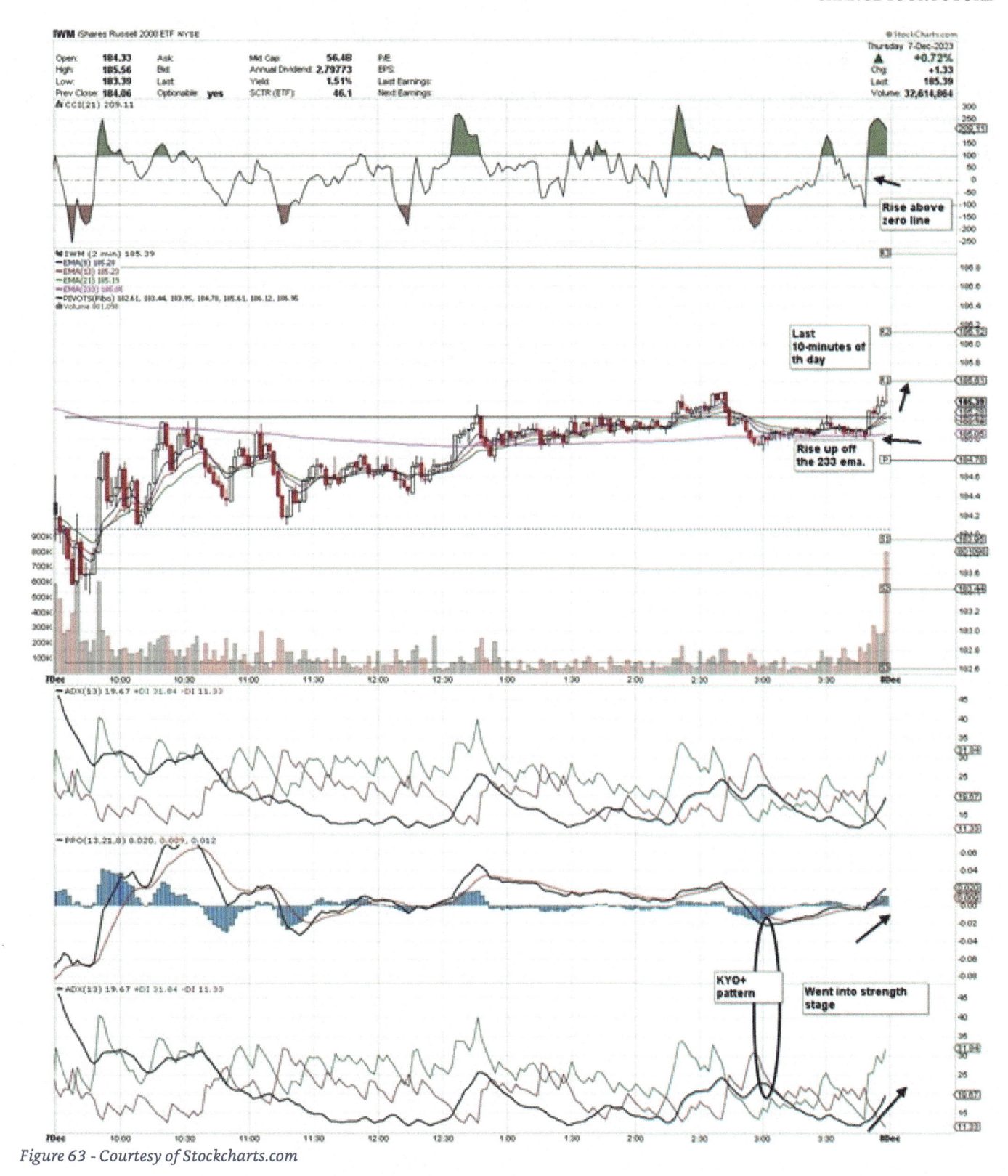

Joy-reminder-

Change Your Future's approach- When we tackle new things like option trading and move deeper into ourselves for the purpose of understanding the self as it relates to the new subject, we discover that our minds are made up of many layers of intricacy that wrap one another like the layers in an onion. To push past one layer of complexity is often to be immediately challenged by another such layer. We should not let this hold us back from our journey into unfamiliar territory or rough seas to know more about what defines our uniqueness as an individual. While it is unlikely that we will ever reach the centermost part of ourselves, we nonetheless grow in our understanding each time we peel back another layer.

In this case, the journey into option trading is often more important than the trading destination itself as our developing knowledge of self as we joyfully approach something new will positively impact our lives forevermore.

Navigating the seas and exploration of self as you embark into option trading will help you discover new vistas in your personal evolution and life's adventure. Maintain joy as your beacon!

BROKERAGE ACCOUNTS

Chances are, if you are interested in the stock market, you already have a broker with whom you are dealing. Many traders want the convenience obtained by establishing an online brokerage account. Once you have the trade form filled in, and you push the "send" button, the trade is instantly filled if it is a market order, or when it hits the amount of a limit order. (I will discuss limit orders and market orders in the next section.)

There are several types of trading accounts.

Cash Versus Margin Account

In the process of opening an online trading account, you will have the choice of opening a Cash or Margin. **Open a Cash Account.** The reason for this is the very restrictive day-trading SEC (Security Exchange Commission) regulations.

Day-trading refers to traders who are in and out of a trade within the same day. Regulations require that day traders with margin accounts always maintain $25,000 in their trading accounts. If their account drops below that amount and they have more than 3 day-trades placed in a 5-day period, the broker often freezes the account for 90 days.

Not everyone has $25,000 to leave sitting in an account to fulfill that requirement, and, though this strategy does not always do round-trip trades each day, it does happen most of the time. The stress of tracking how many roundtrips you have made in the last 5 trading days can be eliminated if you open a Cash account. The SEC's restrictions of 3 round-trip trades in a 5-day period applies only to Margin accounts and not to Cash accounts in the same way.

There may be statements in the broker's application about pattern trading, but day-trades are not monitored in cash accounts.

I also don't advise trading on margin, which is borrowed money, where you then must pay interest. Trade with your own money that has been set aside for trading and not borrowed funds.

FINE TUNING PURCHASE PRICES: PLACING TRADE ORDERS

Market Orders

Market orders trade at the current price. These include both buy or sell orders in which the broker is to execute the order at the best price available, which should be very close to the price shown on the options chain.

If you are trading during market hours (Wall Street hours, and therefore, Eastern Standard Time), there shouldn't be any unexpected surprises if you are using an online broker. If you are calling your broker to place the trade, the price can change during the time it takes to connect with your broker.

Stock prices often change quickly in a hot market where a price moves up and down within seconds. Options prices change a little more slowly, but as you click "Place Order," the option could go up or down a few cents. The sale with a market order online happens in seconds.

With limit-orders, you specify at what price you want to trade, and the duration (trading day or until canceled) they should float the order, that is, try to fill it at the price you requested. If the market never reaches the price you specified during that period, the order will be canceled. This strategy can be useful if you are going to be away.

If you are going to be away and can't personally place an order at the price you'd like, then place a limit order, and leave it in effect for the period that you will be away.

The disadvantage to this is some brokerages demand that you have more in your account than the amount needed to make the purchase. If this happens, place a limit order, and increase the limit amount by a dime or fifteen cents to cover an increase during the moment of execution. The order will be filled in at the lowest amount possible from the available exchanges.

Under normal circumstances, place a market order the moment you are interested in buying and the order will be filled.

Two rules to adhere to:

1. NEVER place a market order after the market closes or before the market opens. If you do, your order will be filled in at the opening price, and that amount very well may be on the initial jump of the market out of the gate. Then, as the market settles after the first 30 minutes or so, you find you could have bought for considerably less, so right off, you are in a position of needing to recover from a loss. If you zero in on a trade overnight or first thing in the morning, watch the stock and evaluate the trade at open. What is happening? Did it gap up/down? Continue to follow it to 10:00-10:15am, an hour after open. Does it still look like a good buy? Can you get in now for less than you would have paid at 9:30 EST? If you are going to be away during the first hour or so of the trading day, then set a limit order by setting the highest price you are willing to pay. The order will fill and close at the lowest price. There will be no unpleasant surprises.

2. NEVER chase an option. I have heard of traders changing limit prices every few seconds as the price of a stock moves above their limit. In the time that it takes to fill in the order form, the equity's price moves beyond their price. If you want to buy, use a market order, grab the position, or set the highest amount you are willing to pay and stick to it. If you chase a stock's price, moment by moment, the essential information you used to base your decision in the first place is changing. The spread may have increased. You want to trade on your researched information or as close to it as possible.

Limit Orders

Limit orders can be used in a variety of ways. You can use a limit order to purchase an option. You can also use a limit-sell order to take profit. There are several reasons that this can work out well.

Let's say that you have a profit target on a particular trade. You would like to sell just before the price reaches a previous resistance level, yet you are going to be out for the afternoon and don't want to close the trade now rather than let it run its expected course. In this case you can set a limit sell order so that the trade is closed when the equity's price reaches the amount you set as a "sell-to-close limit".

Another way to use a limit order is to set a profit dollar amount. Let's say you purchased 10 contracts for $.30 premium per share. $30 times 10 = $300. For this trade, you would like to earn 50%. So, you place a limit sell order for $.45, which will give you $0.15 profit once the bid premium reaches $.45.

I have found that, when I have a profit target in mind, if I use a limit-sell order, I often make more profit. The reason for this is, no matter how fast I am, I am slower than a computer. As an example, let's say I have a profit target in mind. When the stock's price reaches $42.20, just below the resistance level of $42.25, I plan to sell. I am watching the computer screen with the chart, and I have my "market" sell order set up on my online brokerage account.

There you go, just as I expected, the stock sits for a few minutes at $42.17, and then, in a flash, it shot up and tapped $42.25 and immediately started to pullback. I quickly flip over to my sell order and push the button. The trade is closed at $42.15.

Had I placed a limit sell order for $42.20, the position would have been closed when the price ran through that amount on its way to $42.25. The result would have been that I made $0.03 more per share and on 10 contracts that would be $30 (an amount that would have more than covered my trading fees).

Now there is a downside to limit-orders. They can limit profit. In the example above, if the price continued to rise through the $42.25 resistance level, my limit order would have been closed at $42.20, cutting my profit short. But the way I see it, there is nothing short about earning a profit.

If the trade appears to be one that is defying gravity, I can wait for a pullback and other signals for my strategy.

This is one of the areas where our core beliefs can be changed. We need to allow ourselves to be right, no matter what happens. Traders so often set themselves up for criticism no matter the trade result. "Oh, I got out too quick and left money on the table," or "Geez, if I had sold sooner, I would have made another $100 bucks," or "If I had gotten in earlier, I would have paid 7 cents less per share," or "I got in too late and paid an extra $15 per contract."

Allow yourself to get it right. Give yourself a pat on the back for earning money that wasn't in your account yesterday. Change your thinking and give yourself credit for executing a profitable trade. Or for selling and cutting a loss short. Congrats, you followed your trading plan!

FOLLOWING THROUGH AND TRADING THE STRATEGY

Okay, we have covered all the necessary aspects of the Change Your Future trading strategy. The alerts and confirmation signals are laid out for you to practice and follow. Test the strategy on paper or through virtual trading until you have confidence in it. Utilize the Divine Proportion EMAs and the indicators we have discussed until they become close friends.

Apply what you have learned to locate, analyze, and enter profitable trades.

It doesn't matter that you are or have been in prison, you have as much opportunity for success as anyone else. It is all dependent on your attitude, study, and willingness to try. To try, to learn from results, and to proceed.

Did you know that most people who read trading books and go to trading seminars still fail to achieve the success they want?

It's true. The great Napoleon Hill once said that only 2% of those who learned his now legendary success principles used them to become successful.

Only 2%.

Here's why (and, yes, there is a solution).

Even when you know what to do, and even if you really want success, there are many ways you may unconsciously sabotage yourself.

You may quit if you have a setback. You may procrastinate. You may unconsciously make bad decisions or attract people who take you off-track, instead of attracting those who can help you achieve what you want.

You may be nurturing erroneous core beliefs and believe things about success, about yourself, about other people, about money, or about something else . . .

. . . that causes you to get in your own way.

If your behavior is generated by an unconscious part of your mind, you may have trouble taking the successful actions you need to take . . .

. . . even if you know what they are and want to take them.

And, sadly, as I said, 98% of people do this. This includes many, many people who have never been in prison.

What can you do about this? What is the most potent, most effective way to get rid of these unconscious, self-sabotaging thoughts?

Become consciously aware of when negative self-talk is taking place. Stop it. Rethink. Remind yourself that it stems from something that happened in the past, and the past is gone...done...over with. Start new from this moment. Don't bring the past into the current situation. React, not out of habit, but out of what is presented to you right now.

Each trade is a new trade. Apply what you know. Practice until you are comfortable and then apply those same principles to real trades.

Expect the unexpected and expect it to be great!

Follow the stages of the Change Your Future pattern. Identify the stages so you know what to expect next as the pattern unfolds and moves into the strength stage. You have followed the steps leading to this stage, you are prepared to reap the rewards of a great trade as it closes.

I wish you the greatest success. I KNOW it is possible for you. It may sound silly, but when you look at the Divine Proportion EMAs on your chart, let them cast a special hue over the information, so that it reminds you of the all-encompassing plan that wants the very best for you and knows you will succeed where you place your positive-mental energy.

Be happy. Experience joy!

Believe in yourself.

To your success!

Made in United States
North Haven, CT
10 January 2025